WITHDRAWN

MERCENARIES

Also by Guy Arnold

WARS IN THE THIRD WORLD SINCE 1945

BRAINWASH: The Cover-Up Society

KENYATTA AND THE POLITICS OF KENYA

MODERN NIGERIA

THE RESOURCES OF THE THIRD WORLD

* WORLD GOVERNMENT BY STEALTH

BRITAIN SINCE 1945

* THE END OF THE THIRD WORLD

* *From the same publishers*

Mercenaries

The Scourge of the Third World

Guy Arnold

First published in Great Britain 1999 by
MACMILLAN PRESS LTD
Houndmills, Basingstoke, Hampshire RG21 6XS and London
Companies and representatives throughout the world

A catalogue record for this book is available from the British Library.

ISBN 0–333–73387–8

 First published in the United States of America 1999 by
ST. MARTIN'S PRESS, INC.,
Scholarly and Reference Division,
175 Fifth Avenue, New York, N.Y. 10010

ISBN 0–312–22203–3

Library of Congress Cataloging-in-Publication Data
Arnold, Guy.
Mercenaries : the scourge of the Third World / Guy Arnold.
p. cm.
Includes bibliographical references and index.
ISBN 0–312–22203–3 (cloth)
1. Mercenary troops—Developing countries. I. Title.
U42.A78   1999
355.3'54—dc21   99–18562
                                                                  CIP

© Guy Arnold 1999

All rights reserved. No reproduction, copy or transmission of this publication may be made without written permission.

No paragraph of this publication may be reproduced, copied or transmitted save with written permission or in accordance with the provisions of the Copyright, Designs and Patents Act 1988, or under the terms of any licence permitting limited copying issued by the Copyright Licensing Agency, 90 Tottenham Court Road, London W1P 9HE.

Any person who does any unauthorised act in relation to this publication may be liable to criminal prosecution and civil claims for damages.

The author has asserted his right to be identified as the author of this work in accordance with the Copyright, Designs and Patents Act 1988.

This book is printed on paper suitable for recycling and made from fully managed and sustained forest sources.

10 9 8 7 6 5 4 3 2 1
08 07 06 05 04 03 02 01 00 99

Printed and bound in Great Britain by
Antony Rowe Ltd, Chippenham, Wiltshire

Contents

Preface		vi
List of Abbreviations and Acronyms		vii
Introduction		ix
1	The Congo 1960–1965	1
2	The Nigerian Civil War	18
3	Southern Africa (1) Rhodesia	26
4	Southern Africa (2) Angola	33
5	African vulnerability	46
6	Island destabilization: Comoros, Seychelles, Denard	56
7	The British mercenary tradition: The Middle East	65
8	Papua New Guinea and Bougainville	74
9	Nicaragua and Colombia	86
10	Europe	101
11	South Africa and Executive Outcomes	113
12	The new mercenary coporations	123
13	Sierra Leone, Sandline and Britain	132
14	Western attitudes	147
15	The United Nations	159
16	Conclusions – the future	169
Notes		175
Appendix		181
Index		190

Preface

The subject of mercenaries rouses similar emotions to that of arms sales and in a violent, competitive world the demand for the services of the former and the supply of the latter steadily escalates. In the near 40 years from the Congo crisis of the early 1960s to the restoration of President Kabbah in Sierra Leone with the help of the British mercenary company Sandline in 1998, there has been a profound change in the perception and use of mercenaries, from the individual soldiers-of-fortune who turned up in the Congo or Angola to the new corporate mercenary who is leased out by a range of security and military advice companies which claim only to work for legitimate governments. These companies are the result of a new approach to problems by an ever wider range of governments: the 'outsourcing' of tasks to private enterprise which formerly were the sole province of government. There is every indication that sophisticated military advisory security firms will become increasingly powerful, sought after and dangerous. If this proves to be the case they will turn into an independent monster that cannot be controlled and one, moreover, that will have been encouraged by the shortsighted and foolish policies of the world's major military powers.

List of Abbreviations and Acronyms

ADFL	Alliance of Democratic Forces for the Liberation of Congo-Zaire
AFRC	Armed Forces Revolutionary Council
ANC	African National Congress
APC	All People's Congress
BATT	British Army Training Team
CCB	Civil Cooperation Bureau
CIA	Central Intelligence Agency
DCC	Directorate of Covert Collection
DSL	Defence Systems Limited
ECOWAS	Economic Community of West African States
ECOMOG	Economic Community Monitoring Group
ELP	Portuguese Liberation Army
EO	Executive Outcomes
FAPLA	Forças Armadas Populares de Libertação de Angola
FAZ	Forces Armées du Zaire
FMG	Federal Military Government
FNLA	Frente Nacional de Libertação de Angola
MDLP	Democratic Movement for the Liberation of Portugal
MPLA	Movimento Popular de Libertação de Angola
MPRI	Military Professional Resources Inc
NGO	Non-Government Organization
NPFL	National Patriotic Front of Liberia
NPRC	National Provisional Ruling Council
OAU	Organization of African Unity
RUF	Revolutionary United Front
SADF	South Africa Defence Force
SAS	Special Air Services
SDP	Seychelles Democratic Party
SLPP	Sierra Leone People's Party
SPPF	Seychelless People's Progressive Front
SPUP	Seychelles People's United Party
SWAPO	South West Africa People's Organization
UDI	Unilateral Declaration of Independence

UNITA	União Nacional para a Independência Total de Angola
UNSDF	Ukrainian National Self-Defence Forces
ZANU	Zimbabwe African National Union
ZIPA	Zimbabwe People's Army

Introduction

The story of mercenaries goes back almost as far as that of organized armies; they recur throughout recorded history, sometimes playing a relatively honourable role, at others a disreputable one. The most reliable army is that of patriotic volunteers, the least the mercenary corps, while lying between these two extremes is the army of the modern state: that is, one made up largely of conscripts. The fact about the mercenary which should never be forgotten is that he serves for pay; he is not a patriot and he has no loyalty to the cause for which – temporarily – he is fighting. An army composed, wholly or in part, of mercenaries cannot be relied upon in the same way as a national army. The financial motive comes first with the mercenary; as a result his loyalty must always be suspect. Those who employ mercenaries, therefore, must ensure that they are paid and paid regularly. Such pay is often extremely high but unpaid mercenaries are a danger to their employers and not to be trusted. The mercenary bands commonly employed in the sixteenth and seventeenth centuries easily and often turned into a menace both to their former employers and, more generally, to the country in which they would operate as freebooters once the money to pay them had run out – as it frequently did.

Mercenaries first appear in ancient Egypt and Mesopotamia where their services were essential aspects of imperial control. At the height of their military dominance the Carthaginians employed large numbers of mercenaries alongside their regular troops. Some of these regular mercenary forces such as the Nubians serving the Pharoahs or the Janissaries serving the Ottomans were composed of slave regiments. Possibly the most famous mercenary band in history was that celebrated by Xenophon in the *Anabasis*, his story of the 10,000 Greeks who were employed by Cyrus, the pretender to the Persian throne. These Greeks formed a highly efficient fighting force and were available because the long Peloponnesian war between Athens and Sparta had just come to an end.

Mercenaries or potential mercenaries are usually available in large numbers at the conclusion of any major war. When the Roman Empire ceased to rely upon its citizen armies and turned instead to mercenaries it embarked upon a path that led to its eventual disintegration.

The end of the 'Dark Ages' which followed the collapse of the Roman Empire saw the rise of a new kind of mercenary. The medieval Spanish hero, the Cid, whose exploits have been celebrated in over 200 poems and sagas, was a mercenary who hired himself out to both Christian and Moorish rulers in the long struggle then taking place in Spain while Norman knights as early as the eleventh century roamed Europe in search of military employment to end up as mercenaries serving petty kingdoms in Italy or Sicily. In the early fourteenth century the Byzantine Empire hired Spanish *almogavares* or frontiersmen to fight the Turks; this they did successfully but then turned on their patrons to attack the town of Magnesia before going on to ravage Thrace. The end of the 100 Years War in 1453 left large numbers of unemployed soldiers in Europe ready for hire and it was at this time that Swiss, Italian and German soldiers took to hiring themselves out in bands to rulers or the churches; these bands put themselves under *condottieri*, the name by which the mercenary leaders of the time, the contractors, became known. They were well trained professional soldiers who sold their services to the highest bidder. Their livelihood depended upon the military life and their commanders attracted men into their service according to their reputations for success and the booty to be gained under them. They flourished not least because the Italian city states and their medieval rulers feared their own citizens and were loathe to arm them. In general, such mercenaries were undisciplined, greedy and brutal and much easier to hire than subsequently to fire. If it suited them to do so they would desert their paymasters on the eve of battle, especially against a superior enemy, to plunder civilians instead.

Mercenaries were a regular feature of European politics throughout the fifteenth to eighteenth centuries and some of them acquired high reputations for loyalty and steadfastness as did the Swiss Guards employed as bodyguards to the kings of France. The Swiss generally were highly regarded as mercenaries all over Europe and often formed elite corps in the armies to which they were attached. The French revolutionary wars saw the rise of national armies and from the nineteenth century onwards mercenaries tended increasingly to be single soldiers of fortune.

As the major European powers extended their world influence and created their empires through the nineteenth century a new kind of mercenary appeared. Regular soldiers such as Britain's General Gordon would obtain leave of absence from their own armies and instead take service under a foreign power as he did in China. France created one of the most famous of all mercenary bands, the French Foreign Legion, to provide a force to fight in the long war of conquest in Algeria that began in 1830 while Britain, for more than a century, recruited battalions of Gurkhas from Nepal as a regular component of its imperial armies. The rise of the European empires in the nineteenth century also witnessed a new interest in mercenary troops who represented a relatively straightforward way of boosting colonial armies that could not rely upon locally recruited militias. Mercenaries could also meet part of the military requirements of wealthy imperial powers which could afford to hire them and, for example, the annual recruiting of Gurkhas in Nepal by the British became an important social and economic event for a country which was among the poorest in the world.

In the post-1945 world perceptions of mercenaries again shifted. They were to become a factor in a number of newly independent developing countries, especially in Africa, where it has been assumed, often erroneously, that the mercenary would provide a level of skill and professionalism that the country itself was not yet able to produce. As it happened, the end of the European empires and the emergence of many new weak states coincided with the years following World War II when many discharged soldiers who knew little except warfare were available and more than ready to act as mercenaries – for suitable pay. Such mercenaries have become prominent in a number of Third World countries, hiring themselves out to governments or dissident factions or liberation movements, assisting coup attempts and appearing on both sides in civil wars.

The mercenary appears at one crisis after another according to the laws of supply and demand; he is expensive to hire and expendable once the crisis has passed. As a rule nations or factions hire mercenaries 'whenever there exists a gap between a soldier and his ability to operate complicated modern military equipment'.[1] At least this is one explanation for his appearance. It became clear during 1975 in Angola that both the United States through the Central Intelligence Agency (CIA) and France through its intelligence service were directly involved in the recruitment and use of mercenaries to fight against the Marxist *Movimento Popular de Libertação de Angola* (MPLA) which had formed the successor government to the departing Portuguese. Otherwise these mercenaries would not have appeared on the scene. By the second half of 1976, following the capture, trial and execution of a number of European mercenaries in Angola, Lebanon and Rhodesia became the main focal points for mercenary recruiting operations. It was described[2] as symptomatic that one French mercenary, Stephane Zanettaci of the neo-fascist 'Action Jeunesse', and one British mercenary, Gerald Thacker, both lost their lives taking part in the Falangist attacks on the Palestine refugee camp at Tel al-Zaatar. The modern mercenary can be seen as a semi-outlawed professional killer: he is supposed to be good at his job; he cares nothing for his victims and is widely despised and feared by the general population.[3] A fact about the modern mercenary that constantly recurs is the rightwing nature of his politics: a high proportion of mercenaries have shown themselves to be openly racist, anti-communist, and all too often fighting to maintain reactionary regimes in power. In the period since 1960 when mercenaries of the present era first became notorious in the Congo, there have generally been too many mercenaries chasing too few jobs; some have been proficient trained soldiers; others, and all too often, have been little better than killer psychopaths. They have appeared in the Congo, Nigeria, Angola and Rhodesia; in the drug wars in Colombia where an estimated 10,000 drug traffickers have been trained in jungle commando tactics by former members of Britain's SAS or Royal Marines; or in the civil wars in Central America; in Burma and Papua New Guinea and Cambodia. They serve as bodyguards or make up private armies. Sometimes they have been supported clandestinely or relatively openly by western governments which do not want to be directly involved in dubious dissident or revolutionary operations yet are clearly committed to a particular side although political considerations have prevented them declaring their interests. Some names crop up again and again. The British mercenary 'Mad Mike' Hoare first achieved notoriety in the Congo in 1960 and made his last mercenary appearance in a 1981 botched coup attempt to overthrow Albert René, the left-wing President of Seychelles. The French mercenary, Colonel Bob Denard who also featured in the Congo during the early 1960s, made his penultimate appearance in a Paris court which treated him more as a hero than a lawbreaker.

A long article in a 1990 issue of *Defence Today* attempted to justify mercenaries:

> Whatever the opinion each one of us has concerning mercenaries, it is necessary to reflect on the extraordinary flexibility of this profession, which has always known how to adjust itself to meet new market requirements, caused by the evolution of the art of war and of political relations, also in the most backward corners of the earth.'[4]

The article suggests, conveniently forgetting the behaviour of mercenaries in the Congo, that the modern ideological condemnation of mercenaries really only began in the mid-1970s after a number of western mercenaries were put on trial in Angola by its new Marxist government. Individual mercenaries such as Hoare or Denard or the riff-raff who turned up in Angola in 1975 are on a different level to the organized mercenary forces used by Britain (the Gurkha Brigade), France (the Foreign Legion) or even Gadaffi's Islamic Legion which was used in the long war and Libyan intervention in the Aozou region of Chad during the 1980s. It is a moot point whether the Cuban troops used in Angola during the 1970s and 1980s in support of the MPLA government could be described as mercenaries; they were volunteers and much of the cost of the operation was paid for by the USSR rather than Cuba. Britain has positively encouraged former regular army officers to serve as military advisers in such places as Oman or the Gulf Emirates. Former Royal Marines turned up in the low-intensity civil war, waged for several years in Suriname, leading the insurgent forces of Ronny Brunswick against the government of President Buterse. The brutal war that destroyed Yugoslavia between 1991 and 1995 saw the emergence of a new generation of mercenaries and in its aftermath Serbs and Croats appeared in Zaire in 1997 supposedly in support of Mobutu's crumbling empire though when it came to fighting they retreated ingloriously instead.

Though exceptions may be found, the general behaviour of western mercenaries operating during the last 40 years of the twentieth century in what until recently was described as the Third World has been abysmal: brutal, cruel, racist and, more often than not, simply ineffective. The great majority of the mercenaries who feature in this book came from Europe or North America and on the whole they have done far more damage to the reputations of their own countries than they have succeeded in solving the military problems of the countries in which they operated.

1 The Congo 1960–1965

The Congo Crisis which erupted in July 1960, immediately after Belgium had reluctantly conceded independence to its colony of the Belgian Congo, produced the first major upheaval with international dimensions in post-colonial black Africa. The Congo was ill-prepared for independence and the five years which followed witnessed a United Nations intervention that, among other results before it came to an end, saw the death of the Secretary-General, Dag Hammarskjöld; a confrontation between the two Cold War superpowers with the United States and the Soviet Union inevitably backing different sides in the Congo power struggles; an attempted secession by mineral-rich Katanga heavily supported by Belgium and various western (especially British) financial interests; and a separate civil war known as the Simba revolt. Into this complex tangle of rival interests and ideologies appeared a relatively large number of western mercenaries whose activities left behind an indelible impression of greed, brutality and racist viciousness that made their name anathema in Africa and has coloured every perception of mercenaries operating in the Third World from that time until the present.

Although the Congo's para-military *Force Publique* mutinied within days of independence, it was the attempted secession of the mineral-rich province of Katanga under its pro-western leader, Moise Tshombe, that represented the heart of the crisis which followed. Secessionist Katanga existed from July 1960 until the spring of 1963 and throughout this time Tshombe was in the market for arms and mercenaries to prop up his regime. Much of his secessionist war was financed by the lobby of the *Union Miniere du-haut Katanga*, the Belgian mining conglomerate that exercised a financial stranglehold over the Congo. Katanga's gendarmerie was to be reinforced over the secession period with the injection of white mercenaries; at first they were only used to strengthen the local gendarmerie but later they were organized into their own small mercenary battalions which were designated 1, 2, 3, 4, 5 and 6 Commandos. The number of mercenaries employed during the Katanga secession averaged 400 although later, when mercenaries were employed by the central government to fight the Simba revolt, their numbers rose to 1500. The mercenaries were drawn from a range of backgrounds: these included British soldiers from the old British-Indian Army, combat experienced French from

Algeria, WWII RAF pilots from Rhodesia and South Africa and Belgian paratroopers.[1] Some of these mercenaries attempted to maintain a certain *esprit de corps* and claimed that they acted from idealistic motives; others were of a different stamp including drug addicts, adventurers, racists, the bored and the rootless, psychopaths and killers. Many signed on for excitement and danger in reaction to a humdrum life following WWII. In the Congo and later the majority of these mercenaries consisted of British, Dutch, Belgian, Polish, Czech, Egyptian, German, South African, Rhodesian, Greek, Swiss, Algerian (former italics), Portuguese. Whatever their backgrounds and however they justified their arrival in the Congo, they signed on for money. A raw recruit was offered US$500 a month as well as incentive pay for dangerous assignments; they were insured for US$20,000 and were also attracted by the possibilities of loot. An officer with combat experience could earn as much as US$2,800 a month as well as any loot he could lay his hands on. Pilots were the most valued mercenaries and could command US$1,000 a flying mission.[2] The Congo represented the first occasion since the end of WWII that mercenaries came to be employed as fighting units and as whites fighting in a black country they provided a conspicuous and explosive combination in what was becoming an increasingly race conscious world.

Belgium, a reluctant decolonizer with huge financial stakes in Katanga, played a significant role introducing mercenaries to the Congo. Following the revolt of the *Force Publique* the Belgian government built up a Katanga base from which to challenge the Congolese Central Government. At independence there were about 100 Belgian officers with the *Force Publique*; by December 1960 there were some 500 'volunteers' as well as large-scale military aid in the form of arms and equipment supplied to the Katanga leader, Moise Tshombe. As early as October 1960 the United Nations forces in the Congo had stopped two military incursions from Katanga into Kasai Province; these were led by European officers supported by Belgian arms and on one occasion supplied by helicopters.[3] As the confusion in the Congo escalated with the UN forces trying to maintain order, the Belgians pursuing their own pro-Katanga agenda, and mounting chaos in much of the rest of the huge country, the opening for mercenary activity became steadily more apparent. On 7 February 1961, South African technicians and pilots were being recruited to serve in the Katanga Air Force. On 10 April 1961, UN Ethiopian troops captured and disarmed 32 Katanga white mercenaries in the north Katanga town of Kabalo.

The UN forces subsequently seized a charter aircraft bringing in seven tons of arms and ammunition to Kabalo. The German crew of the plane were not detained as they claimed to be unaware of the nature of the cargo they were carrying until they were airborne! Despite demands by 'President' Tshombe for the return of the plane, UN Indian troops continued to hold it as well as the arms it had carried at a base in West Katanga. A conference of Congolese leaders authorized President Joseph Kasavubu to take 'immediate necessary measures to rid Katanga of occupation by mercenaries and armies' which meant all units not recognizing the authority of the Commander-in-Chief of the National Army, General Joseph Mobutu.[4] The Central Government then requested UN help to disarm Tshombe's gendarmerie and to get rid of foreign soldiers and advisers in Katanga. The damage done was already of major proportions:

> Politically Tshombe has done immense harm by bolstering up an anti-Congolese State by European army officers and advisers. Whether or not he is a Belgian puppet he has behaved like one, and relations between Black and White in Africa are so delicate that any suspicion of European domination in a new form serves only to prevent true cooperation between the races coming about.[5]

An agreement was reached at Leopoldville (later Kinshasa) on 7 June 1961, whereby French-speaking officers of the UN command would take control of the Katanga Army of 7,000 men and replace the 300 to 350 Belgian, French and Polish officers then running it. This was to be done under a UN Security-Council resolution of 21 February 1961, and with the approval of the Central Congolese Government. The Katanga Minister, Munongo, who negotiated the agreement with General McKeown of the United Nations force, also agreed to dispense with the 100-strong corps of mercenaries then still in Katanga. The agreement was not implemented. In August 1961 UN forces operating in Katanga moved to expel all foreign military personnel. Colonel Bjorn Egge, the Norwegian officer in charge, said that about 100 Belgian, French and British officers had been rounded up out of 500.[6] Then, over 24 hours, a majority of the estimated 512 British and other foreign officers serving with the Katanga gendarmerie were rounded up by UN forces, leaving the 12,000 strong gendarmerie in a chaotic condition with only 100 partly trained Katangan officers.[7] At the end of September the United Nations gave President Tshombe 'a matter of days' to expel those white mercenaries still serving with the Katanga forces. Tshombe however continued to defy the United Nations.

On 5 November 1961, Katanga parachute commandos led by European officers repulsed Central Government forces. As a result of this and other mercenary activity a United Nations Security Council resolution on the Congo of November 24, 1961, included the following clause (d)

> to secure the immediate withdrawal and evacuation from the Congo of all foreign military, para-military, and advisory personnel not under the United Nations command, and all mercenaries.

The resolution further stated that the Security Council

> Authorizes the Secretary-General to take vigorous action, including the use of requisite measure of force, if necessary, for the immediate apprehension, detention pending legal action, and/or deportation of all foreign military and para-military personnel and political advisers not under United Nations command and mercenaries, as laid down in the Security Council resolution of February 21, 1961.

and

> Further requests the Secretary-General to take all necessary measures to prevent the entry or return of such elements under whatever guise, and also of arms, equipment or other material in support of such activities.

The United Nations went on to ask that all states should refrain from either supplying arms or allowing their nationals to do so or allowing such people or equipment passage across their territories. During all the complex manoeuvres in the Congo the mercenary factor – whether in the form of individuals or groups who were hired directly as mercenaries or the more formal supply by governments of advisers and arms – always had to be taken into account by the United Nations as one of the principal problems with which it had to deal.

The British Labour MP, Philip Noel-Baker, calculated that Union Miniere and the British company Tanganyika Concessions (TANKS) had together paid during 1960–61 some £15m to the Katanga government. He asked:

> If Mr Tshombe had not been paid this money, could he have paid his white mercenaries, his Katangese gendarmerie, and the foreign arms firms who have supplied him with aircraft, weapons and ammunition. Could he have started, or continued, the movement

which has so greatly increased the cost of the United Nations operation?[8]

He suggested that Britain had diverted money that ought to have gone to the Congo central government to Tshombe in order to help his secession. On 24 January 1962, Tshombe gave another of his assurances to the United Nations: that French mercenaries had been paid off.

There was much discussion of the role of mercenaries at the time. In April 1962 a special correspondent for the *Observer* described *Mission Marissal* (MM), a Belgian organization that recruited mercenaries for Katanga. Colonel Adelin Marissal had been a wartime Belgian hero.

> Following the departure of Belgian troops and many Belgian technical personnel in 1960, Mr Tshombe felt a vacuum, particularly a military vacuum, and asked Marissal, who had strong connexions with Katanga, to assist in filling it. According to the M. M. they accomplished three things. They recruited about half the mercenaries who fought in Katanga beginning in September 1960. The last mercenary of those known by the M. M. did not leave Katanga until February 1962. They brought 40 Katanga soldiers to Belgium, where they gave them 'moral and physical training'... They acted as unofficial advisers to Mr Tshombe and two of their members were in Brazzaville, across the river from Leopoldville, during the recent Tshombe-Adoula talks. The M. M. attempted to make clear to me what they were not. They were not, they said, connected with the Belgian Government, or in the employ of Union Miniere. Neither were they being paid by the Katanga Government – work was voluntary. Their members lived in Belgium and had no large financial holdings in Katanga. They were neither fascist nor right-wing, nor anything particular politically. The M. M. describe their motivation as ideological and idealistic. They believe devoutly that by opposing the U.N. they are fighting communism...

Certainly, the anti-communist motive is the only consistent ideological one that was advanced periodically by mercenaries, some of whom, for example, argued that they would take on any job except fighting, for the communists although at that time it was clear that the communists would not employ Western mercenaries anyway. To continue:

> According to the M.M. there were, all told, 560 European mercenaries. They came principally from Belgium, but there were also French, Southern Rhodesians, English and South Africans. (The

South Africans were ultimately asked to leave because of their anti-black feelings.) The M.M. recruited about 100 Belgian mercenaries and also had an office in Paris to recruit French irregulars. They went to Katanga in small groups by regular commercial planes.

I asked them why they had wanted to fight, and they gave two reasons. One was that they wanted adventure. The other was the ideological reason – anti-communism, pro-Tshombeism etc. ...All rejected the suggestion that they had fought for money... After weeks in the bush, they said, 'We looked so terrible that we began calling ourselves *les affreux* – the horribles...

This title *les affreux* stuck to the mercenaries though with a different connotation than that used by the *Observer* correspondent's mercenary informant.

The M.M. claim that the forces opposing the U.N. in December consisted of 200 loyal Katanga soldiers, 45 mercenaries, and some civilian snipers who seemed to have been disliked by the mercenaries almost as much as by the U.N.

The versions of the U.N. and the mercenaries about what happened in the September and December fighting are radically different, and one is forced to accept that of the U.N. as a broader picture. According to the mercenaries their small band held off a U.N. force of 4,000–8,000 men by being better, braver soldiers and by employing a sort of *Beau Geste* tactic – that is, by constantly moving mortars around to create the impression that they were a much stronger force than they actually were. What may be important about the M.M.'s view of the fighting is their faith in the expertise of the mercenaries and in their clear superiority over the U.N. It follows from the M.M.'s thinking that if 45 *affreux* could stand off 8,000 U.N. soldiers, then a larger force of mercenaries could drive the U.N. out of Katanga...

The M.M. say they do not stand for a separate Katanga but for a federation, and they mention Switzerland as a model. They think the country should have one customs, one foreign affairs head and, eventually, one army. But they want to reserve strong local rights, and would not recommend that the Katanga army be disbanded or merged with that of the Central Government until it becomes clear that Katanga will not be put in the hands of a Central Government who, in the M.M.'s view, are at best inept, and at worst, headed towards communism and barbarism.

The Congo 1960–1965 7

This, stated as objectively as possible, is the M.M.'s view, and one must assume that it is not too different from the position Mr Tshombe took at Leopoldville. They seemed certain that Mr Tshombe would succeed in getting out, because, having no faith in the U.N. guarantees, they had insisted that Mr Tshombe get guarantees of safety from the Americans and British in writing. The M.M. say that Mr Tshombe got those guarantees. The M.M. did not say that they would recruit more mercenaries to go to Katanga should a third war break out – a war, which in their view, would be started by the U.N. They did say, however, that there were at least 2,000 mercenaries who would 'be ready to fight'.[9]

This long quote provides one of the rare instances when mercenaries, despite their claim that they had no particular political motivation, advanced a political programme to justify their activities. It is also one of the few occasions when a spokesman for mercenaries attempts to persuade a leading western newspaper, the London *Observer*, that they were highly ideologically motivated. Over succeeding years the kind of arguments advanced above either do not recur or are only briefly advanced in bowdlerized versions.

The United Nations chief representative in the Congo, Robert Gardiner, said the United Nations had a complete file with names and addresses and photographs of mercenaries who had arrived in Katanga. President Tshombe, however, said that reports of mercenaries returning to join the Katanga forces were similar to 'the story of the sea serpents or the abominable snowman'. In his report to the UN Secretary-General Robert Gardiner pointed out that the build-up of the Katangese armed forces was contrary to the Kitona Declaration of 21 December 1961, and the specific pledge to eliminate mercenaries from Katanga. He reported that the United Nations possessed documentary evidence of the presence of at least 115 mercenaries in Katanga during the period from the beginning of 1962 to September of that year, and additional evidence pointing to a total figure of between 300 and 500 mercenaries. On the significant build-up in air power of the Katanga gendarmerie, Gardiner reported that information on the arrival of new aircraft in Katanga had been confirmed by aerial photography which had also revealed the extension and construction of airstrips and runways.

As the Congo crisis deepened at the end of 1962 with the position of breakaway Katanga still unresolved it became clear that the United Nations was finally preparing to use force. Writing on 17 November in the *Guardian*[10] Patrick Keatley said that Katanga with a population of only 1.5 million was supporting an army of 40,000 men and a military budget above £20m while the number of mercenaries had risen to 1500, three times the numbers which had taken part in the battles of 1961. The United Nations finally moved its forces into Katanga at the end of December 1962. Commenting upon the UN action a *Times* editorial[11] said that although Tshombe had not called off his threat of a scorched earth policy and guerrilla warfare:

> But his troops and white mercenaries have not shown much stomach for the war. If they do fight on, and do destroy installations, then, in the long-term interests of the Katanga people and the Congo as a whole, the U.N. will step by step be drawn into the reduction and pacification of the province, or at least of its key areas. This was always the predicted outcome of a 'third round' fought to a finish.

Tshombe fled to Spain following the UN occupation of Katanga at the beginning of 1963 though his political career in the Congo was far from over. He was to be recalled under obscure circumstances by President Kasavubu in 1964 to be prime minister of the Congo and take control of the war against the Simbas. In March 1964 reports reached the United Nations that 400 former members of the Katanga gendarmerie, employed by the mining companies at Kolwezi and Jadotville, had crossed into Angola 'in response to a mobilization order'. They were under the orders of former active mercenaries and were training near Teixeira de Sousa with mercenaries recently recruited from Europe. According to the *Financial Times*[12]

> There is now little doubt that Mr Tshombe's mercenaries are training rebel Katangese forces somewhere in Angola or Northern Rhodesia, and that he may be preparing to return by force if the Central Government cannot exert its authority in Katanga after the withdrawal of the U.N. troops.

The UN Secretary-General quoted reports that mercenaries had been recruited in Europe on behalf of Tshombe and instructed to proceed to Vila Luso in Angola where a mercenary camp had been established. Tshombe said the report was 'absurd' and 'incorrect' but General Mobutu said the massed forces in Angola were 'the greatest external danger facing my country'.[13]

The situation had changed radically by mid-1964 as the Simba revolt in the eastern part of the country led to violent fighting that threatened the collapse of the government. By July 1964 when about a fifth of the country was in rebel hands President Kasavubu invited Tshombe to return to become prime minister, in place of Cyrile Adoula, to take control of the war against the Simba rebels. Tshombe did so and at once raised a new force of European mercenaries; he possessed the necessary contacts and there were plenty of willing mercenaries waiting for work. In the meantime the 30,000 strong Congolese army had virtually disintegrated and was reduced to 5,000 effective troops. Both the United States and Belgium committed their support to the new Tshombe government not least because it was reported that China, operating from its embassy in Burundi, was supporting the Simba revolt. The Chinese General Kin Me, a guerrilla specialist, was said to be responsible for the tactics and strategy that had produced sweeping victories for the rebels in eastern Congo. This new development meant that the Central Congolese Government in its turn had begun to recruit white mercenaries in big cities in southern Africa; these new recruits were to form a 'shock brigade' to strengthen the Congolese army against the rebels. Large numbers of would-be mercenaries responded to this appeal in both South Africa and Southern Rhodesia and the South African government, in response to a Congolese request for non-military aid, lifted its ban on South Africans enlisting as mercenaries. Recruiting got under way in Johannesburg; in Salisbury (Harare) the *Rhodesia Herald* offered 'more than £100 a month to young men seeking something different in the way of employment'.

According to his Belgian military adviser, Colonel van der Walle, Tshombe intended to create five or six columns, each of 300 Congolese soldiers with white officers, plus a spearhead group of 50 whites. They would be used to recapture rebel-held towns.[14] However, these reports were denied by a Congolese Government spokesman. M. Emmanuel Msinda said: 'We know nothing about a special force. There is no truth to this story. We do not need foreign mercenaries. Our own army can do the job'.[15] The fighting between government forces and the rebels was on a substantial scale over the period September to November 1964 and by the latter month there were between 400 and 500 mercenaries in the Congo. Some were reported to be training at the Kamina base in Katanga although the majority of them were taking part in military operations in eastern and northern Congo. Although, at this time, most of the mercenaries came from South Africa and Southern Rhodesia, they also included British, French, German, Greek, Italian and Belgian mercenaries.[16]

The mercenaries played their most effective role in the two months of October and November 1964 when the Simba rebellion was effectively crushed. On 25 October Congo Government forces reinforced by white mercenaries recaptured from the rebels the important road and river junction of Boende in north-west Congo. On 5 November the Congolese army, led by 300 white mercenaries, captured Kindu which acts as the gateway to Stanleyville (Kisangani) 250 miles further north and was then the provisional capital of the rebel People's Republic. There was little resistance in the town and 84 Belgians and 140 Greek, Pakistani and Indian merchants were found to be unharmed. Stanleyville, the last main stronghold of the People's Republic of the Congo fell to the Congolese National Army (ANC) on 24 November. However, before the Congolese army arrived, a dawn attack was launched by Belgian paratroopers which broke the rebel resistance. Some of the 1,200 white hostages then held by the rebels had been shot in Lumumba Square before the Congolese army arrived though most of these 1,200 Europeans were traced and flown to Leopoldville (Kinshasa). Those killed were from the 250 Belgians and Americans and both Belgium and the USA defended their intervention on humanitarian grounds – the United States had provided military aircraft to move the Belgian paratroopers. Following the fall of Stanleyville, mercenary forces under the command of the British mercenary, Major Hoare, and the Congolese army, advanced to rescue other Europeans held by the rebels in other towns. By the end of December 1964 an estimated 185 whites had been killed since mid-November.

According to Derek Wilson of the *Sunday Times*, the murdering of white hostages had been overshadowed by the revelation of the systematic extermination over the preceding three months of Congolese Government officers by the rebels. Refugees had given horrific eye-witness accounts of how about 7,000 non-rebels were put to death. There had also been reports of indiscriminate killings by some of the mercenaries; using machine guns and hand grenades they had killed people in nearly every village they passed through on their way to Stanleyville.[17] In the immediate aftermath of this phase of the war, another journalist, Colin Legum wrote:

> A new approach must start with the recognition that there can be no military solution for the Congo's problems. A country the size of all Europe ... cannot be coerced by a Government with limited authority with an administration of the sketchiest kind, and with an army

so deplorable that it can fight only when led by a handful of White mercenaries.[18]

As the rebel-led civil war continued into 1965 mercenaries were still a key factor and whatever the rights and wrongs of the Congo crisis, the presence of white mercenaries, especially those from South Africa, was universally condemned by the rest of Africa. By January 1965 Tshombe's mercenaries were thin on the ground and the rebels invariably recaptured places that had been left to be held by black troops alone. Yet recruitment of mercenaries continued and in Johannesburg it was reported that 300 had been signed up to be trained at Kamina in Katanga for three weeks before replacing other mercenaries in February whose contracts had expired. Unmarried privates were being paid £200 a month, including danger money, as well as amounts up to £7,000 to be paid to relatives of the men who were killed. In addition, about 300 Cuban exiles were reported to have enlisted as mercenaries for service in the Congo at a Congo enlistment centre in Miami.[19]

The revolt was not yet over and during February an ambush of a mixed column of Congolese army forces and mercenaries 150 miles northeast of Stanleyville came as a shock to the government; two mercenaries and eight Congolese soldiers were killed and 10 mercenaries and 25 Congolese soldiers wounded while 15 vehicles were destroyed. This was a substantial setback since the column included 100 French, Belgian and other mercenaries. It was one of the last rebel successes and by March the revolt was beginning to disintegrate. A comment upon the revolt and the role of the mercenaries came from the *Times*[20]:

> The collapse of the rebellion, like its spread, has been surprisingly swift. It grew and melted like a snowball. It was nourished by hatred of an ineffectual Government and its undisciplined soldiery, by withcraft, by drugs, by lure of loot, by shared guilt in murder and mayhem, by its progressive capture of transport and territory until the fleshpots of Leopoldville seemed in its grasp. Mr. Tshombe halted it when he called in his Katanga gendarmes and white volunteers – mercenaries – from South Africa, Rhodesia, Belgium and France to stiffen his demoralised troops.
>
> This case-hardened spear-point of the regular army broke rebel resistance everywhere. Mr. Tshombe's army and air force, with some American airlift, relieved the countryside from the thrall and uncovered the sabotage done by the rebels, of which the extermination of educated Congolese was the worst.

Meanwhile, Colonel Michael Hoare and his mobile fifth commando unit had sealed the borders with Sudan and Uganda behind the rebels and claimed that the people were returning to their villages from the bush while rebels were surrendering in large groups. Writing in the *Observer* Colin Legum said of the mercenaries:

> The Belgians have provided the nucleus for a force of 600 French-speaking mercenaries who are inferior as a fighting force to Colonel Hoare's men, but equal to them as safebreakers and looters, and the Congo Nationalist Army of 38,000 men is a dead loss, except for two battalions which have shown some capacity for fighting[21]

One of the most damning revelations about mercenary behaviour was uncovered in another *Observer* story when a senior mercenary produced a series of photographs showing atrocities committed by his men. The pictures (two were printed by the *Observer*) showed how mercenaries not only shot and hanged their prisoners after torturing them, but used them for target practice and gambled over the number of shots needed to kill one. The officer, who by then had returned to South Africa, said he took the pictures 'for the men to send home to their families'. Then, he claimed, he became so disgusted at the atrocities that he decided to expose them. He said the majority of the mercenaries refused to participate in the grosser cruelties indulged in by the warped minority. But they were powerless, he argued, to prevent 95 per cent of all their prisoners from being killed, often horribly.[22]

On 13 October 1965, President Kasavubu dismissed Tshombe and that represented the end of his influence in the Congo. The President then announced that he intended to dismiss the mercenary force; however, the dismissal of 800 white mercenaries then attached to the Congolese army might allow the rebels to launch new attacks. Instead, a mercenary presence in the Congo was to continue for a further two years. A final confrontation with the mercenaries took place in August 1967 by which time a partially rejuvenated Congolese army was attempting to round them up and expel them from the country. The mercenaries were concentrated round Lake Kivu near the Rwanda border which was closed. They were trying to break out of the encircling Congolese army. The mercenaries led a mixed group that, apart from themselves, consisted of some government units which had mutinied at Bukavu, Kisangani and Kindu the previous July, Katangan gendarmes and 150 European civilians. The government rebels had regrouped in the plantation of Major Jean Schramme near Punia and he was now to feature prominently as the leader of this group.

On 9 August these mercenaries captured Bukavu and then announced that they were ready to negotiate with President Mobutu who by this time had seized power. Major Jean Schramme, the Belgian planter, said his conditions included the liberation of Mr Tshombe and a place for him in the Congo government. Schramme threatened that if Mobutu refused to talk his forces might move into Katanga, a clear threat to renew Katangan secession. He claimed he had attacked Bukavu to enable the white civilians accompanying him to cross into Rwanda. Schramme had acted after the Congo Army HQ had ordered the French mercenary, Colonel Robert Denard, to disarm 10 Commando, the mercenary group under Schramme's command. These two mercenaries – Schramme and Denard – had decided that were Schramme to be disarmed the Congolese army would then feel strong enough to turn on Denard's 6 Commando unit. And so another drama had to be played out between the remaining mercenaries, who saw that their time was running out, and the government forces.

Schramme and his force of mutinous mercenaries were seen as sufficient a threat that Mobutu asked for help from the UN Security Council though this was refused. On the other hand, Mobutu was receiving logistic aid from the United States which adopted him after the fall of Tshombe and Kasavubu and was to support him, more or less, for the next 30 years. In Brussels the Burundi Ambassador asked the Belgian Government to prevent Major Schramme from extending violence to Burundi's soil but Belgium denied any responsibility for Schramme's actions. Western comments upon Schramme were bemused and from being, apparently, a major threat he became a would-be fugitive. Writing in the *Financial Times*, Ian Davidson said:

> Solid information on the events in the Congo is considerably more rare in Brussels than speculation or one-sided propaganda by the Kinshasa government. Yet it seems established that Major Schramme, who, only a fortnight ago threatened to set up a rival Government in the Congo and has never seriously been embarrassed by the efforts of the Congolese Army, is now merely asking for a safe-conduct out of the Congo for himself and the mercenaries, and for a promise of a general amnesty. What is not at all clear is why he has so abruptly back-tracked in the past few days, after having openly allied himself with the rebel 'Government of public safety' set up by Colonel Monga. One theory is that he had been counting on help from outside the Congo, most probably from

Angola. At all events there are reports that a plane from Angola visited Bukavu over the week-end, before the start of the truce.[23]

Perhaps the explanation for the change was that given by John de St Jorre from Bukavu:

> In the normal run of Congo warfare the mercenaries and the Katangese would be more than a match for the numerically stronger Congolese. But morale among these soldiers of fortune has hit an all time low. They have not been paid for three months; they neither trust nor respect their leader, the idealistic but fundamentally weak Major Schramme[24]

Some mercenaries deserted to Rwanda, another brutally murdered an Indian trader. The mercenaries recovered somewhat at the beginning of September when they took the initiative against government forces and some mercenary reinforcements joined Schramme. Then, at the Organization of African Unity (OAU) conference held in Kinshasa, it was agreed that the mercenaries should be given the opportunity to leave the country under the supervision of an international organization, and President Mobutu gave them three days in which to accept an offer of evacuation under the supervision of the International Red Cross. Meanwhile, interviewed by Radio Luxembourg, Major Schramme claimed that his aim in the Congo was stability and pacification and that he and his men were idealists and not interested in money. He said that while Mobutu thought only of his own position Tshombe lived for his people.

On 9 November 1967, the UN Security Council met at the request of the Congo to condemn the actions of mercenaries which had 'caused ruin and devastation' within the country. M. di Lutete for the Congo said the mercenaries had acquired French, Spanish and Swiss arms some of which had been delivered to Angola by Air France. The Portuguese delegate denied that his country was involved with mercenaries and invited the United Nations to appoint an inquiry. Lord Caradon for Britain described the mercenaries as 'the curse of the Congo' and said the Security Council had the clear duty to eliminate the evil that they represented. The US delegate said it was difficult to understand how foreign mercenaries could be in Angola preparing to enter the Congo without the Portuguese authorities' agreement or knowledge.

The International Red Cross, meanwhile, had reached an agreement with the Congo government to fly the 140 mercenaries to Malta and the 950 Katangese and their dependents – 650 women and children – to Zambia where they could either settle or return to the Congo under amnesty. Colonel Schramme then raised objections to the Red Cross plan and it was suspected that he was deliberately delaying in the hope of receiving aid from Colonel Denard who was then in Angola with his own mercenary force. At this point the Congolese Army intensified its attack and refused the IRC appeal for a ceasefire. It captured Bukavu on 4 November and the mercenaries then fled to Rwanda. In Geneva the IRC said that about 130 white mercenaries and 900 dissident Katangese gendarmes laid down their arms when they crossed into Rwanda. About 100 had been wounded, some seriously.

In the south the group of mercenaries under the command of Bob Denard crossed into Katanaga from Angola although Portugal denied this. Some of the mercenaries with Schramme then left him to join Denard but within a few days the latter had withdrawn from Katanga and returned to Angola. On 6 November Justin Bomboko, the Congolese Foreign Minister, said that the evacuation of European mercenaries was no longer desired. The situation had changed after the fall of Bukavu and the fresh mercenary incursion into Katanga. In Rwanda President Kayibanda was brought under strong pressure by Belgium and other western governments to allow the evacuation of the mercenaries who had fled to his country. On 7 November President Mobutu demanded their extradition to the Congo. Zambia withdrew its offer to help airlift Colonel Schramme's mercenaries and rebel gendarmes to safety. International sympathy for Schramme, posing as an idealist, had added to the complications of the situation in eastern Congo while Mobutu's position had been greatly strengthened with the fall of Bukavu.

In the end Schramme agreed to a plan advanced by Diallo Telli, the Secretary-General of the OAU. The White mercenaries and the Katanganese gendarmes were asked to sign a guarantee: 'I solemnly undertake towards the O.A.U. and every individual state in Africa to cease definitely all activities as a mercenary and never to return to Africa.' The Katanganese gendarmes were to be granted an amnesty if they returned to the Congo. The International Red Cross then withdrew from the operation while the OAU stated that before the mercenaries were allowed to depart their countries should compensate the Congo for the damage they had caused.

The evacuation of the mercenaries to Europe ended with a series of accusations and evasions though it was apparent – as it had been throughout the Congo story – that powerful interests in Europe, including governments, had been behind the mercenary interventions. The final push into Katanga by Denard and his mercenaries was assumed to have been a diversion to assist Schramme when he was trapped in Bukavu:

> It is not clear who is financing the Denard force. The strongest indications from usually reliable sources in Europe and Africa agree that there is some form of French involvement with the obvious cooperation of the Portuguese who are not stopping Denard from using his Angolan base.[25]

The Belgian government announced that mercenaries who were Belgian citizens would lose their passports if they returned to Belgium. The French Foreign Minister, Couve de Murville, denied that his government had any responsibility for mercenaries who, like Denard, were French citizens. However, a spokesman for the Congo Foreign Ministry said French consular officials had given Denard protection and that by dissociating itself from the mercenaries the French government was trying to get out of an awkward situation. Yet Denard's dealings with the French Ambassador in Kinshasa were known to everyone.[26] When eventually Schramme appeared in a Belgian court he was treated with great leniency and was seen as a hero of the right.

The Congo crisis produced high emotions in Africa and Europe. In Africa (1960 was the so-called *annus mirabilis* of the continent when 17 former colonies became independent) the activities of the mercenaries, inevitably, were seen as a form of neo-colonialism while their brutality served only to reinforce anti-white and anti-imperialist views. Mercenary conduct in the Congo did great damage to the White image in Africa which, in any case, was coming under increasingly close and adverse scrutiny as a result of the race policies being pursued in the southern part of the continent. Moreover, direct and indirect evidence of western government support for the mercenaries ensured that they were regarded as an arm of western policy and not simply as maverick individuals who could not be controlled. The image of *les affreux* coloured the African response to mercenaries for years to come.

In Europe the Congo crisis had more complex repercussions. The political right – those who opposed African independence (or opposed it at that time) and racists whose starting point was an automatic assumption of white racial superiority – saw the mercenaries as heroes and this attitude was greatly reinforced when the lives of whites in the

Congo were at risk. Many press articles at the time talked of a return to barbarism and the word Congo became synonymous with the belief among this group that Western control was needed in Africa for a long time to come. Such attitudes also greatly reinforced support for white minority rule in the south of the continent and the continuation of apartheid in South Africa. On the other hand, the brutality, overt racism and greed of the mercenaries awoke a sense of shame in liberal opinion and contrasts were made between the small number of white casualties and the relatively huge number of black ones during the five years of Congo strife. Final estimates of casualties in the Congo suggested that a total of only 175 Europeans had been killed (though media publicity at the time suggested much higher figures) and 20,000 Congolese. What also emerged clearly was the fact that none of the principal European countries involved – Belgium, France, Britain and Portugal – could escape responsibility for the actions of the mercenaries. Their governments knew what was happening, they sometimes gave overt support and too often turned a blind eye to what they could have prevented. Finally, the experience of the United Nations in the Congo must have significantly reinforced the opposition of the world organization to any form of mercenary activity though it was not until 1989 that the *International Convention against the Recruitment, Use, Financing and Training of Mercenaries* was to be adopted without a vote.

2 The Nigerian Civil War

The Nigerian Civil War, unlike the Congo crisis, represented a setpiece confrontation between two sides both of which, though with varying degrees of reluctance, hired mercenaries. The war lasted for 30 months from the declaration of an independent Biafra at the end of May 1967 until its final defeat by the forces of Federal Nigeria in January 1970. It was the first occasion since the Carlist wars in Spain when mercenaries fought one another from opposite sides.[1] When the civil war began Africa had set its face against mercenaries whose activities in the Congo had been roundly condemned with Zambia's President Kaunda, for example, describing them as 'human vermin'. It was, therefore, a political risk that might prove counter- productive to enlist mercenaries at all. Once the civil war was underway the Federal Military Government in Lagos wanted to demonstrate its capacity to deal with the Biafran secession without calling in outside help; to use mercenaries would undermine this position. Biafra, on the other hand, would promote through its propaganda the picture of an embattled 'underdog' fighting for its existence and, as such, would justify turning outside for assistance, including the enlistment of mercenaries. In the event both sides employed mercenaries though in each case exercising far greater control over their activities than had been possible in the Congo.

In July 1967 the Federal Government hired British, Rhodesian and South African pilots at a reported fee of US$2,800 a month tax free to be paid into numbered Swiss bank accounts. Their recruitment was arranged by the British mercenary, John Peters, who obtained a lucrative contract from the Federal Government to supply pilots; Peters, who did not fly himself, received a big commission for each recruit. Following Britain's refusal to supply the Federal side with war planes Soviet and Czech planes were purchased although Russia would not permit its pilots to fly these in the war with the result that Czech and Egyptian mercenary pilots were hired to do so. Bad relations ensued more or less at once between these Czech and Egyptian mercenaries and also between them and the English-speaking mercenaries.[2] The English-speakers were dubbed the 'whiskey pilots' on account of their drinking habits; one of their number, Boozy Bonzo from South Africa, a former RAF pilot, was reputed to consume a bottle a flight. The Federal Government employed between 12 and 20 mercenary pilots throughout the war (there was a rapid turnover) and in the end used them to fly the Russian MiG 15s since the Egyptian pilots proved totally inadequate. Biafra first hired 83 French mercenaries under Colonel Roger Faulqes in November 1967; their initial task was to train Biafran troops. Faulqes was a former Foreign Legionary with fighting experience from WWII, Indo-China and Algeria (where he had opposed de Gaulle's policy); then he had fought as a mercenary in both Yemen and Katanga before arriving in Nigeria. Faulqes was joined by Colonel Bob Denard with a further 200 mercenaries; Denard arrived in Biafra fresh from his last escapade in Angola and Katanga where he had been until the final retreat of the mercenaries into Rwanda in November 1967. Later, a third group of French mercenaries under Michel Declary joined Faulqes and Denard. The decision to recruit French mercenaries apparently was made only after Colonel Michael Hoare had declined a Biafran offer (he wanted too much money). Originally, Hoare had been contacted in South Africa by Pierre Lorez who was the Biafran leader, Colonel Chukwuemeka Ojukwu's arms buyer in Lisbon. On 25 October 1967, after a meeting with Lorez in Lisbon, Hoare flew to Biafra for a meeting with Ojukwu who offered him a personal fee of £30,000 to lead a shock corps of 100 men. It was tentatively suggested that Hoare should take charge of one mercenary unit while Denard's group, on its arrival from Angola, would assume the defence of Port Harcourt, and a third group of mercenaries under the Frenchman Declary (also an old Congo hand) would be in charge of Ojukwu's personal safety. These three units were to be under the overall command of the Portuguese Lorez. At this point in the recruiting saga, John Peters, the British ex-mercenary from the Congo then acting as a military adviser to the Federal Government, contacted Hoare who went to Lagos where, for whatever reasons, he was persuaded to keep out of the Nigerian war. It was suggested that English-speaking mercenaries had scruples about fighting against one another although this did not apply to English and French mercenaries![3]

Many of the French mercenaries were later to quit when they found that the equipment needed for training the Biafrans was not forthcoming so that by the summer of 1968 the considerable French contingent had been reduced to five for by then it was clear to the mercenaries (if not to the Biafrans) that their secession was doomed.[4] In December 1967 French mercenaries had led a Biafran force in a costly and unsuccessful attempt to capture the Federal toehold at Calabar which had been gained by the redoubtable Federal soldier,

Brigadier Benjamin Adekunle (the Black Scorpion), who went on to capture Port Harcourt in May 1968. In any case, it became plain during 1968 that Biafra's most compelling need was for pilots to ferry in supplies to its one remaining airstrip at Ulli. As the Federal net closed ever tighter round Biafra the air lifeline to Ulli became the sole means of maintaining the war against the Federal government. Some of the supplies for Biafra were in the form of humanitarian aid which was provided by a number of non-government organizations (NGOs) such as Caritas, the World Council of Churches or the International Red Cross; other military supplies were flown in by mercenaries.

A typical blockade runner was Captain Henry Warton who operated as the North American Aircraft Trading Company at a rate of US$12,000 a flight or six flights for $60,000 and he transported food, medical supplies and arms. He made large profits. A rival American was Captain Lucien Pickett of USAIR and these two competed for contracts from the European relief organizations. Pickett's number two was the notorious Nazi war hero, Colonel Otto Skorzeny, who had liberated Mussolini when he was initially captured by the allies. Such pilots might be classified as the more daring and skillful adventure addicts among the mercenaries though many other mercenaries had similar backgrounds. When in October 1967 the Federal air defences shot down a plane over Lagos which at only 300 feet appeared to be making a run on the supreme military headquarters the dead crew consisted of four mercenaries and four Biafrans and, it was claimed, this represented a loss for the Biafran leader Ojukwu of 20 per cent of his mercenary pilots. They were drunk.

In December 1967 the Federal Government in Lagos claimed that 150 South African mercenaries had been enlisted by Biafra which, it said, had also acquired three French helicopters with one German, one Canadian and one French pilot. On 23 December four white mercenaries were killed by Federal troops in South-East Nigeria. General Yakubu Gowon, the Federal head of state, also accused Portugal of supplying Biafra with arms.[5] At this time Biafra was believed to have 12 T6 planes carrying two bombs each, two B26 bombers from Portugal and eight French helicopters taken from commercial firms in Biafra and then armed with 20mm cannon and rockets. In addition, Biafra had installed six radar-controlled Bofors anti-aircraft guns (costing £80,000 each) and had also acquired ground-to-air heat-seeking missiles. It was not known where Biafra was obtaining its ready money for such arms: 'But with such rich pickings, the mercenaries promised to have a field day. When Ojukwu met Hoare he talked in terms of 1,000 mercenaries.'[6]

Prior to the real military onslaught on Biafra by Federal forces General Gowon issued a 'Code of Conduct' to his troops in which it was stressed that the Ibo people were not the enemies. At the same time it was laid down that mercenaries 'will not be spared: they are the worst enemies'. During the early stages of the war in 1967 propaganda from both sides referred to the use of mercenaries and it was assumed, whatever principles were laid down, that mercenaries were likely to be employed and to the end of the war there were to be stories of mercenary involvement on both sides that often exceeded the reality. The stated reluctance to employ mercenaries despite the fact that both sides did so was in part because senior Nigerian officers on either side in the civil war had formerly served with the United Nations in the Congo and come up against mercenaries there. Any reference to mercenaries made headlines since Africa – and the Western media – were both still very much influenced by the stories of mercenary behaviour resulting from the Congo crisis. Furthermore, the special OAU meeting convened in Kinshasa, Congo, during September 1967 which was concerned with the ongoing activities of mercenaries in that country, at that time dominated by the behaviour of 'Black Jack Schramme' who with his mercenaries and mutinous Katanga gendarmes was then holding out in Bukavu, also discussed the question of mercenaries in Nigeria.

When mercenaries were engaged the assumption was that they possessed military skills that the Federal or Biafran armies lacked; in the end this special advantage came down to pilots. Three kinds of mercenary were employed in the civil war: pilots on the Federal side; pilots and soldiers in Biafra; and relief pilots employed by the humanitarian organizations assisting Biafra. Combat mercenaries charged huge fees but gave poor returns and were rarely worth the money they were paid. Furthermore, the much vaunted reputation of the mercenaries suffered a significant decline during the course of the war which destroyed any idea of their invincibility as special forces. It became clear that the imported white soldier – man for man – was no better than the black soldier and, furthermore, he wanted maximum pay and minimum risks for his services. Apart from pilots and despite high publicity the white mercenaries played a relatively minor role in the civil war.

Most of the leading mercenaries engaged on either side knew one another and clearly feared that their antagonistic activities might bring strife to the mercenary brotherhood which provided all of them a living. They made determined efforts, therefore, to ensure that the mercenaries on one side would not be responsible for killing mercenaries on the other side. Thus, for example, the British mercenary Colonel John Peters who had made his name in the Congo and was employed as a military adviser by the Federal Government telephoned another English mercenary, Alistair Wicks, on the Biafran side, to warn him: 'Don't recruit for Biafra. I don't want my boys fighting yours'. On the other hand, national antagonisms among the mercenaries meant quite different attitudes emerged. During the civil war Britain and British mercenaries supported the Federal side while France and French mercenaries supported Biafra. A Belgian mercenary, Marc Goosens, who died near Onitsha, said before his death: 'One good thing about this war is that we're fighting the English on the other side.'[7]

Control of mercenary activity was much more closely exercised by the Nigerians than it had been in the Congo and famous mercenaries who had made their name in the Congo or Yemen – Roger Faulques, 'Mad' Mike Hoare, Bob Denard and John Peters – found themselves far more circumscribed as to what they were allowed to do as both the Federal and the Biafran governments maintained careful supervision over their mercenaries and what they permitted them to do. At the same time the two sides made extraordinary propaganda attacks upon each other for the degree to which they supposedly depended upon mercenaries.

The story of the Ulli airstrip[8] which became the lifeline for beleaguered Biafra over the last eighteen months of the war illustrates both the capacity and the unreliability of mercenaries. A principal task for the mercenary pilots employed by the Federal Government was to force the closure of Ulli airport which became the sole port of entry for arms and ammunition for Biafra (as well as humanitarian supplies) following the fall of Port Harcourt in May 1968. Yet it was not knocked out by the Federal air force and survived for the final eighteen months of the war, being much used throughout this time and indeed becoming famous in the various accounts of the war. As de St Jorre says: 'Without Ulli Biafra would have collapsed in a matter of weeks, perhaps days.'[9] The problem was that Ulli presented a dilemma for the mercenaries who at the time were the only pilots with the skills to destroy the runway. If they destroyed it as they undoubtedly could have done the war would have been brought to an end and with it their jobs. Moreover, to close it and keep it closed meant killing mercenaries on the other side. As a result, since the mercenaries did not wish to forego their lucrative jobs or kill others of the brotherhood, they determined that Ulli should not be closed by their efforts and a 'pact' was entered upon by the two sides. This represented a huge benefit to Biafra which was enabled to hold out for at least a year longer than otherwise would have been the case. Count von Rosen, the Swedish mercenary who flew in relief supplies to Ulli for the churches, said: 'They (bomber pilots) told us on the radio once that they were bombing Ulli for the money and they wouldn't shoot up another mercenary in the air.' Thus the Federal mercenary pilots were prepared to bomb Ulli to show they were trying but they made certain that their actions were not sufficiently effective to scare away the relief pilots. The general mercenary rule was that 'dog doesn't eat dog' but there was an exception that nearly destroyed this mercenary pact. A forty year old ex-RAF pilot signed on for the Federal side and went on several missions that made him realize how the other mercenaries were deliberately not hitting the target. Then he flew a mission with an all-Nigerian crew and destroyed several planes on the Ulli runway. Subsequently his brother mercenaries forced him to leave Nigeria so that he could not upset their pact and the Ulli runway could be kept open and the war continue. Otherwise, in the whole course of the war only one Biafran arms freight plane was shot down.

As in the Congo, Western governments either played active roles in support of their mercenaries or were quiescent about their activities. The French government, for example, played an active role in recruiting mercenaries for Biafra. At the beginning of the war Biafra was in two minds about using mercenaries but was persuaded to do so by the French secret service chief, Jacques Foccart. It was Foccart's office which recruited Roger Faulques with the task of providing a ground force for Biafra which he only visited on one occasion. He was paid £100,000 through a Paris Bank to supply 100 men for six months; in fact he only produced 49 men. These were the mercenaries who attempted to dislodge Adekunle from Calabar in December 1967; instead, they were ambushed, five were killed and a number were seriously wounded. It was a disastrous showing for the mercenaries at the beginning of the war and effectively meant the collapse of the Faulques group of mercenaries. By February all but four had left Nigeria: the group was only 49 strong instead of 100 and had contributed six weeks of service rather than the promised six months but they kept all the money advanced to them which they had at most only quarter earned. France which had supported their recruitment, embarrassed, ordered all its nationals to leave Nigeria.

Two of the Faulques group who remained behind were Rolf Steiner, a German, and 'Taffa' Williams, a Welsh South African, and they were joined in mid-1968 by a fresh group of mercenaries from Rhodesia and the Congo. This group which became known as the Steiner group trained Biafrans in guerrilla tactics; the Biafrans had no guerrilla skills and the Steiner effort in this aspect of warfare was probably one of the more effective mercenary contributions to the Biafra war effort. Under Steiner's command the Biafran 4th Commando Brigade which had a strength of 3,000 turned into an elite force. The mercenaries leading it were all treated as officers and paid US$1,000 a month in dollar bills. A second mercenary group consisted of 15 Frenchmen under Maurice Lucien-Brun (alias Paul Leroy in Biafra) who convinced Ojukwu that he should create Vietcong-style units to operate behind the Federal lines. However, unlike Steiner's group, Leroy's proved a costly failure; he quarrelled with senior Biafran officers over supplies and with the Steiner group as well and suddenly withdrew from Biafra, first to Gabon and then back to Europe. Each member of the group had been paid for two months but they had only spent a week in Biafra. In the end Steiner also became a liability, quarrelling with Biafran officers, attempting to operate independently and putting forward increasingly impracticable schemes. Finally, drunk, Steiner went to see Ojukwu and got into a fight with his bodyguards; he and five other mercenaries were hastily expelled from Biafra. Steiner then went to join the rebels in the south of Sudan but was later arrested in Uganda. The rest of the Steiner group led an assault on Onitsha that turned into a disaster which spelt the end to mercenary activity in Biafra (apart from pilots) and at the end of their contract period early in 1969 they too left Biafra.

Other peculiar mercenary figures came and went in the Nigerian war. One of these was a 70-year old black American, Colonel Hubert Fauntleroy Julian, who called himself the 'Black Eagle' from Harlem. He offered his services to the Federal Government in Lagos but was declined. The Swedish pilot, Count von Rosen, who had already spent some time flying supplies into Biafra returned in August 1969 with a new supply of aircraft; these according to the Swedish paper *Aftonbladet* were of Swedish type, manufactured under licence in Germany, armed in France and then flown to Biafra by Count von Rosen and his associates.[10] Alistair Wicks was another contractor who did a deal with Ojukwu and used a small Rhodesian airline to bring in supplies but in the end one of his mercenary pilots took off with US$250,000 and brought the enterprise to an end.

In real terms, whether in fighting or training, Biafra got very little value out of the mercenaries upon whom it spent vast sums of money, the greater part of which was wasted. Moreover, despite continuing support for mercenary activity, especially from France, they did little to retrieve the reputation which they had acquired in the Congo.

3 Southern Africa (1) Rhodesia

The decade of the 1970s witnessed a major change in the position of the white minority governments in Southern Africa. The military coup of April 1974 which brought an end to the long-lived Caetano government in Portugal also signalled the end of the Portuguese African empire. The short-lived Portuguese government of General Antonio Spinola who led the military overthrow of Caetano did not favour rapid decolonization but he was replaced in September 1974 by the more radical General Francisco da Costa Gomes who determined to grant rapid independence to Angola and Mozambique and was prepared to override the wishes of the white settlers in those two colonies in order to do so. Mozambique was to become independent on 25 June 1975, and Angola on 11 November of that year.

Meanwile, by mid-1973, Rhodesians had come to accept the guerrilla war as a permanent part of their lives and while defence expenditure in 1972–73 accounted for 12.6 per cent of the budget, for 1973–74 it had risen to 17.4 per cent and from this time onwards the regime of Ian Smith and the white minority which had declared independence illegally (UDI) in November 1965 became increasingly embattled as more and more of the country came under guerrilla threat. In his 1974 New Year's speech Smith had warned that the guerrilla campaign would get worse and by May of that year the South African *Star* said: 'The options [for Rhodesia] are no longer fully open. Rhodesians must shake themselves out of their dream of perpetual white supremacy.' These developments, and especially independence in Angola and Mozambique, contributed to black unrest in South Africa which helped trigger the June 1976 Soweto uprising; this produced the most serious racial violence in that country since the Union in 1910.

South Africa and Rhodesia had already become recruiting grounds for mercenaries during the 1960s when these had gone to take part in both the Congo crisis of 1960–65 and the Nigerian civil war of 1967–1970. Now, however, South Africa was to be increasingly involved on its own doorstep. The collapse of Portuguese control in Angola and Mozambique had effectively destroyed the white controlled 'cordon' that lay between South Africa and independent black Africa to the north. From 1975 onwards South Africa became overtly involved in

Angola where it intervened on behalf of the forces opposed to the Marxist *Movimento Popular de Libertação de Angola* (MPLA) and also found itself, reluctantly, obliged to continue supporting the embattled government of Ian Smith in Rhodesia although in August it had withdrawn the last of the military forces which had been stationed there for several years. South African mercenaries were now to play an increasing role in both these countries.

By the beginning of 1975 it was clear that the Rhodesian regime needed a fresh injection of military strength in face of the escalating guerrilla threat, especially as a growing number of young white Rhodesians were determined to avoid military service if they could do so. Wider military call-up commitments for whites, Coloured and Asian men were announced in September 1975; earlier the government had cancelled exemption from national service of university entrants and, as an incentive for all the forces, had announced 40 per cent pay rises for combat soldiers of every rank and race. The pressures of the war increased even as such measures were announced. In the circumstances the government sought to bolster its security forces by the recruitment of mercenaries and a substantial number of these were to be found without great difficulty in South Africa and from farther afield. There were reports in June 1975 of American mercenaries fighting in the Rhodesian army against the black guerrillas and a State Department official said there were 'certainly indications' that the description of mercenary recruiting given by Tapson Mawere, the representative of the Zimbabwe African National Union (ZANU) in the United States, was accurate.[1]

As an increasing number of rural districts in Rhodesia became 'no go' areas at night because of guerrilla activities and the war waged against the nationalist guerrillas became ever more savage so the mercenary factor became more important. By 1976 it had become clear that the Rhodesian security forces were not even holding their own against the guerrillas and the underlying political question was what South Africa would do if Rhodesia was in serious danger of collapsing. The South African government refused to make any commitments to Rhodesia though it was clearly deeply concerned about the direction the war was taking. The 'communist' threat was constantly cited by the white minority governments as one of their principal justifications for fighting the liberation movements which were provided with military aid, training and finances by both the Soviet Union and China. It suited South Africa, in particular, to represent itself to the West as a bastion against the spread of communism in southern Africa, and the West, especially Britain and the United States, was ready enough to seize upon the communist threat as an excuse, first for not helping the liberation movements and second for supporting the white minority governments, at the very least by a policy of quiescence. The West preferred white governments in southern Africa since these would preserve and encourage western economic interests while any incoming black government was, at the least, regarded as likely to pose a threat to such interests. On the other hand, because of the changed climate of the time, the West did not wish to appear overtly racist and, as a result, routinely condemned apartheid and other excesses of white minority rule while claiming its inability to do anything to bring such minority governments to an end.

Yet, if Western governments were incapable of using their power to bring pressures to bear upon the white minority regimes in order to force them to change their policies, they were believed by their African critics to be only too ready to turn a blind eye to the activities of their own citizens when these decided to enlist as mercenaries in Rhodesia and Angola. One advertisement for foreign volunteers at this time read: 'Would you like to work in fun? Then come and join the Rhodesian Army'. The influx of volunteers or mercenaries to join the Rhodesian army and the failure of Western governments to do anything to prevent them enlisting created a new problem for Western–African relations. In essence, and this was true of most African perceptions of the Western response to events in Southern Africa, the problem was a racial one: Western governments were not prepared to stop their citizens enlisting as mercenaries on behalf of the white minority regimes, provided they were supposed to be fighting against 'communists' or, in other words, governments (as in Angola) or liberation movements whose long term objectives were thought to be antithetical to Western interests. Had large numbers of East European volunteers turned up to fight for the liberation movements the furore in the Western media would have been indescribable.

One possibility at the time was for South Africa to allow its soldiers to enlist in the Rhodesian army so that they would not appear fighting the guerrillas in South African uniforms. In any case, by mid-1976 there was evidence of substantial numbers of Western 'volunteers' in the Rhodesian army: rates of pay then stood at US$4,000 a year for privates, US$6,400 a year for sergeants and US$7,600 a year for junior officers.[2] The size of the regular Rhodesian army in 1976 was about 6,000 and according to a British deserter from it, Hugh Lynn, there were then some 2,000 British volunteers, many of them former paratroopers, serving with it as well as about 100 Americans who were mostly veterans from Vietnam. Further evidence from other deserters who were interviewd by Botswana Radio suggested that about a third of the regular Rhodesian forces were composed of foreign volunteers. In another report to the *International Herald Tribune*[3] Robin Wright put the number of foreign recruits at 1,000 and these were drawn from Germany, Canada, Greece, Holland, Australia, Portugal, France, New Zealand, Britain and Sweden while there was an American contingent of 400, a figure which was confirmed by a South African reporter, Paul Smurthwaite, who also suggested the overall figure was 1,000 volunteers.[4]

South Africa's prime minister, B. J. Vorster, wanted to bring an end to the war in Rhodesia but was not prepared to exert too much overt pressure upon the Smith government which in racial- power terms was seen in white South Africa as an extension of its own problem. At the same time the continuing war in Rhodesia was bound to influence events in Namibia where the South West Africa People's Organization (SWAPO) had been engaged in guerrilla warfare against the South Africans along the Caprivi Strip since 1966 while independence for Angola now meant that SWAPO could operate from bases in Angola along the length of the Angolan–Namibian border. South Africa saw Angola becoming the base country for SWAPO as newly independent Mozambique had become the base country for the Zimbabwe People's Army (ZIPA). Estimates of South Africans being recruited for service in Rhodesia were unreliable although the Lisbon paper, *Diario de Lisboa* of December 1976, had a story that recruits for the Rhodesian forces were being trained at Iscar in northern Spain near Valladolid; units were being trained there to operate from Rhodesia against Zimbabwe African National Union (ZANU) bases in Mozambique. Other stories of recruitment all indicated that a sizeable component of the Rhodesia army was of mercenary origin.

An important aspect of mercenary recruitment was highlighted by the Tanzanian *Daily News*, which was a government controlled paper, that 1,500 mercenaries had been recruited abroad and that it was unlikely such large numbers could have been enlisted without the prior knowledge of their governments. Radio Moscow regularly referred to Western mercenaries in Rhodesia. On the other hand, Major Nick Lamprecht, the chief army recruiting officer for Rhodesia, denied that foreigners in the Rhodesian forces were mercenaries. He claimed, instead, that their motive for enlisting was 'enthusiasm about fighting communism – they don't want to see a repeat of what happened in Vietnam.'[5]

Ironically, the Major's own son, contradicted his father from South Africa. Having completed his Rhodesian national service he had emigrated to South Africa; he said: 'I think the situation in Rhodesia is getting out of hand' and he argued that constant call-ups, shortages and 'all-out drives to wipe out the terrorist menace' were not fooling the people as to the seriousness of the situation and he concluded: 'It becomes difficult to fight for something you don't think has a hope of succeeding.'[6]

Continuous guerrilla activity had first got underway in the northeast of Rhodesia at the end of 1972; by 1976 the guerrilla influx had become a steady stream and instead of guerrillas entering Rhodesia in small groups of two or three they were coming in large numbers from Mozambique, Botswana and Zambia and whereas the offical estimate for 1975 had been only 50 guerrillas operating in the country, by the end of 1976 the figure was 1,500. Moreover, by this time the conflict was affecting a number of small towns and was moving close to Salisbury while travel was often only safe when in convoy. As the Minister of Defence, Reg Cowper, said: 'Government has decided that the stage has been reached where the needs of the security forces must be paramount.' The shortage of manpower was again emphasized when at the end of January 1977 the regime decided to call up men between the ages of 38 and 50 for military service. In such circumstances Rhodesia was only too ready to recruit and welcome volunteers or mercenaries from outside the country, the 'enthusiasts for fighting communism'.

In relation to both Rhodesia and Angola Western governments, and particularly those of the United States and Britain which had laws governing the enlistment of their citizens as mercenaries to fight in overseas wars, managed to find endless excuses to do nothing about such mercenaries because it suited them to turn a blind eye. Although during 1977 an estimated 200 to 300 Americans, mainly military veterans, fought for the Rhodesian army they escaped prosecution in the United States or the loss of their passports primarily because Rhodesia, in the eyes of the US government, remained a territory of indeterminate status and was not defined as a state.[7] This convenient quibble allowed the State Department to ignore what it could easily have acted to prevent. By the end of 1977 two Americans had been killed fighting in Rhodesia and about a dozen had deserted. A clear indication of the political sympathies of mercenary recruits was perhaps highlighted by the fact that two rightwing US political organizations, the John Birch Society and the American Nazi Party, established chapters in Rhodesia. At the same time the rebellious colony appeared to have become a haven for American refugees from criminal justice. Whatever the real figures the number of mercenaries attached to the Rhodesian forces by the late 1970s was sufficiently large that it attracted fairly constant media attention. Even so, shortages of manpower led the Smith government to increase the recruitment of black soldiers during 1977, many probably enlisting because of the high rates of unemployment. Estimates of 1,000 to 2,000 foreign mercenaries in Rhodesia which had been made in 1976 were subsequently thought to have been too low. At the end of 1977 it was reported that 100 former French Legionnaires had enlisted under two majors.[8] Joshua Nkomo, in what appeared to be a massive exaggeration, claimed on 6 February 1978, that there were about 11,200 mercenaries then operating in Rhodesia and that they were concentrated on the Zambian border. His claim was widely rejected by local diplomatic sources. According to Nkomo the mercenaries included 600 Israeli commandos, 4,500 South Africans, 2,000 British, 2,300 Americans, 1,000 French and unspecified numbers of Portuguese and West Germans. He was contradicted by Western intelligence sources in Lusaka which claimed the total number of foreigners in the Rhodesian army was about 1,400.

The precise figures do not matter. What did matter was the extent to which the Rhodesian army had become dependent upon foreign mercenaries and what mattered still more from an African viewpoint was the perceived political attitude of these mercenaries. They were whites who had come to support a hated white minority regime which was steadily becoming more brutal in its efforts to hold on to power. Furthermore, the failure of Western governments to prevent recruitment of mercenaries and the suspicion that their presence in Rhodesia was not unwelcome as Western ministers constantly referred to the spread of communism were seen as a convenient camouflage for western attitudes that were persistently more sympathetic to the white than to the black cause. The end for the Smith regime was clearly signalled in 1977 when major cross-border raids by Rhodesian forces into Mozambique and the bombing of Zambia failed to slow down guerrilla operations and the Rhodesian Commander of Combined Operations, Lt-Gen Peter Walls, then argued publicly for negotiations, saying the whites could not win the war. This prompted the white minority government to attempt an internal settlement with Bishop Muzorewa of the Zimbabwe ANC in March 1978 when Smith agreed to introduce a form of majority rule although with provisions that would ensure the effective continuation of white minority control. This internal agreement did nothing, however, to lessen the scale of the fighting. It was only following the Commonwealth Heads of Government Meeting (CHOGM) which was held in Lusaka during August 1979 that a formula was finally found which brought Rhodesia to the settlement of 1980 and saw the birth of an independent Zimbabwe. The need for mercenaries fell away and by the time Zimbabwe had become independent in April 1980 the mercenaries had moved on to other activities.

4 Southern Africa (2) Angola

Mercenaries were to make headline news in Angola immediately after that country achieved independence in 1975 because the capture of a number of them by the MPLA government allowed it to stage a model trial and highlight the evil they were seen to represent in Africa. The CIA was already heavily involved supporting the pro-Western opponents of the MPLA before Angola became independent; then, on 19 December 1975, the US Senate by a vote of 54 to 22 banned the Ford Administration from continuing undercover military assistance to the two liberation groups opposed to the Angolan government – the *Frente Nacional de Libertação de Angola* (FNLA) and the *União Nacional para a Independência Total de Angola* (UNITA) – in reaction to the recent US debacle in Vietnam. Prior to its vote of 19 December the Senate had also voted to ban the employment of US combat personnel in Angola or the provision of any assistance to groups there 'without the full authorization of Congress'. This was at a time when the CIA had earmarked US$33m for operations in Angola. The failure of the South African military intervention in Angola at the end of 1975 and the public attitude of the US Senate made it all the more likely that the CIA would turn instead to the use of mercenaries for at the time both the United States and South Africa were determined to provide support for the anti-MPLA forces in Angola.

The collapse of the FNLA at the end of 1975 reinforced the need for an alternative to continue opposition to the MPLA; the CIA with the complicit support of Britain, Belgium and Portugal now undertook to recruit and finance mercenaries for Angola. It was to become a complex and sordid story involving some of the least savoury characters in the mercenary world. One of these, for example, was the British former private soldier Nicholas Hall who had served two years in prison for selling arms to the Ulster Loyalists and now undertook to recruit mercenaries to serve the leader of the FNLA, Holden Roberto.[1] A good deal of the recruiting in England was done from the Surrey town of Camberley close to Sandhurst, the premier British officer training establishment. A *Daily Telegraph* article of January 1976 reported that six British Angola-bound mercenaries were ex-members of the SAS.[2]

Accounts of British mercenary recruitment appeared in the press and were widely known yet the government did nothing either to dissuade or prevent them going to Angola. They were able to go from Britain to Belgium, thence to Zaire and across the border into Angola without facing even normal border formalities. Most of the British mercenaries, it appeared, had few skills, some had never handled a rifle before, each one represented a £200 commission for the recruiting officer. Their story is told in *The Whores of War*[3] and what comes across vividly is the third rate quality of the men recruited as well as the general incompetence of the whole operation. Holden Roberto, the leader of the FNLA, was an unlikely candidate to lead any serious military operation:

> Holden Roberto was a fabrication of the late President John Kennedy at a time when he was looking around for some compliant potential leaders ready to implement an 'African policy' which Kennedy perceived the United States was going to need.[4]

This unflattering, though largely accurate, judgement of both Roberto and Kennedy helps explain the fiasco which was to come. In January 1975, at the beginning of Portugal's last year in Angola, the CIA gave Roberto $300,000 to reactivate the armed wing of his FNLA which at that time was largely moribund; according to the *New York Times* of 20 December 1975, Roberto had been on the CIA payroll since 1961. As the faction fighting in Angola between the MPLA, the FNLA and UNITA escalated in early 1976, the *Daily Telegraph* reported: 'In Johannesburg, about 600 mercenaries are assembling, apparently awaiting contracts to fly into Southern Angola to join Dr. Jonas Savimbi's hard-pressed UNITA forces'.[5]

A detailed account of the American involvement in Angola at this time has been provided by the former Chief CIA Angola Task Force officer, John Stockwell.[6] Following the Portuguese withdrawal from Angola in 1975, the United States, working through Zaire, backed Roberto's FNLA whose forces moved on Luanda only to be devastatingly repulsed by the MPLA, now aided by its new Cuban allies. This was the point when the CIA decided to employ mercenaries. Initially the CIA turned to France and Portugal and began by employing French 'Hoods' as they were known, the CIA working through the French intelligence service. Bob Denard was the agent of the French service and had already made his name in the Congo before falling out with Mobutu in 1967. The CIA believed that French mercenaries would be more acceptable in Angola than Portuguese and that sponsorship by the French intelligence service would reduce the possibility of sadists and misfits being recruited. It was agreed at French insistence that Bob Denard would handle all the recruiting and that only he would have contact with the CIA. French intelligence would facilitate obtaining passports and visas for the mercenaries; UNITA would be responsible for housing the mercenaries in Kinshasa and Savimbi would supervise their activities in Angola.

French intelligence certainly knew how to deal with the CIA which was desperate to demonstrate that it was active in Angola. At first the French demanded $250,000 to cover the costs of the mercenary operation but then increased the figure to $350,000: Bob Denard would field 20 mercenaries for five months and deliver them to Kinshasa 30 days after the $350,000 had been paid over by the CIA. As Stockwell argued, it was absurd to pay mercenaries in advance since 'their code is money and their only loyalty is to money.'[7] The haggling between the CIA and Paris continued and in the end Denard got $500,000. The first 11 'Hoods' arrived in Kinshasa on 10 January 1976, where they underwent two days of CIA weapons training before being flown by CIA Task Force planes to Silva Ponto in Angola; the remainder of the French mercenaries arrived in Angola on 27 January and included among their numbers a French agent.

The saga of the Portuguese mercenaries paid for by the CIA is even more absurd than that of the French for Denard at least was a highly professional operator. The Portuguese having lost their colonial war and seen the vast majority of their settlers quit Angola at speed at the time of independence decided to mount a mercenary programme of their own (with CIA finances) in opposition to the MPLA successor government. A CIA officer met the Portuguese Colonel Santos Castro in Madrid early in December 1975 to work out the details of recruiting a Portuguese mercenary force of 300 men. The CIA began by opening a Berne bank account for Castro with $55,000 working expenses. Castro then agreed to recruit, pay and direct 300 Portuguese 'commandos' who were refugees from Angola and would fight alongside the FNLA. Castro himself was to be reimbursed for all his recruiting expenses; the 300 return fares to Kinshasa; salaries, bonuses, maintenance in Angola, medical expenses. The contract for the 300 who were to fight in Angola for five months would total $1.5m. The salary bill for these mercenaries was similar to the rates paid for Congo mercenaries a few years before: a private would receive $500 a month, a sergeant $650, a second lieutenant $800, a first lieutenant $1000, a captain $1400 and a major $2500. The CIA was committed to pay a gross monthly salary bill of $172,700 over five months. In addition, the mercenaries would receive monthly separation allowances of $100 per wife and $50 per child which added a further $600,000 bill to the CIA payroll. Other costs included $200,000 for travel, $50,000 for medical costs, $100,000 for bonuses and $75,000 for subsistence. These bloated figures become all the more important when the actual effectiveness of the operation is judged. Colonel Castro himself was to receive a commission of $25,000 and was free to take whatever else he could extract from the total budget.

Castro claimed, while these negotiations were in progress, that 600 men were awaiting his call; in fact recruiting was slow and he then said that it was difficult over the Christmas holidays. In addition, he had to create an infrastructure for his small army. He then demanded additional funds while refusing to account for the $110,000 he had already received. He provided the names of only a few dozen recruits and the first mercenary, a sergeant, arrived in Kinshasa on 1 January 1976; he was followed by 12 further mercenaries on 28 January by which time the FNLA forces in Angola were in retreat and disintegrating. The CIA then told Castro to suspend recruiting and the 13 men who had turned up in Kinshasa were returned to Europe. They never saw Angola.

By any standards the CIA operation was a hastily concocted mess. Holden Roberto's FNLA had been largely ineffective for years and Roberto himself was corrupt and incompetent, a fact the CIA had no excuse for not knowing since he had been on their payroll since 1961. The Portuguese, who had been fighting the Angolan population for fifteen years and had then quit the country *en masse*, were clearly the wrong source from which to recruit willing mercenaries while any elementary knowledge of mercenary behaviour should have inhibited the CIA from dispensing large sums of money to such figures as Castro and Denard. The whole operation demonstrated a desperate determination on the part of the CIA (no doubt fuelled by current anti-communist hysteria) to do something and to be seen to be doing something to hold back the spread of communism as perceived in Washington and to prevent what in fact was already a *fait accompli*: that is, the emergence of a Marxist style government in Angola. The story did not end here however.

A third force of 150 British and American mercenaries was recruited by Roberto himself and though originally separate from the CIA operation the two soon became intertwined with each other. US planes were to transport these mercenaries into Angola; they were provided with US weapons by the CIA and received CIA briefings in Kinshasa. Two Britons, Nick Hall and Doctor Bedford, were responsible for recruiting mercenaries in England and these began to arrive in Kinshasa in late December 1975; by January 1976 over 100 English mercenaries were in Angola attached (loosely) to the FNLA. Although there was a considerable amount of publicity in the United States only a handful of American mercenaries actually turned up in Angola. The CIA attempted to make Roberto account for the funds he had received from it but he refused to do so. The British mercenaries, meanwhile, were being paid in new US $100 bills which were the currency that had been paid to Roberto.

At this point an especially unpleasant mercenary figure advances into the limelight: George Cullen was appointed Roberto's field general in Angola. He was reputed to have ambushed and routed a small MPLA column virtually singlehanded. He came from Leeds in Yorkshire and had been a parachute commando and served as a mercenary in Oman. He spoke Greek (his real name was Costa Georgiu), Arabic and some Portuguese. He appeared to have the right qualifications of a tough soldier but he had not been in Angola long before stories of his racism and brutality began to emerge: he murdered or humiliated black soldiers serving with him and then was responsible for shooting a number of his own ill-assorted mercenaries. On 1 February 1976, a patrol of 25 mercenaries on a reconnaissance near Sao Salvadore in the north of Angola attacked a forward post of their own men by mistake. They fled back to Sao Salvadore but Cullen came after them and had 14 of them lined up at the roadside where he shot them, subsequently leaving their naked bodies as a warning to others. Following this episode Roberto sent another British mercenary, MacLeese, and an American to deal with Cullen; they shot Cullen's assistant after a summary trial. It was plain from these and other incidents that this new group of largely British mercenaries were ill-disciplined, lawless and brutal and were unlikely to assist Roberto's crumbling cause. Fifteen mercenaries seized a plane and flew to Kinshasa with arms to claim their pay from Roberto. A CIA officer managed to persuade them not to go into town with their weapons or they would have fallen foul of Mobutu's bodyguards. In mid-February Cullen and 12 other mercenaries were captured by the MPLA and this group which included three Americans was shortly to be put on trial in Luanda.

The remnants of the FNLA fled across the border into Zaire at the beginning of March 1976 and the rest of Roberto's mercenaries travelled overland to Kinshasa and from there returned to Britain. A group of 30 Portuguese who had been with Roberto now dispersed either to South Africa or returned to Europe. The French 'Hoods' who had been recruited to assist UNITA deserted long before their contract expired and when their services were most needed: of 22 'Hoods' two were killed while the rest returned to France three months before the expiry of their contracts. The British and American mercenaries who included Cullen and other psychopaths had managed to make the general reputation of mercenaries in Africa even worse than it was already while the whole operation had created much adverse publicity for the CIA. The British mercenaries earned an especially unsavoury reputation for themselves in Angola and in June 1976, appearing on British television, John Banks, one of the mercenary recruiters, boasted: 'Our guys killed more than a thousand Angolans. We had a kill ratio of more than twenty to one.'[8] The whole CIA Angola programme had degenerated into a disaster with both the Portuguese Colonel Castro and the already notorious Frenchman, Colonel Denard, extracting large sums of money from the CIA for minimal returns.

Given the generally inflammable situation in southern Africa at the time the CIA involvement with mercenaries was a double disaster. At the Angolan level the use of mercenaries had achieved none of its objectives and the programme had to be abandoned. In any case the CIA had backed a loser in Holden Roberto and after dealing with him over fifteen years ought to have known his limitations. More important than this failure, the appearance of white mercenaries in Angola at the changeover from Portuguese rule to independence simply emphasized, as far as African opinion was concerned, the determination of the West to go on manipulating weak African states wherever it was possible to do so. The overt American and French support for these mercenary operations only served to damage still further the reputation of the West in southern Africa at a time when it was always seen to support right-wing, reactionary or racist regimes in the region.

The CIA which used the euphemism of 'foreign military advisers' for mercenaries sought to recruit them from Portugal, France, Brazil, the Philippines and South Africa. Its effort to recruit mercenaries in Brazil whose Portuguese speaking black Brazilians were acceptable to both Roberto and Savimbi was a failure: Brazil would not permit any recruitment to take place. The CIA also attempted to recruit Filipinos but again without success for when the Americans had quit

Vietnam they had abandoned to their fate 250 of their Filippino employees.[9]

THE LUANDA TRIAL

The capture of 13 white mercenaries by advancing MPLA troops during the first two weeks of February 1976, as the retreating FNLA forces collapsed, provided the new Angolan government with a unique opportunity to focus attention upon the mercenary threat to Africa. The thirteen mercenaries consisted of nine Britons, one Irish and three Americans. They were brought to trial in Luanda on 11 June 1976, before the Angolan People's Revolutionary Tribunal (the court had been established by decree the previous month); the main object of the trial was to focus world attention upon the menace of Mercenarism. As Angola's Justice Minister Diogenes Boavida said:

> Yesterday in the Congo, today in Angola, tomorrow in Zimbabwe or Namibia, these sordid agents of international gangsterism, recruited from all geographical and political directions, do not hesitate to sell their supposed fighting superiority, without following any ideal but merely pursuing wretched personal gain.[10]

Thousands of Angolans marched through Luanda in a demonstration before the trial began demanding the death sentence for the mercenaries. The 13 mercenaries were charged with a total of 139 counts of armed combat against the forces of the Angolan People's Republic, with violation of frontiers, acts against civilians, destruction of civilian and military equipment and 'crimes against peace'. In addition, the indictment charged 'acquiescence and complicity of various Governments, particularly those of Britain and America, in the preparation and development' of the mercenary operation.[11] Lengthy individual counts were laid against two British mercenaries, 'Colonel Callan' and Andrew McKenzie who were accused of responsibility for the massacre of 14 British mercenaries on 1 February at Maquela do Zombo. Four of the defendants – Costas Georgiu (Colonel Callan), Andrew McKenzie, Daniel Gearheart and John Barker – were sentenced to death by firing squad and the remaining nine were sentenced to long prison terms ranging from 16 to 30 years. The death sentences were confirmed by President Agostinho Neto on 9 July and were carried out two days later. Prior to the trial the Angolan government had invited a number of eminent jurists and had set up a 50-member International

Commission of Inquiry on Mercenaries in Luanda to observe the trial and prepare a draft convention to secure an international ban on mercenary activities.

THE CABINDA ENCLAVE

The Cabinda enclave is a geographic anomaly: a tiny territory sandwiched between the northern bank of the Congo (Zaire) river, the Atlantic and Congo (Brazzaville) and yet a part of Angola, attached to it by the Portuguese for administrative convenience though in other circumstances it might have been treated as a separate colony. Rich oilfields made Cabinda essential to the economic survival of the MPLA government; they also made it a prime target for destabilization while both Zaire and Congo were tempted to seize it. Separatists hoped to take advantage of the chaos in Angola and establish an independent Cabindan state and in August 1975 two groups made competing claims: The President of the Front for the Liberation of the Enclave of Cabinda (FLEC) which was based in Kinshasa, Luis Ranque Franque, declared the territory independent at a press conference in Kinshasa on 1 August; six days later a rival separatist, N'Zita Henrique Tiago, announced from Paris that he had set up a Provisional Revolutionary Government for Cabinda. Since MPLA troops were firmly in control of Cabinda these pronouncements had little impact, except that they suggested complications to come.

Zaire, while supporting the FNLA which opposed Cabindan separatism, was also aiding FLEC and on a number of occasions Mobutu insisted that Cabinda was a separate entity from the rest of Angola; he suggested that its future status should be determined by a referendum. Gabon also recognised FLEC. The Congo, while aiding the MPLA, gave limited suport to the separatists opposed to the Ranque Franque faction and Congo's Foreign Minister, Henri Lopes, said on 29 April 1975, that 'Cabinda exists as a reality and is historically and geographically different from Angola.' He, like Mobutu, proposed a referendum. In October 1975 Mobutu thought he saw his chance to annex Cabinda as Angola, then in a state of near chaos, prepared for independence. He approached the CIA which promptly flew in 'a one-thousand-man arms package for use in the invasion' while CIA officers in Kinshasa visited the FLEC training camp to coordinate the invasion:

On November 2, a joint invasion force launched a three-column attack against the MPLA defenders, who were reinforced with Cuban advisors. They were accompanied by a half-dozen French mercenaries, not that they made any difference. The Cuban/MPLA force easily held Cabinda.[12]

Following this abortive invasion, President Ngouabi of Congo (Brazzaville) came out fully in support of the MPLA and said that Congo would intervene on behalf of the MPLA 'if mercenaries' entered Cabinda.[13]

During 1976 Cabindan separatist groups carried out guerrilla raids against MPLA forces and an MPLA commander admitted in April that he faced strong pressure from the guerrillas who, he claimed, were backed by mercenaries. On 24 November 1976, the Provincial Commissar of Cabinda, Evarista Domingo Quimba, accused Mobutu of trying to keep the Cabinda enclave 'in a permanent state of alert, confronted by an enemy as powerful as Zaire, which received direct aid from Imperialism'. He said that FLEC and Zairean forces were being trained for an offensive by mercenaries in border zones and at the Zairean base of Kitona.[14]

In a speech of 25 February 1977, President Agostinho Neto of Angola accused Zaire of threatening Angola's security. He said:

> On our northern border we have two neighbours – the People's Republic of Congo (PRC) and the Republic of Zaire. We have excellent relations of cooperation, friendship and close alliance with the PRC; but this is not the case with the Zairean Republic.

He then gave details of Zairean hijacking of Angolan planes and listed bases from which 'puppets' of Zaire as well as elements of its army threatened Angola's security. He claimed that a major action had been planned for September/October of that year, known as Operation Cobra, and was to be run jointly by the FNLA and FLEC although the commander was a Frenchman, Colonel Mouton Pierre. There were a number of foreign enlisted officers under him who included an American, Colonel Michael Brown with a unit of 30 men; a second American, Colonel Johnson who allegedly had led the Green Berets in the Bolivian guerrilla war; and a Colonel William Thompson, in charge of an airborne division of 1,200 men. Neto said that 'These were irrefutable facts'.[15]

In March 1977 when about 1,500 'Katanga gendarmes' crossed from Angola into Zaire and occupied a number of key towns of Western

Shaba (Katanga) Province and forced the demoralised Zaire army to retreat, Mobutu said that the incursion was led by Cuban and Soviet mercenaries but he was never to substantiate this claim although the rebels did have Soviet and East European arms. Subsequently, France airlifted Moroccan troops to Kolwezi and the rebellion was defeated. France also sent a small number of military instructors to Zaire. Mobutu had played the anti-communist card to which the West responded all too readily while France had an agenda of its own which was to increase its influence in French-speaking Zaire.

Some fighting occurred in Cabinda at the end of May 1977 with guerrillas crossing into the enclave from Zaire. The Neto government in Luanda accused both France and Zaire of providing assistance to FLEC. A Defence Ministry communique issued in Luanda on 4 May warned 'international opinion that Paris is nearly always the source of the attacks against the People's Republic of Angola and that Kinshasa is the sanctuary of desperate puppets and mercenaries of every origin in a vain attempt to destroy the Angolan revolution'. FLEC, however, was seriously weakened by factionalism and from this time onwards never really presented any realistic threat to the MPLA government. Gulf Oil, under pressure from Washington, had temporarily stopped production in Cabinda; now, in mid-1976, it came to an agreement with the Luanda government and resumed output and this was soon to achieve 75 per cent of the pre-independence level while, subsequently, oil revenues would provide the principal source of finance for the Angolan government throughout the troubled 1980s.

NEW PERSPECTIVES OF THE 1990s

During the 1980s, as part of its general policy of destabilizing its neighbours, South Africa repeatedly launched substantial military raids into Angola, allegedly to 'take out' SWAPO bases but also in support of UNITA which waged a civil war against the MPLA government throughout the decade. These South African incursions culminated in the year long battle of Cuito Cuanavale (1987–88) in southern Angola when up to 9,000 South African troops supporting UNITA forces were trapped by FAPLA (the MPLA army) and its Cuban allies. The stalemate at Cuito Cuanavale, which was close to a defeat for South Africa, played a significant part in bringing the different sides to the negotiating table during 1988, leading to the agreement which was signed in New York at the end of the year. As a consequence of this agreement, South Africa withdrew its forces from Angola, Namibia became independent in March 1990, the Cubans withdrew their estimated 50,000 troops from Angola over 30 months, and the African National Congress (ANC) moved its cadres out of Angola; unfortunately, however, the civil war between the government of Angola and UNITA continued, with broken truces and peace accords, into the mid-1990s.

UNITA was able to finance its war during the 1990s because it controlled the the greater part of the country's diamond producing region and now, in what must be seen as one of the great ironies in the mercenary story, the government of President Eduardo dos Santos, whose predecessor Agostinho Neto had staged the famous mercenary trial of 1976, hired South African mercenaries to assist in ousting UNITA forces from the diamond fields. A further irony consisted in the fact that the mercenaries came from the new South Africa which was presided over by the world acclaimed figure of Nelson Mandela and that many of them had already served in Angola supporting UNITA during the height of Pretoria's policy of destabilization against its northern neighbours.

In July 1994 a group of South African mercenaries were flown to Saurimo in Lunda South province in the northeast of Angola to fight UNITA; dressed in khaki with no insignia except for a small flash of Angolan colours they insisted, as is the wont of mercenaries, that they were only instructors. Their arrival represented a paradox since South Africa had supported UNITA throughout the 1980s, often by supplying some of its best trained soldiers, similar to these, to assist Savimbi. Some of the men who disembarked at Saurimo on this occasion had fought against the dos Santos government in the 1980s. Now their objective was to capture the diamond fields of Lunda South and Lunda North provinces from UNITA for the government. The decison of the government to employ South African mercenaries followed the seizure a year earlier by UNITA of the oil town of Soyo, also with the help of mercenaries.

In January 1993, after suffering a series of reverses at the hands of government forces, UNITA with the help of white English-speaking mercenaries had captured Soyo on the coast just south of the Congo river, Angola's strategically vital oil town and refinery, taking 17 foreign oil workers prisoner at the same time. Western intelligence sources claimed that UNITA had used mercenaries in three days of fighting for Soyo which is not only the most important oil town in Angola but also the logistics base for operations in Cabinda. 'We have complete proof of the activities of white mercenaries in Soyo, but it does not appear that they were running the operation as commanders' a diplomat in Luanda said.[16] The Angolan government had been claiming for several weeks that UNITA was using white mercenaries; this was the first independent confirmation of their claim. Shortly after this incident the Luanda government itself engaged South African mercenaries to protect the vital installations in Soyo after the town had been retaken from the UNITA rebels by the army. Soyo had then been captured a second time by UNITA forces and this persuaded the government to step up its recruitment of South African mercenaries. Thus, by the middle of 1994, there were an estimated 500 black and white South African mercenaries in Angola; they had been recruited by Executive Outcomes, the increasingly high profile South African firm with offices in Pretoria which deals in mercenaries.

The director of Executive Outcomes, Lafras Luitingh, was a former member of the Civil Co-operation Bureau (CCB) of South Africa which formerly had been responsible for special military operations and had been quietly dissolved three years earlier by President F W de Klerk; Luitingh was assisted by Eeben Barlow, the former commanding officer of 32 battalion which in the apartheid years had acted as the spearhead of South African interventions in Angola and, in its turn, had been dissolved in 1993. Now the men from these organizations were to reappear in Angola as mercenaries. Another white mercenary officer who similarly returned to Angola was Major Wynand du Toit who had made headlines in 1985 for carrying out a sabotage mission in Cabinda. As these former South African soldiers, now mercenaries, returned to fight in Angola, this time on the side of those they had attempted to destabilize through the 1980s, they insisted that it was 'strictly business'. Their budget was reported to be US$40m.[17] UNITA, understandably, announced on a number of occasions that any of these mercenaries who fell into its hands would be summarily executed and at the end of July 1994 announced that some 25 of them had been killed.

In January 1998 the Angolan government ordered all foreigners working for the London-based security company Defence Systems Limited to leave the country immediately. Defence Systems Limited (DSL) had been founded by former officers of the elite British Special Air Service (SAS). The 103 foreigners who were forced to leave included 45 Gurkhas from Nepal. DSL was the largest private security firm in Angola and undertook to guard top expatriate officials from embassies, oil and mining companies. The security business is another form of mercenary activity, though strictly defensive in its role. Some 90 security companies operate in Angola and, according to a western diplomat, 'This is a nightmare, not only in terms of who will protect our houses and offices, but also for any foreign company planning to invest in Angola.'[18]

According to a Reuters report from Johannesburg,

The Interior Ministry said DSL, which operated as DSL Angola since 1992 when it became illegal for foreigners to own security companies in the country, had kept its top management exclusively for foreigners. Most foreign security companies in Angola have joint ventures with Angolan partners, usually army generals who are paid hefty dollar salaries.

This kind of security activity represents a half-way house between legitimate policing and full deployment of mercenary recruits. The demand by the rich and vulnerable for private security firms in Africa has become a major growth industry and many of the firms involved tend to be laws unto themselves. The activities of a firm such as DSL with its ex-SAS directors and Gurkhas comes very close to being a mercenary force.

Early in 1998, despite repeated efforts at reconciliation, it was clear that Savimbi had no intention of joining the government as second vice-president, the post he had been offered, although some of his followers had done so. The government, meanwhile, was employing mercenaries supplied by Executive Outcomes who were trained in the use of Russian-built SAM-14 ground to air missiles to bring down planes flying into Savimbi's headquarters at Bailundu in Huambo region. In January 1998 a DC-4 cargo plane was forced down; it was carrying diamond mining equipment and munitions and had a flight plan from Johannesburg to the Democratic Republic of Congo although it was heading for a Savimbi (UNITA) enclave in Angola. South Africa asked for the return of its plane. In February President Mandela of South Africa had a meeting with Savimbi and said he was trying to persuade him to accept the Angolan peace settlement. There were no indications in mid-1998 that the low-intensity war in Angola would cease or that mercenaries would not continue to be used, for the time being at any rate, as employees of the legitimate government.

5 African Vulnerability

African vulnerability to outside pressures of many kinds was amply demonstrated through the 1990s: mercenaries are simply one of the various instruments deployed to make such pressures effective. Three major Western powers are the most persistent source of these pressures: these are Britain and France, the two most important of the former colonial powers, both with large economic interests to defend on the continent; and the United States which has increasing economic interests in Africa but also sees its role as that of a peacemaker, though only when peacekeeping interventions suit its policy-makers. In the civil wars and liberation struggles already examined above – the Congo (1960–65), Nigeria (1967–70), Rhodesia during the 1970s and Angola from independence in 1975 to the 1990s – the Western powers exerted pressures in a number of ways. These included the supply of arms and military instructors, the provision of finance, the recruitment and deployment of mercenaries, the application of sanctions, and a range of diplomatic pressures and sometimes threats to persuade governments to change their policies. In addition, they have worked through proxy governments or movements, the United States for example providing support throughout the 1980s to Savimbi's UNITA to ensure that it did not relax its war upon the forces of the Angolan government. Where mercenaries have been concerned Western governments have permitted recruitment by default: that is, according to their own laws or commitments to the United Nations they ought to have prevented such recruitment taking place but in fact did nothing to prevent it, instead turning a blind eye and disclaiming responsibility because they favoured the faction or government for whom the mercenaries were being employed.

The end of the Cold War did not, as optimists hoped and briefly predicted, bring about a new world order; rather, it witnessed a reversion to an even older order of a deeply destabilised world in which civil wars and the collapse of small weak states became the norm in an international system that lacked either the rigid parameters of the super-power controlled world that disappeared with the disintegration of the USSR or the imposed law-and-order of a largely colonial dominated world order which had preceded the Cold War era. As a consequence, there is no automatic formula for interventions to end violence most of which now takes place within the framework of single countries; instead, the big powers intervene or not depending upon the interests they have to defend. In such circumstances the use of mercenaries is likely to become more rather than less prevalent and they will be used in two broad ways: as the instruments of a major power (Britain in Sierra Leone during 1998, for example); or they will be invited in by weak governments to guard installations or assist overstretched or incompetent armed forces maintain control or fight a civil war (as in Angola during the 1990s).

African countries which suffered from civil war or inter-communal violence on a substantial scale during the 1990s included: Liberia and Sierra Leone in West Africa; Eritrea, Ethiopia, Somalia and Sudan in the troubled Horn of the continent; Burundi, Rwanda, Uganda, Zaire (now the Democratic Republic of Congo) and Congo (Brazzaville) in Central Africa; and Angola, Mozambique and South Africa in the southern part of the continent. In a majority of these cases significant external interventions altered the course of the internal struggles taking place. Britain, France and the United States were each to be involved in several of these conflicts, usually indirectly and by proxy although the indirectness was fairly relative; the United Nations tried hard enough but too often was denied any meaningful role because of the big power jealousies which destroyed its possible effectiveness; and, significantly for Africa, both Nigeria and South Africa began to assume responsibilities as regional peacemakers. The mercenary was never far from the scene of action though there were important changes in the mode of mercenary operation while a noticeable effort had been made to invest the mercenary with a certain legitimacy which poses a number of problems for the future. The emergence into the public eye of mercenary organizations or companies – Executive Outcomes of South Africa or the British organization Sandline, for example–suggests both a new public acceptance of the role that mercenaries are expected to play and an increasingly brash certainty on the part of the mercenary community that its services are needed and that its members will continue to be lucratively employed round the world. Indeed, as the twentieth century drew to an end and the governments of more and more states appeared less and less able to maintain law and order so the openings for mercenaries and organized mercenary interventions multiplied.

Events in Congo (Brazzaville) and disintegrating Zaire during 1997 are worth study because in both cases mercenaries were either directly involved or else hovering in the background. In the case of Congo (Brazzaville) it seems almost extraordinary that mercenaries did not appear openly on the side of former- President Sassou-Nguesso whose insurrection was so obviously supported by both France and the oil companies.

Earlier in the decade Israeli mercenaries made an appearance in Congo. Pascal Lissouba had won a presidential election in August 1992 against the former military general, Denis Sassou-Nguesso, who had been in power since 1979 but had been forced by popular pressure to abandon Marxism and the one-party state and hold open elections. In order to make himself more secure – since the regular army was dominated by officers from Sassou-Nguesso's Mbochi tribe who were loyal to the former president – Lissouba formed his own militia from the loyal Zoulou and these were trained by Israeli mercenaries. Following indecisive legislative elections in May 1993 violence erupted and continued through into 1994 and by February of that year an estimated 300 people had been killed. At this point the role of the Israelis in Congo came under question. The Israeli military training team was headed by a retired Brigadier General Zeev Zachrin, a former parachute officer who previously had served in southern Lebanon, while his team of 25 former Israeli Defence Force personnel had been members of Israeli army special units. A further 40 Israeli mercenaries who were being paid salaries of $2,500 a month were on standby in Israel to go to the Congo when attempts were made in the Knesset (Israeli parliament) to stop further Israeli involvement in Congo.

A member of the left-wing Meretz Party, Benny Temkin, raised the mercenary issue:

> I became involved in this issue after parents complained that their sons were going straight from the army into a conflict in Africa. Israel is today an accepted member of the international community. We do not need to involve ourselves in other conflicts. It is bad for the young men involved and bad for Israel.[1]

A second Meretz MP, Naomi Chazan, also campaigning to halt Israeli military involvement abroad, said that opposition groups in Congo were in their turn seeking to engage Israeli mercenaries: 'We could have an absurd situation where Israelis will be fighting each other on both sides of a civil war.'

Levdan, the Israeli security company which obtained the contract to supply military experts to Congo, had received the approval of the Minister of Defence Yitzhak Rabin (also Israeli Prime Minister); he confirmed that he had approved the Levdan contract but insisted that

Israel was not involved in the arrangement. By then former Israeli army veterans had been engaged as mercenaries for some years and in Africa had served in Liberia, Zaire and Angola. In the 1980s they had also been involved training Colombian death squads for the drug barons and assisting the former Panamanian ruler, General Noriega.[2]

In June 1997 a full-scale civil war broke out between supporters of the incumbent President Pascal Lissouba, and supporters of former President Denis Sassou-Nguesso, with all the appearance of a determined power bid by the former president. The situation was complicated by the fact that French troops were already in Brazzaville ready to evacuate expatriates from Zaire where the long-lasting Mobutu regime was finally collapsing in chaos. Fighting broke out in Brazzaville on 5 June after the army had cordoned off Sassou-Nguesso's house in an apparent attempt to disarm his independent Cobra militia. On 7 June Lissouba accepted an offer by the Mayor of Brazzaville, Bernard Kolelas (another contender for power), to attempt to find a solution to the crisis. President Omar Bongo of Gabon also offered to mediate. Meanwhile the fighting continued. Then, following the death of a French soldier on 7 June, the French government announced that it would send additional forces to Brazzaville to reinforce the 450 French troops who were there already as part of the military buildup to evacuate French and other expatriate nationals from Kinshasa across the Congo river in Zaire. By 9 June Brazzaville had been cut in two by the rival groups both of which were using heavy weapons. A further 400 French troops arrived in Brazzaville and President Jacques Chirac appealed to Lissouba and Sassou-Nguesso to end the fighting. On 11 June both men ordered ceasefires but these broke down the following day.

Meanwhile, the foreigners in Brazzaville were evacuated in French air force planes and by 15 June some 5,000 foreign civilians had left, most of them being ferried to Gabon. On 17 June a three-day ceasefire (later extended) was agreed to allow the French troops to withdraw. On 21 June the UN Secretary-General, Kofi Annan, asked the Security Council to approve a force of 1,600 international troops to secure Brazzaville airport. The fighting continued despite the ceasefire amid growing reports of atrocities by both sides against civilians as well as looting. French military sources suggested 2,000 deaths by the end of June with overall casualties at 10,000. The fighting continued through July and on July 23 it was reported that more than 4,000 people had been killed since the violence erupted on June 5.

While peace talks were held in Libreville, Gabon, Lissouba asked the Constitutional Court to postpone the presidential elections due on 27 July and to extend his mandate to its expiry date on 31 August. Sassou-Nguesso opposed any extension which he said would lead to further fighting. He demanded, instead, the formation of a national government. The Libreville talks broke down on 19 July and when on 22 July the Constitutional Court postponed the presidential poll this produced a furious response from the Sassou-Nguesso camp. Fighting between the two sides escalated through August and spread to the north of the country and on 19 August Sassou-Nguesso's forces captured Ouesso, the main town of northern Congo. Meanwhile, the new president of Democratic Republic of Congo, Laurent Kabila, called for fresh talks and intervention by neutral African countries. A peace plan advanced by President Omar Bongo of Gabon was rejected first by Sassou-Nguesso and then by the government delegation (21 and 23 August) and the government radio accused Bongo of favouring Sassou-Nguesso who was his son-in-law.

Thirty-nine parties and groups supporting President Lissouba or the opposition Congolese Movement for Democracy and Full Development (MDDI) signed a power-sharing agreement even as heavy fighting continued in Brazzaville although Sassou-Nguesso's United Democratic Forces did not sign. The agreement came into force on 31 August, the expiry date of Lissouba's presidency, and provided for a government of national unity and the continuation of existing political institutions for an indefinite transitional period. Lissouba then appointed Bernard Kolelas who was Mayor of Brazzaville and leader of the opposition Congolese Movement for Democracy and Integral Development as Prime Minister with a mandate to form a government and bring an end to the three month old civil war. By mid-September casualties were estimated at between 4,000 and 7,000 dead while 800,000 people had fled the devastated capital of Brazzaville.

On a visit to Paris Lissouba announced that he would not negotiate with Sassou-Nguesso whom he dubbed a 'common rebel' while Sassou-Nguesso confirmed that his Cobra forces were fighting government supporters in the north of the country; interviewed on *Radio France Internationale* he said he believed there had to be a transitional government to reorganize the state and 'organize credible elections'. A summit of eight African leaders met in Gabon and called for a UN-peacekeeping force; they made another appeal to the warring sides to cease fighting. President Lissouba did not attend the summit to which he sent Kolelas; instead, he went to Kinshasa to meet President

Kabila. Sassou-Nguesso would not agree a ceasefire. Kolelas' new government began in inauspicious circumstances: fighting in Brazzaville kept the ministers away from their offices. Five seats in the new coalition government were offered to members of Sassou-Nguesso's party but they refused to participate. Prime Minister Kolelas outlined to the National Assembly three aims of his government: restoration of peace, post-war reconstruction and new presidential elections.

The civil war came to a climax in mid-October when forces loyal to Sassou-Nguesso launched a large-scale offensive in Brazzaville and as key points in the devastated city fell to them the transitional government set up by Lissouba collapsed. The Cobra militia – Sassou-Nguesso's forces – celebrated the fall of Brazzaville with a massive orgy of looting in a city strewn with corpses. Sassou-Nguesso explained the civil war in terms of 'tribalism, regionalism, intolerance and political violence. In order that history does not repeat itself, we ought to attack the problem at the root and henceforth work for national reconciliation and unity to finally give birth to an indivisible and happy democratic Congo' he told his first press conference.[3] The immediate problem appeared to be the necessity of dismantling the different ethnic and political militias which had appeared over the preceding years as the power struggle between the country's various elite groups had developed. The Executive Secretariat of the Democratic and Patriotic Forces (FDP) announced that Major-General Denis Sassou-Nguesso would be sworn in as President of the Republic of Congo on 25 October 1997. This ceremony took place in the Parliament building which was one of the few public buildings left standing in Brazzaville.

In fact Sassou-Nguesso's quick victory was almost certainly the result of intervention on his behalf by Angola whose President, Eduardo dos Santos, sent troops that helped him capture Congo's second city, Pointe Noire, which is the centre of the country's oil industry and vital to economic control. Dos Santos acted in the expectation of a 'return' from a victorious Sassou-Nguesso in the suppression of UNITA bases in Congo as well as those of the separatists from the Cabinda enclave. Following the earlier fall of Mobutu in Zaire, Congo had become the last fuel and weapons base for UNITA. By this time the vast majority of Brazzaville's population of 800,000 was dispersed in the bush and forests of Congo or they had become refugees in Kinshasa.

France denied having intervened in the civil war on behalf of Sassou-Nguesso and insisted that its sole object throughout the four months of fighting had been to support the mediation efforts of President Omar Bongo of Gabon. Elf, the French oil multinational which plays a leading role in exploiting Congo's oil, was also believed to favour a return to power of Sassou-Nguesso. French denials of support for Sassou-Nguesso were hardly matched by the official reaction to his installation as president when a Foreign Ministry spokesman, Jacques Pummelhardt, said 'It is a good thing' and it is 'essential for war-ravaged Congo to commit itself wholeheartedly to the path of nation.' However, promoting a scapegoat so as to divert attention from France's role, he went on to denounce the 'savage occupation' of the country by the Angolan forces which had backed Sassou- Nguesso.[4] Angolan troops took control of the ruined capital on behalf of Sassou-Nguesso and one of these claimed 'My Government has sent me as some kind of mercenary.'[5] The Angolan intervention was part of a determined effort to eliminate all outside sources of assistance for UNITA. Towards the end of the struggle it was reported that Lissouba was hiring UNITA mercenaries. At the same time a number of experienced African mercenaries with a long connexion with French intelligence were reported to have been leading Sassou-Nguesso's Cobra militia.[6]

The restored president had always been seen as a reliable ally of France, even in his Marxist days, and had been accorded VIP treatment when visiting France while in opposition to Lissouba. France at once sent medical aid to Brazzaville after the revolution on the direct orders of President Chirac and clearly signalled its support for the new government. The oil company Elf reportedly supported Sassou-Nguesso throughout the war. Ex-President Lissouba was granted asylum by Togo. On 28 October, just three days after Sassou-Nguesso's inauguration as President, his ally President dos Santos of Angola announced that Angolan troops would be withdrawn from Congo only after an agreement with the Congo government. Early in November when he announced his new government Sassou-Nguesso also claimed that UNITA troops as well as other mercenaries had assisted Lissouba. It was a tangled story and one of the first problems facing the new government was the existence of the various militias. On 21 November the Minister of the Interior, Pierre Oba, banned all militia groups and announced that only the security forces would be allowed to carry arms. There were reports of the Cobra forces of Sassou-Nguesso getting out of hand and demonstrating in Brazzaville to demand integration into the regular army. The Zoulous, Lissouba's personal militia, were given an ultimatum to lay down their arms and return from the bush.

The complexities of the Congo story illustrate some of the powerful external influences that come into play whenever a small African country with important resources (in this case oil) is in danger of subversion. When, following months of tension prior to the elections, President Lissouba moved to disarm the various militias, Sassou-Nguesso refused to comply and so Lissouba attempted to disarm the Cobras by force. This sparked off the civil war which, it would seem, Sassou-Nguesso was determined to launch anyway. In the event his Cobras were supported by 1,000 crack Angolan troops as well as war *materiel* supplied by the Angolan government. The Angolan troops were still in the country in April 1998 despite a call for their withdrawal by the US Congress. Britain and the United States which had been loud in their condemnation of the illegal 1997 coup in Sierra Leone kept remarkably quiet about what in real terms was a coup by warfare carried out in Congo by Sassou-Nguesso; clearly, they did not want to upset France and its President, Jacques Chirac, or interfere in a region which they considered to come under France's influence. Lissouba blamed Chirac for his political fall.

Lissouba's problem related to Congo's oil. Elf Aquitaine dominated the country's oil industry which it controlled with other French companies with Congo receiving only 15 per cent of oil revenues; the rest being retained by the companies. After he had become President, Lissouba set about changing the system: first he increased competition by persuading other oil giants such as Exxon and Shell to come in or increase their stakes in the country; then he negotaited a 33 per cent revenue take for the Congo government. Elf, the main beneficiary of the previous system, set out to destroy the new one and, according to Lissouba, used Sassou-Nguesso and enlisted the support of President Chirac of France. Shortly after Lissouba's overthrow the oil companies renegotiated the Lissouba oil deal with the new government and had the 33 per cent national share of revenues reduced to 20 per cent. While the fighting was taking place Chirac telephoned Lissouba from Paris and demanded that he appoint Sassou-Nguesso as vice-president and head of the armed forces and when Lissouba demurred on constitutional grounds he reportedly said 'Chuck your bloody constitution in the dustbin.[7]'

Again according to Lissouba, a pan-African peace-keeping force prepared by the French Prime Minister, Michel Rocard, was set to intervene when pressure from Chirac aborted the plan. Oil and French economic and political interests in Congo ensured French support for Sassou-Nguesso and the destruction of the democratic process which had been inaugurated in 1992 after 14 years of Sassou-Nguesso's autocratic rule. Much of the story had yet to be revealed in 1998; what remains clear is the level of external manipulation which ensured the downfall of the Lissouba government.

THE END OF MOBUTU'S ZAIRE

The corruption and greed of President Mobutu Sese Sheko of Zaire was on such a scale that he and his supporters were deemed to be responsible for the new political term of kleptocracy or rule by theft. As the rebellion which got underway in 1996 gathered momentum at the beginning of 1997 it was perhaps fitting that Mobutu sought to bolster his crumbling regime with the assistance of mercenaries. On 7 January 1997, reports in the French press said former senior French officers were recruiting a 'white legion' of mercenaries to fight alongside Zaire government forces. The officers involved included Colonel Alain Le Carro, the former head of security at the Elysée Palace under President Mitterand, and Robert Montoya, a gendarmerie officer who had served at the presidency. It was also reported that more than a dozen former French officers had already made their appearance in the north of Zaire with a force of between 300 and 400 men. These included Angolans, Belgians, French, South Africans and Britons and they were all mercenaries. Later reports claimed that mercenaries from Serbia and Croatia had also been recruited. They were being paid directly by Mobutu. Then, on 31 January 1997, Laurent Kabila, the Chairman of the Alliance of Democratic Forces for the Liberation of Congo-Zaire (ADFL), claimed that a mercenary led Zairean army advancing on his rebel-held territory had been stopped. In February 1997, as the ADFL forces advanced on Kisangani, it was reported that the town was garrisoned by FAZ units (the Zaire regular army) bolstered by Serbian mercenaries and that jets based on Kisangani and piloted by mercenaries were bombing ADFL held towns in eastern Zaire including Bukavu, Walikale and Shabundu and killing civilians (February 16–17). In early March, as the ADFL forces closed in on Kisangani, the demoralised FAZ troops and the mercenaries deserted the town and many of the latter were reported to have left the country during March. This inglorious retreat of the mercenaries was not the end of the story for in May 1997 Kabila was reported to be recruiting mercenaries for security duties after he had come to power in Kinshasa. Back in Belgium Jean-Claude Wavreille was investigated by the Belgium police for his role in recruiting mercenaries; he had former Katanga connections and was a member of the little known Moise Tshombe Association. Towards the end of 1997 Kabila sought help from an Israeli security firm, Silver Shadow, which was headed by a retired Colonel Amos Golan, to provide a personal bodyguard but the deal collapsed because the Israeli government opposes contracts with unstable regimes! As the story of the independent Congo had begun in instability which was made for worse by mercenaries so once more they reappeared as Mobutu's regime finally collapsed. His successor Kabila, judging by his efforts to engage mercenaries, had learnt nothing from the story of the Congo/Zaire and its previous reliance upon mercenaries.

6 Island destabilization: Comoros, Seychelles, Denard

No other mercenary figure crops up so often as does the Frenchman, Colonel Bob Denard, from his first appearance and taste of notoriety in the Congo during the early 1960s to his final exit from the Comoros' story in 1997. In France where governments have always been cynically ambivalent about the use of mercenaries Denard was seen more as a mythical hero figure from the pages of *Beau Geste* than as a ruthless peddler of violence and subversion for money. In 1967, at the tail end of the Congo mercenary story, Denard led 16 mercenaries on bicycles across the Angola border into Katanga Province and bluffed his way 300km to the Kolwezi mine in an attempt to make the Katanga gendarmes rise up against Mobutu. Then he was forced to withdraw to France.[1] In 1975 he was again in Central Africa but this time recruiting mercenaries to assist Mobutu's planned invasion of the Cabinda enclave of Angola. Later he became involved in his first operation in the Comoros. In 1977 he was involved in a curious mercenary 'invasion' of Benin in West Africa. He became a key figure in the Comoros from the 1970s through to the 1990s until in June 1997 the prosecutor's office in Paris ordered Denard and two others to appear in court to answer charges relating to the assassination in Moroni of Ahmed Abdallah Abderrahman, the President of Comoros, on 27 November 1989. Denard denied any involvement in the 1989 assassination but he had reappeared in Comoros in 1995 when he led a coup against President Said Mohamed Djohar.

The Benin 'invasion' of January 1977 stands out as one of the more bizarre mercenary actions of that time, an apparent attempt to overthrow the Marxist government of President Ahmed Kerekou. Cotonou Radio announced that a group of mercenaries had been repulsed in an attack on the country. On 16 January 1977, a group of nearly 100 mercenaries, 60 Europeans and about 30 Africans, landed at Cotonou in an unmarked aircraft, seized control of the airport and then drove into the town where they spent the morning firing indiscriminately at any building that looked important; they killed six Beninois and lost two mercenaries in fighting before Denard ordered his men to retreat. They then flew away. In the haste of their departure the mercenaries left behind one mercenary, a Guinean called Ba Alpha Oumarou, and documents which included detailed plans of the operation as well as the names and bank accounts of all the mercenaries whose leader was identified as Gilbert Bourgeaud (in fact Bob Denard's real name) who was acting at the time as a French special adviser to President Omar Bongo of Gabon. The captured documents apparently linked the mercenary invasion to France, Morocco and Gabon: the mercenaries appeared to have flown back and forth between Paris and Morocco, to have been trained in Morocco and then to have been assembled in Gabon and flown from there to Benin. The group, codenamed Force Omega, had as its ostensible aim the imposition of a new president on Benin. A subsequent investigation by the United Nations omitted any reference to the countries Benin accused of complicity – France, Gabon and Morocco; it accepted that the attackers had been recruited by a group calling itself the Dahomey Liberation Front. No satisfactory explanation for this curious attack – Benin claimed the mercenaries had done the equivalent of $28m worth of damage in Cotonou – was forthcoming at the time though revelations of French complicity became apparent during Denard's trial sixteen years later.[2]

A referendum of 1974 in the Comoros which had been under French control since 1909 resulted in a 96 per cent vote in favour of independence although on the island of Mayotte there was a 64 per cent vote for the status of a French overseas department rather than full independence. French pressures for decentralization which would favour the desire of Mayotte to retain its links with France were rejected by the Comoran chamber of deputies and on 6 July 1975, the chamber voted for a unilateral declaration of independence (UDI) and appointed Ahmed Abdallah as president of the newly independent state. This decision which led to an independent Comoran state of three islands – Grande-Comore, Anjouan and Moheli – and a French overseas department of Mayotte set the scene for years of difficult relations with France and tensions which on several occasions led to mercenary interventions. Although France recognized the independence of the Comoros (less Mayottte) at the end of 1975, relations between France and the new state were suspended. In January 1976 Ali Solih became president and initiated a programme of radical reforms. The excesses of the Solih regime were deeply resented, however, and he was finally overthrown, after four attempted coups, in May 1978. The successful coup was assisted by about 50 European mercenaries led by Bob Denard on behalf of the exiled first president Ahmed Abdallah and Solih himself was killed two weeks later. The new regime was ruled by a 'politico-military directory' in which Ahmed Abdallah was reduced to the role of co-president with his former deputy, Muhammed Ahmed. A new constitution was promised and Abdallah attempted to restore relations with members of the Arab League. However, members of the OAU to which Comoros belonged objected to the role the mercenaries had played in the coup – it remained official OAU policy to oppose any use of mercenaries in African affairs – and expelled the Comoros delegation from the ministerial council of the OAU. Denard and his mercenaries remained in Comoros, causing the government increasing embarrassment by their presence, until they were asked to leave in September. The new regime had restored diplomatic relations with France and though Paris insisted it had not given any help or encouragement to the mercenaries it was clearly pleased with the results of their action since it now found a government in Moroni that was more sympathetic and pliant to French interests in the Indian Ocean.

The next skirmish with mercenaries, a minor one, occurred in December 1983 when a plot to overthrow the government was discovered: a group of British mercenaries in Australia were apparently preparing to carry out a coup in Comoros on behalf of Said Ali Kemal, a former Comoran diplomat. However, the plot was uncovered, the mercenary leaders were arrested and later prosecuted by the Australian attorney-general for plotting to overthrow a lawful government recognized by Australia.

In 1987, when President Abdallah was abroad to attend the annual Francophone summit a coup attempt against him was mounted by a small number of former members of his presidential guard and members of the armed forces. On this occasion the coup was thwarted by French mercenaries and South African military advisers who were then in Comoros acting as presidential guards.

A serious coup was mounted in 1989 when President Abdallah was killed during an attack on the presidential palace on the night of 26/27 November. The accusation was later made that members of the presidential guard had been responsible for Abdallah's assassination; these included a number of European advisers (mercenaries) who were under the command of Colonel Bob Denard. According to the constitution the president of the supreme court, Said Mohamed Djohar, became interim head of state but at this point Denard (whatever part he had played in the earlier assassination of Abdallah) intervened to carry out a coup of his own: the regular army was disarmed and 27 policemen were reported killed. Both France and South Africa became embarrassed at the international outcry which followed Denard's coup. The French at the time were providing 16 per cent of the Comoran budget while South Africa was paying the mercenaries £2m a year to run the presidential guard. It is believed that President Abdallah had decided to refuse to negotiate a new contract with the mercenaries and this may have sealed his fate. Having disarmed the regular army Denard rapidly gained complete control over the three islands, deploying some 650 presidential guards and a further 150 new reservists at strategic points. France rapidly assembled a naval task force at Mayotte, supposedly to evacuate French citizens from Comoros. In an interview in *Le Figaro* – 'Offer me an honourable way out' – Denard hinted at his readiness to leave as France and South Africa collaborated to oust him. About 30 of the mercenaries had been in Comoros since independence. Although on Mayotte island France had the military means to oust Denard, in fact negotiations were carried on to discover how much compensation would persuade Denard to leave peacefully. In his interview with *Le Figaro* Denard who had helped Abdallah to power in 1975, deposed him a few weeks later and then restored him to power in 1978, insisted that he was not responsible for his death in 1989.

Denard, with the braggadoccio of a successful mercenary, claimed not to be in political control of the islands, but only in charge of security arrangements; he then went on to say that the interim president, Said Djohar, was having difficulty making his presence felt. When asked why there had been firing on the night President Abdallah was killed, Denard replied 'Because President Abdallah had requested that the regular army be disarmed'. But to the further question 'And then the President was killed?' Denard replied 'I have nothing to say'.[3] South African financial support for the mercenaries (the Pretoria government had contributed $5m a year since 1984 in support of the Presidential Guard in exchange for the use of Comoros as a staging post for ferrying arms to the Renamo rebels in Mozambique) had made possible Denard's presence in the Comoros over these years; however, in 1988 Pretoria had begun to wind down its Mozambique operation and ceased paying for the mercenaries in 1989 with the result that in April 1989 Denard forced the quasi-official South African attache to leave Comoros. In yet another extraordinary exchange in his *Le Figaro* interview Denard replied to the question that the French President had been putting pressure upon President

Abdallah to dispense with Denard as follows: 'Abdallah told me that he had spoken to President Mitterand about me and President Mitterand had said each time: "I have confidence in this man, you must hang on to him".'[4] Although there had been student demonstrations demanding 'Murderer get out' Denard claimed that he was the one element of stability in Comoros. Denard and the other mercenaries had, over the years, built up substantial personal economic interests in the islands. The French clearly wanted Denard to go peacefully for if they had to arrest him he would have been forced to face charges in France of 'associating with criminals' that resulted from the mercenary invasion of Benin 12 years earlier.

Finally, on 15 December, Denard and the other mercenaries left Comoros after handing over power by arrangement to French military officials; French military helicopters and transport planes had brought in a large contingent of French troops. Then, in a brief ceremony, a French military attache ordered the mercenaries to leave. Denard was said to be angry that his 'conditions' had not been met: he had demanded an 'honourable exit' and some form of payment for the mercenaries. The French and Belgian mercenaries were flown out on a South African military transport. According to Mr Dries Venter, a South African Foreign Ministry official, the mercenaries would be transferred at once on to flights to Europe. 'We want them out of here as soon as possible' he said; their sidearms, which they had been allowed to wear as they embarked on the transport plane in Comoros, had been taken from them when they disembarked in South Africa.[5] The reign of Denard in Comoros was summed up by Ali Mahmoud, a teacher, who said: 'He killed our President and terrorized our people. The only thing he developed here was the graveyard.'[6] Most of the mercenaries left South Africa almost at once (after a day long bout of drinking) but Denard and three others were allowed to remain while Pretoria consulted Paris about a 'suitable destination' for him. A degree of complicity by France and South Africa in the mercenary activities in Comoros was made evident by the way in which he was treated at the end: he ought simply to have been arrested and either put on trial in Paris or handed over to the legitimate authorities in Comoros but neither course of action was followed. Instead, Denard was to remain in voluntary exile in South Africa for three years. In Comoros it was agreed that a French military presence should remain for two years to retrain the local security forces.

In 1993 Denard decided to leave his exile in South Africa and return to France to face trial for his Benin adventure of 1977. He was arrested on his arrival in Paris and also charged with complicity in the murder of the Comoros President, Ahmed Abdallah, in 1989. He said that the political changes then taking place in South Africa stopped him making his living as a mercenary. By this time Denard, at 64, had been linked with mercenary activities in the Congo, Yemen, Biafra, Angola, Benin and Comoros.[7] In his subsequent trial French military, diplomatic and intelligence chiefs broke their normal cover to admit in the Paris court that the state had backed or tacitly approved overseas coup attempts by Denard. General Maurice Robert, a former head of the French external spy service SDEC, said that the Benin coup attempt was the kind of action 'where France closes its eyes but supports the operation where it serves French interests'.[8] In his trial Denard was portrayed as a patriot and even the prosecutor asked for leniency while a parade of retired generals, intelligence chiefs and politicians testified that Denard had never betrayed French interests. He was given a five-year suspended sentence and walked free after two months behind bars awaiting his trial. Speaking after his trial Denard said: 'One can be a mercenary and a gentleman, you know.' He went on to claim, speaking of his eight children from seven wives: 'All my roots, all my family, all my children are in France. I could no longer stay away. I couldn't continue living like a pariah. I had to come home.'[9] France apparently did not want him to continue as a pariah either.

In personal revelations which told at least as much about official French attitudes to and use of mercenaries as they did of Denard himself, he said of his mercenary activities:

> For a long time it was the fight against communism. For us, wherever there was communism, it had to be eliminated. And since in all these rebellions, the two blocs, East and West, were always confronted, well, we were the soldiers of the West.

However, Denard claimed, before embarking on any action he always checked with Paris – with French military intelligence or with the official in charge of African affairs in the Elysée Palace: 'I would receive the yellow light which meant there was no opposition.'[10] Denard also insisted that he never saw his role as defending whites or 'civilizing' Africa. 'That was the excuse for colonialism' he said 'and so many mistakes were made. If we have lots of African immigrants here today, it is because we took their raw materials and never created jobs. Now we're paying for it.' Denard's reflections after his much-publicized trial project the image of a philosophical guardian of

Western interests rather than a mercenary. This spectacular court appearance was not quite the end of Denard's mercenary career.

Said Mohamed Djohar was elected President of Comoros in March 1990 taking 55.3 per cent of the votes cast compared with 44.7 per cent cast for his rival, the president of the national assembly, Muhamed Taki. Djohar soon found that his presidency was also to be troubled by the activities of mercenaries. In mid-August 1990 a coup attempt was mounted by armed rebels who attacked various French installations in Anjouan; two of the plotters who were later arrested were supposed to be supporters of Taki while the revolt was sponsored, according to the government, by a small number of European mercenaries who hoped by forcing the removal of French forces from the islands to bring about Djohar's downfall.

The following month the minister of the interior, Ibrahim Halidi, was accused of complicitry in the plot and dismissed and by mid-September some 20 people had been detained on grounds of involvement in the plot. The leader of the conspirators, Max Veillard, was killed by security forces in October.

In September 1995 Colonel Bob Denard with a number of mercenary followers returned once more to Comoros to mount yet another coup; the mercenaries were joined by between 300 and 700 Comorans and the Prime Minister, Caabi el Yachroutou, was forced to take refuge in the French embassy from where he appealed for help. A week later French special forces arrived from Mayotte to reverse the coup. Denard negotiated his surrender and he and his mercenaries were then flown off the island. The unpopularity of the octogenarian President Djohar had created the background for the coup. Opposition groups called for an early election and when Djohar went to Reunion in October for medical treatment Yachroutou declared himself 'interim president' and the year ended in political confusion.

Talks between Djohar and Yachroutou under the aegis of the OAU were held in Madagascar and it was agreed that Djohar could return to Comoros in a 'symbolic' role while a new election code laid down that presidential candidates should be aged between 40 and 70. The subsequent elections brought Mohamed Taki and his National Union for Democracy in the Comoros (UNDC) to power. The new president said he wanted French troops to remain in Comoros and for France to take responsibility for the external defence of the Islands. Although President Taki promised greater autonomy to the three islands two of them – Anjouan and Moheli – attempted to secede in August 1997 and said they wished to re-establish their connection with France. The

French government reaffirmed its support for the territorial integrity of the Comoros while the OAU said secession by Anjouan, the principal malcontent, was 'totally unacceptable'. After the failure of peace talks the government sent 300 troops from Moroni to regain control of Anjouan but they were fiercely resisted and in the end the government admitted defeat while attacking France for failing to provide support. The government also complained to the United Nations Security Council that foreign mercenaries had been involved on the side of the Anjouan secessionists.

Bob Denard and his mercenaries could not bring themselves to leave the Comoros alone: partly, this was because the islands were so small and insecure that mercenary intervention was easy; and partly, perhaps, because the ageing mercenaries had invested in Comoran enterprises and hoped to spend their declining years there in the comfort of a pleasant climate where they could also exercise some form of guardian capacity that would give them both power and security: for a time they appeared to have achieved this aim.

THE SEYCHELLES

The Republic of Seychelles had become independent on 29 June 1976 with James Mancham as President and Albert René as Prime Minister. The two men were incompatible. An armed coup by supporters of René's Seychelles People's United Party (SPUP), which had joined a coalition with Mancham's Seychelles Democratic Party (SDP) at independence, was mounted in 1977 when Mancham was on a visit to London and though René denied knowledge of the coup he was its beneficiary and became President in June 1977, just a year after independence. René's party, the SPUP, renamed itself the Seychelles People's Progressive Front (SPPF) in 1979 and then held elections which it won. René pursued a socialist programme which created antagonism among the small but influential middle class which saw its position under threat. There had been two plots to overthrow René in 1978 though these had made little impact. A third, more serious, coup attempt was launched in 1981 with the assistance of a group of mercenaries who came from South Africa.

On 25 November 1981, some 50 mercenaries from South Africa, under the guise of rugby players, arrived at Victoria, Seychelles, in an attempt to overthrow the René government on behalf of the exiled Mancham. A gun was detected in the luggage of one of them at the airport and during a subsequent gun battle 45 of them hijacked an Indian airliner and flew it back to Durban, South Africa. There five of them were arrested on kidnapping charges though the remainder were set free. Among the arrested was the man in charge of the exploit, Mike Hoare, who had first come to prominence as a mercenary back in the early 1960s in the Congo. In Seychelles the government claimed to have captured another five of the mercenaries though three were still at large. The government of Seychelles accused South Africa of complicity in the coup attempt. An embarrassed South Africa was to deny any involvement in this semi-farcical 'rugby' coup attempt despite the fact that one of the mercenaries was found to be a South African intelligence officer. Seychelles exiles in London, supporters of James Mancham, claimed responsibility for the aborted coup. Seven mercenaries who were eventually rounded up in Seychelles included four South Africans, two white Zimbabweans, and a Briton. Six of them pleaded guilty and four of them were sentenced to death. In South Africa the 45 mercenaries who had returned there on the hijacked Indian plane were put on trial in March, 1982, and their leader, Colonel Mike Hoare, was given a ten year sentence for hijacking. In October 1982 the British Foreign Office informed the Government of Seychelles of a further plot which it had uncovered in London for another coup attempt, which apparently would also depend upon support from South Africa. In December 1983 the South African Government claimed to have uncovered a new plot to overthrow the government of Seychelles and five people were detained in connection with it.

In the end both Denard and Hoare appeared as slightly absurd, pathetic figures in their final mercenary appearances. Both were in their sixties: Denard, wearing a Muslim cap, hair greying and sporting a bulging waistline, was bundled out of the Comoros by the French; Hoare, in his Seychelles venture, was no longer up to it, he was a sick man. But though they looked absurd their actions cost other people's lives.

7 The British mercenary tradition: The Middle East

The two figures who captured the public imagination above all others in the course of Queen Victoria's long reign were those of the missionary–explorer David Livingstone and the Christian soldier General Charles Gordon whose death at Khartoum in January 1885 set the whole nation grieving. On two notable occasions in the course of his colourful career Gordon served a foreign power and though his job was described in other terms he was in fact a mercenary. In the first instance he was given leave of absence by the British Army according to an Order in Council which permitted army officers to take temporary service under the Emperor of China. In China Gordon was not an adventurer like other Englishmen serving the Emperor at that time but under orders from the War Office: 'Although on loan to the Chinese government he remained a British officer, conscious that he represented the Crown while loyally serving China.'[1] Such service, a temporary attachment to a foreign power with permission to take extended leave from his regular military employment, has been the pattern for many British officers until recent times. Gordon distinguished himself as the leader of the Ever Victorious Army of the Chinese Emperor, helping to put down the Taiping rebellion and in the process winning the sobriquet by which he was known thereafter of 'Chinese' Gordon.

For an ambitious soldier temporary service in the employ of a foreign power when there was no exciting action to be had in the British army was the way to fame and fortune. After China, Gordon was famous and though only aged 32 and a captain in his regiment, the Royal Engineers, in China he had been a general and given temporary British rank of lieutenant-colonel. Gordon's second momentous appointment outside the British army was to serve the Khedive of Egypt, Ismail, as his governor of the newly annexed territory of Southern Sudan. The Khedive, we are told, was charmed by Gordon: 'What an extraordinary Englishman! He doesn't want money.'[2] The Khedive gave Gordan a *firman* which made him Governor-General of the greater part of Sudan with powers more extensive than those wielded by the Viceroy of India. This, of course, was in the heyday of Empire when British world power and influence was at its height. He might have accepted a third appointment of this kind and, indeed, was on the point of becoming the personal empire builder of King Leopold of the Belgians in what became the Congo (the job ultimately carried out by Henry Morton Stanley) when at the last moment the Gladstone government sent him on his ill-fated mission to the Sudan in which he lost his life.

The tradition of secondment or taking temporary service under a foreign ruler with the active support of the British government fitted an imperial tradition that included generations of political advisers and resident commissioners, the *éminences grises* of Empire, who pulled the strings of political power and persuaded nominally independent rulers to act in the British interest. During the last years of empire in the 1950s and 1960s such military and political advisers, including considerable numbers of seconded or retired army officers, became a British speciality in the Arabian peninsula and Gulf region.

In the years after 1945, following the end of WWII, when Britain found its world-wide power rapidly declining, successive governments succumbed to the lures of a semi-fantasy world in which British influence could be prolonged with the help of political advisers and the use of mercenaries. British influence had been extended to the Gulf region from British India in the nineteenth century and substantially consolidated in the immediate aftermath of WWI when Britain obtained mandates over Palestine, Trans-Jordan and Iraq. The small emirates and sheikdoms of the Gulf with which Britain had established special treaty arrangements or protectorate status were ruled over by more or less absolute monarchs whose often medieval behaviour was excused by the British with such adjectives as quaint; they were ideally suited to the operations of a certain kind of British adviser or military officer who saw service in Oman or Yemen as a continuation of imperialism under another guise. Indeed, a school of thought emerged in Britain during the 1950s which argued (partly the result of *force majeure* since the Empire was rapidly disappearing anyway) that it was more profitable and more exciting to 'manage' small states by advising and pulling strings in the background rather than exercising overt colonial control which by then was going out of fashion. This adaptation to a changing world constituted the genesis of what was soon to be called neo-colonialism.

One of the great paradoxes of British history is the dichotomy between Britain the guardian of liberties and freedom, as her propagandists so loved to portray the country during the nineteenth and early twentieth centuries, and Britain the world's greatest imperial power. Imperialism by its nature is the antithesis of liberty and freedom and when in the aftermath of WWII it became impossible to hold on to empire any longer the British establishment was torn between the dictates of reality and the need to disengage from Empire as smoothly as possible so as to create ongoing good relations with former subject peoples and the temptation to hold on to power wherever this seemed a practical possibility. Unfortunately for Britain's international image (though the ever-present excuse of combating communism during the Cold War era served its purpose well) when support was provided for governments that sought Britain's aid, almost without exception these proved to be reactionary anti-democratic regimes whose rulers were determined to resist the forces of progress since the most likely outcome of such progress would be to deprive them of their hereditary authority. Fighting rearguard actions on the wrong side in a rapidly changing world became the preoccupation of what might be described as official British mercenaries and nowhere was this more so than in the Gulf.

David Stirling, the creator of the Special Air Service (SAS), was a hero of WWII whose idea of highly mobile light forces striking behind enemy lines was invaluable to the British campaign in North Africa and came to be copied by other military establishments both during the war and later. In his seminal book, *Arabia Without Sultans*[3] Fred Halliday whose perspective was very much from the left none the less provides an interesting and fair portrait of Stirling as the prototype of the modern mercenary, at least as they would like to see themselves. The SAS, whose success in WWII made Stirling a famous personality, has in subsequent years provided a substantial proportion of British mercenaries whose operations have been based upon the idea of an elite, highly skilled force which can be used to enter a specific war situation, accomplish a mission and then retire. Growing out of the SAS is the concept behind a number of modern security or mercenary business ventures which operate on the principle of providing a secret, highly trained force which is available for operations anywhere in the world. Stirling led the way by establishing his own firm Watchguard (International) Ltd which was designed to supply Asian and African rulers with military advisers. The services it offered included military surveys and advice, head of state security and the training of special forces to combat insurgency and guerrilla warfare.

Between 1962 and 1970 Stirling's organization supplied recruits (both British and French mercenaries) to fight in the civil war in North Yemen; their activities were supported by Britain from Aden, which it controlled until 1967, and from bases in Saudi Arabia, with the connivance of the Saudi government. In 1970 Stirling became involved in an abortive attempt to oust Gaddafi from power in Libya. And, inevitably, the mercenary business often found itself intertwined with the arms-selling business with mercenaries being hired to demonstrate the use of new weapons in Third World countries. Stirling was an elitist whose Capricorn Society which he established in East Africa after the war had as its aim the creation of a new African Dominion that would be white-dominated, though suitable blacks would also have a role to play, and an elitist/racist approach is an essential component of the post-1945 mercenary world. Stirling and other mercenaries, or senior army officers who in retirement sold their services to Gulf rulers, saw the Third World as their natural theatre of operations: skilled white soldiers would sort out the military (and sometimes the political) problems of developing Asian and African countries which had yet to acquire the proper political and military know-how. Mercenary services offered to Third World countries in this way implied a relationship that was superior/inferior or neo-colonialist although, it has to be said, little different in concept from either official aid or the operations of Non-Government Organizations (NGOs).

Burchett and Roebuck, the joint authors of *The Whores of War*, make a clear distinction between the kind of mercenaries who appeared in the Congo or Angola and the officer class who operated as advisers in the Gulf:

> They move from the clubs of Westminster to the palaces of the sheiks and sultans and back, without need for clandestine methods. They are an integral, if not too visible, part of Britain's military and political establishment. They certainly despise the bunglers and headline-grabbers like Banks and Aspin and are delighted that public attention is diverted from their own activities to those of the mountebanks.[4]

The Dhofar rebellion against the Sultan of Oman over the years 1963–75 was about modernization and saw the radicals of Dhofar pitted against the ultra-conservative Sultan, Said ibn Taymar. The Sultan was backed by the British who had long exercised a protectionist colonial role over Oman and at a time when Britain, generally, was in retreat in the Arab world it none the less determined to support a Sultan who almost universally was regarded as one of the least progressive rulers anywhere in the world. The British, it is true, supported the coup of

1970 which brought his more progressive son, Sultan Qabus, to power though their motives were less about progress than pliability and appearances. The rebellion took a more radical and pro-Marxist turn in 1967 after Aden became independent as the People's Democratic Republic of Yemen (PDRY) and provided back-up for the rebels. Britain was interested primarily in Oman's oil and its strategic position for, lingering years after the end of empire, the British remained fascinated by strategic toeholds round the world. Oman's ability to carry on the war against the rebels depended upon British help and much of this support came in the form of seconded officers and men – mercenaries hired out to the Sultan. The 1970 Defence White Paper described Britain's involvement in Oman in the following brief terms:

> The Sultan of Muscat's armed forces, most of whose officers are British, have continued to be engaged in operations against the Dhofar rebels in the rugged hill country north of Salala. The Sultan has made awards for bravery to some British officers for their conduct in these operations.[5]

Halliday says the number of British military personnel serving in Oman was a close secret but that by the end of 1972 there were about 1,000 men; it was, he says, essentially a counter- insurgency war run by an imperialist power through a puppet government and army.[6] It is not easy to determine where seconded soldiers merge into mercenaries and officially Britain only admitted that one military category was to be found in Oman: serving military personnel who had been seconded to the Sultan's Armed Forces (SAF). Halliday, however, identifies three categories as follows: British serving personnel in Oman who were not seconded and included RAF personnel manning the Salala and Masirah bases; members of the British Army Training Team (BATT); and British officers no longer serving in the British army. He adds that the mercenaries, described as 'contract officers', were under the overall British-SAF command.

Some of the mercenaries who appeared in Oman had already served in Katanga and North Yemen and for many it was a chance to amass tax-free savings. The *Sunday Times* listed the pay rates for seconded and mercenary officers as follows: flight lieutenant £5,000pa; contract captains £3,665; majors £4,721; they had no expenses and no income tax to pay.[7] Sultan Qabus was said to prefer British to American mercenaries because they came cheaper! The attitude of many of these mercenaries was summed up accurately and honestly enough by Major Ray Barker-Scofield, head of the Dhofar gendarmerie, who said Dhofar was the last place in the world 'where an Englishman was still called sahib'. He went on to say:

> I am a mercenary and a professional soldier and I've done twenty-five years abroad in such places as India, Burma, South Africa, Egypt, Somalia, Mogadishu, Libya and Germany. This is my profession. Basically I am on the market.[8]

The British involvement in North Yemen during the 1960s was somewhat different for Britain had no 'colonial' foothold there as in Oman. British and French mercenaries operated in North Yemen on the royalist side during these years and both countries turned a blind eye to the mercenary activities of their nationals. Among those who served in North Yemen was David Stirling and British military advisers ran the radio network and carried out sabotage activities. The best known French mercenary to serve there was Colonel Roger Faulques who had already served in the Congo and would shortly appear on the Biafran side in the Nigerian civil war. There was rivalry between the British and French mercenaries but they also cooperated with one another. A French correspondent for *Le Monde*, Eric Rouleau, visited North Yemen in 1967 and found that the British mercenaries were paid by 'a mysterious centre in London, which is called by the elliptical name of the Organization. This is supposed to be run by... Colonel Stirling and Major Brooke.' When Rouleau asked a tribal leader about a British mercenary he was told: 'He is one of the many British historians who are enquiring from us about contemporary events in the Yemen.'[9]

Since Colonel Nasser of Egypt was supporting the rebellion in North Yemen it is, perhaps, unsurprising that Britain was prepared to assist the royalist cause against him. In the 1960s Nasser was still loathed by the British for his 'triumph' during the Suez crisis of 1956 and though by the mid-1960s his charisma in the Arab world had become tarnished his anti-Western nationalism had infinitely greater appeal through the region generally than the conservatism represented by the regimes which Britain insisted upon backing. In 1967 David Stirling offered to provide a 'task force' for Saudi Arabia to use for purposes of sabotage in Yemen and, he claimed, this would have access to the SAS Regiment of the British Army. In a series of articles which appeared in the *Daily Telegraph* during February 1970, an ex-SAS officer, Colonel 'Jim' Johnson, described the British operation in North Yemen, romantically, with the heading 'Second "Lawrence" Foiled Nasser's Army in Yemen'. As with French mercenary operations in other parts of the world the involvement of British mercenaries in North Yemen and Oman was only possible because it received official backing.

Not all the Middle East was susceptible to this kind of slightly old-fashioned mercenary activity. The civil war in Lebanon which got underway in the mid-1970s attracted a steady stream of French mercenaries from a rightwing background in support of the Falangists as well as some of the more brutal kind from Britain who were not interested in Arabs calling them 'sahib'. The British journalist Peter Niesewand interviewed the mercenary known as 'Blue' Kelly who described the technique used to wipe out Palestinians in the Sabra area of Beirut. Was it costly, he was asked.

Not if you do it methodically, building by building, going down both sides of the street. Just dynamite them, and then move on to the next. Shoot everyone – men, women, and children: no problem.[10]

The bitter Gulf War between Iran and Iraq that raged from 1980 to 1988 produced major arms selling scandals in the West – the Irangate affair in the United States and the Matrix–Churchill affair in Britain – and it saw the emergence of another kind of mercenary job. A story which appeared in the *Observer* in 1987 was about veterans of the Falklands War who were acting as 'safety advisers' aboard oil tankers or other vessels running the gauntlet of attack in the Gulf's so-called 'Exocet Alley'. Typical of these was Peter Tully, who had been a troop sergeant in the Falklands but in the Gulf had become part of an elite team drawn from former members of the Royal Marines and the Special Boat Squadron; his task aboard the tanker was to help thwart successful attacks or, if that failed, help to restrict fires and secondary explosions. He was provided by Defence Analysts Ltd. of Wincanton, Somerset; the company claimed that tanker owners approached it for advice which would include the installation of chaff 'guns' to decoy missiles and ways of reducing the radar signature. The safety adviser, who was not armed, would be put on board. The firm claimed that it had saved insurers millions of pounds. The firm was run by two senior Falklands veterans – Commander 'Sharky' Ward and General Sir Jeremy Moore, both with impeccable military credentials.[11]

In 1991 Arab mercenaries appeared alongside Saddam Hussein's Republican Guards fighting to suppress the Kurdish and Shi'ite rebellions in Iraq. Kurdish rebels fighting the Iraqi army in the northern mountains claimed to have encountered Sudanese, Yemeni and Palestinian militiamen. Ann Clywd, then Labour's spokeswoman for foreign affairs in Parliament who had spent time with the Kurdish resistance fighters under Jalal Talabani, confirmed that he was fighting Palestinians and Sudanese as well as the regular Republican Guards and that captured Iraqi soldiers also confirmed that large numbers of Arab nationals were being used as mercenaries. At the beginning of the Iran–Iraq Gulf War Western reporters had been taken to a militia training ground outside Baghdad where they were shown Sudanese, Yemeni, Palestinian, Jordanian and North African nationals being trained. They were volunteers. A US official said that such non-Iraqi nationals were mainly used in support roles and that their impact on the fighting was minimal: 'These are not mercenaries in the soldier-of-fortune sense' he claimed. The presence of mercenaries in the Kurdish war was also attested by a visiting French doctor, Marcel Roux, who later testified before the Congressional Human Rights Caucus. In an interview after the hearing Dr Roux said: 'The rebels said they were fighting Republican Guards and mercenaries. They said Sudanese, Jordanian and Yemeni mercenaries were being paid thousands of dollars to fight the Kurds.' These claims were borne out by a representative of the Democratic Party of Kurdistan, Mohammed Shokat, while another rebel told *Agence France-Presse* that he had killed a Sudanese helicopter pilot during the battle for Kirkuk in late March 1991.[12]

The mercenary world is constantly changing and those who wish to sell their military skills – whether at the top end of the scale as advisers to governments or at the bottom end of the scale as available cannon fodder – must adjust to the new demands and expectations of would-be employers. The anachronistic ideal expressed by Major Ray Barker-Scofield in Dhofar that it was one of the last places where an Englishman (presumably an officer and gentleman) could still be addressed as 'sahib' must finally have disappeared. Instead, Falklands veterans with very different skills appear in the Gulf to assist in the protection of tankers and an increasing number of Arab 'cannon fodder' mercenaries have been used by Saddam Hussein. Many of the Libyan troops deployed during the 1980s by Gaddafi in the war he fought to gain control of the Aozou Region of Chad turned out not to be Libyans at all, but members of the Islamic Pan-African Legion, often mercenaries press-ganged from among those who had gone to seek work in Libya from other Islamic countries.

During the discussions that followed the British government's far reaching Strategic Defence Review and the White Paper which was launched by the prime minister, Tony Blair, in July 1998 commentators

The British mercenary tradition 73

pointed out that while modern soldiers receive complex training in military matters such skills are often useless when they return to civilian life at a comparatively early age and have to begin a new career. If they are not provided with alternative civilian skills before leaving the army, what are they going to do? The answer, which has become part of the modern and violent age in which we live, is to offer the military skills which they do have on the open market and become potential mercenaries and the proliferation of security and other firms offering special protection and other services abroad would suggest that there is a substantial and growing market waiting for them.

8 Papua New Guinea and Bougainville

Papua New Guinea (PNG) which includes the island of Bougainville and the Bismarck Arhchipelago had been administered as a colony by Australia until it became independent as a full member of the Commonwealth in 1975 and was thereafter treated as a country of concentration for Australian aid. Bougainville has large resources of copper and the development of these resources, inevitably leading to major changes in the lifestyle of the island, created demands for secession which came to a head in 1989. The Prime Minister of Papua New Guinea at the time, Rabbie Namaliu, ordered the security forces which were sent to Bougainville 'to act with caution, understanding and patience'[1] while they tried to cope with the demands of the secessionist-inclined landowners under the leadership of Fred Ona. The rebels succeeded in closing down the giant copper mine thereby depriving the government of vital revenues. The government then took tougher action which included evacuating people from villages near the mine and moving them into camps. The police and military were given power to search, seize, arrest and evacuate people from designated areas. This was the beginning of ten years confrontation between the government and the islanders.

The crisis worsened in 1990: the copper mine remained closed and as a result the kina was devalued by 10 per cent in January. The following month guerrillas of the Bougainville Revolutionary Army (BRA) attacked plantations and forced plantation workers, government workers and expatriates to evacuate. In March government troops and police were withdrawn from the island and in May the BRA declared Bougainville independent. The government then blockaded Bougainville island until an agreement brokered by New Zealand persuaded it to lift the blockade and restore communications. A peace treaty between the government and representatives of Bougainville was signed in January 1991 but this did not resolve the dispute since the guerrillas of the BRA remained in readiness to resume the fighting while conditions on the island appeared to get worse. In April 1992 the Bougainville leader, Tony Anugu, who had been responsible for negotiating the creation of the South Bougainville Interim Authority with two representative of the Papua New

Guinea government, Sir Michael Somare and Father John Momis, was murdered. In October a frustrated government launched a major offensive against the rebels on Bougainville and government troops captured the rebel stronghold of Arawa at the end of the month. Following elections that were held the previous June Paias Wingit had replaced Rabbie Namaliu as prime minister.

Little changed in relation to Bougainville during 1993 although Papua New Guinea faced difficulty in attracting foreign investment and this was made worse by general violence and poor law enforcement. After a long period of stand-off, during which the number of BRA guerrillas occupying the copper mine steadily dropped, government forces recaptured the mine in September 1994 after the remaining guerrillas had withdrawn to the hills. The government hoped to reopen the mine as soon as it was in a position to guarantee worker access to it on a daily basis.

Despite guarantees to the BRA guerrilla leaders the government was unable to persuade them to come down from the hills to negotiate a peace. Continuing unrest in Bougainville during 1995 overshadowed the country's celebration of 20 years of independence. Nine soldiers of the Papua New Guinea army were killed fighting the rebels. Talks to resolve the dispute were held in Cairns, Australia, between a spokesman for the Bougainville Revolutionary Army (BRA) and three other rebel representatives but the talks were abandoned on November 10 by the Prime Minister of Papua New Guinea, now Sir Julius Chan, and nothing was resolved.

The copper mine, the world's largest, lay at the heart of the dispute: for the government it represented a major source of annual revenues; for the BRA it stood for a fundamental alteration in the lifestyle of the island from which its members did not feel they were benefiting. Claims for compensation for environmental damage by villagers were being opposed by the Australian mining resources company BHP. The Prime Minister warned the villagers against unrealistic expectations of compensation while the minister for mining and petroleum, John Giheno, accused BHP of blatant interference in the affairs of Papua New Guinea, claiming that it had helped draft legislation that would outlaw individual claims for compensation against mining companies. BHP denied these charges.

The crisis grew worse in 1996 by which time the confrontation had lasted for eight years. Government forces now employed Iroquois helicopters in the fight against the BRA guerrillas and this led to a row with Australia which had supplied them; the Australian Foreign

Minister, Alexander Downer, threatened to review the A$12m defence cooperation agreement between the two countries on the grounds that it had been violated when the helicopters were used against the Bougainville rebels. In October the possibility of a breakthrough was destroyed when Theodore Miriung, a leading advocate of peace, was assassinated. He had been the head of the Bougainville Transitional Government.

THE HIRING OF MERCENARIES

In February 1997 the Australian government turned down a request from Papua New Guinea for military assistance to fight the Bougainville Revolutionary Army rebels. The government had asked for assistance with electronic intelligence to pinpoint the rebel radio broadcasts and body armour. The Australian position, however, was that there had to be a politically negotiated settlement to the crisis. By this time, according to unofficial figures compiled for a United Nations Commission on Human Rights report, some 10,000 people, mainly civilians, had already been killed in the nine-year old civil war. The dispute was a classic example of a local community pitted against the power of major international mining companies. The indigenous landowners who headed the revolt complained that their land had been stolen from them and that the mine caused deadly pollution. The copper mine was the largest in the world; its Australian operators were Conzine Riotinto Australia (CRA) which is one of Australia's biggest mining companies, in its turn 49 per cent owned by Britain's giant Rio Tinto company. The rebel forces, despite being ill-armed and relying upon home-made rifles, salvaged machine-guns from WWII aircraft and sometimes bows and arrows, had yet managed to force the mine to close and the government army (temporarily) to withdraw from the island. Subsequently, the PNG army was accused by both natives of Bougainville and human rights organizations of atrocities which included burning villages, rape and torture.

According to Australian newspaper reports the PNG government set aside £22m to pay for a covert mercenary operation to end the rebellion. Two Russian aircraft were employed ferrying personel and equipment between Jackson Airport at Port Moresby and the northern coastal town of Wewak where the mercenaries were being trained in Moem Barracks, the point from which an offensive against the BRA would be launched. At that time five PNG soldiers had been held captive by the rebels for the preceding six months. The Prime Minister, Sir Julius Chan, denied that his government planned to use mercenaries but confirmed that it had hired the services of Sandline International to assist in training government soldiers. The PNG Defence Force Chief-of-Staff, Colonel Jack Tuta, said the latest (Sandline) training was no different from that involving Australia, New Zealand or the United States: 'We are occasionally bringing in people to train our guys on the use of new and specific equipment' he said. The news that the PNG government had decided to call in mercenaries led to a crisis with Australia whose Prime Minister, John Howard, told the Australian parliament: 'We would regard the use of mercenaries as an extremely unwelcome development in the South Pacific.'[2] The Australian Foreign Minister, Alexander Downer, reinforced his Prime Minister's opposition to the use of mercenaries, arguing that their employment would damage the international standing of PNG: 'I will use any vehicle which is reasonable that I possibly can to try to stop this operation going ahead' he said. He added that any resumption of military activity in Bougainville would be regarded by Australia 'as absolutely disastrous'. The fact that PNG was prepared to spend £22m on hiring mercenaries was also likely to raise questions among the country's aid donors. Despite this opposition the Chan government went ahead and contracted Sandline International which is a Bahamas registered company with offices in London and Washington DC.

Sandline denied that it consisted of mercenaries. Its chief executive officer, Lt-Col. Tim Spicer, told the British newspaper, *The Independent*: 'We are an international military consultancy company specialising in the provision of advice and problem resolution for legitimate governments and international organisations'. Spicer had been a lieutenant- colonel in the Scots Guards with experience in the Falklands, Bosnia, Cyprus, the Gulf War and Northern Ireland and had acted as military attache to General Sir Michael Rose in Bosnia. His headquarters were offices in the King's Road, Chelsea, in London. The PNG government approached Sandline during 1996 for advice and training for its army and a contract worth £22m was signed in January 1997. After nine years of rebellion and periodic fighting the PNG National Defence Force had failed to bring the BRA rebels under control. Sandline refused to reveal details of its agreement with the PNG government although Australian newspapers reported that up to 150 foreign soldiers (mercenaries) were to be brought in to capture or kill the leaders of the secessionist BRA. The Prime Minister, Sir Julius Chan, then admitted:

> The team we have hired to train our security force members are not cowboys, they are a reputable professional company who are part of our many-faceted strategy to reach a lasting solution to this particular crisis, as well as other matters of national security.[3]

According to Lt-Col Spicer, Sandline was established in the early 1990s in order:

> to fill a vacuum in the post-Cold War era, to offer governments specialist military expertise at a time when Western nations' desire to provide active support to resolve overseas conflicts has materially decreased, as has their capability to do so.

He said Sandline was entirely privately owned by senior ex-military personnel from the UK and US armed forces. Sandline calls upon the resources of a number of different specialist sub- contractors in Britain, the United States and South Africa which include ex-members of the UK, US and South African special forces. Sandline does not like to be described as mercenary and claims it will only accept projects that 'receive the endorsement of the international community'. It declares that it has four operating principles: it will only undertake projects acceptable to key Western governments such as the US and UK; it will only undertake operations that are legal and moral; it works on behalf of internationally recognized government regimes; and its operations must be conducted within the boundaries of client governments.[4]

These Sandline claims are interesting given the vehement opposition to their involvement in PNG by the Australian government. Did Sandline think that Canberra's views did not matter? Or was it acting in PNG because Britain had a stake in the mining business through Rio Tinto which, from Sandline's viewpoint, overrode any Australian objection. Such considerations pose intriguing questions about the real motives and intentions of such security companies.

The South African company, Executive Outcomes, now became involved in PNG claiming that it had been sub-contracted by Sandline to provide aircraft, equipment and specialized training for the PNG forces. Executive Outcomes acknowledged that the training it was to provide was part of PNG government strategy 'to reach a lasting solution to the... crisis in Bougainville.' The Prime Minister, Sir Julius Chan, said of Executive Outcomes: 'They are out here to build up the capabilities of our defence force.' He added: 'They would be taken in only as an advisory team, but we would not use them in the front line. We are no fools. We are a government, and no government would allow their citizens to be killed by foreigners.'[5] Despite this assurance by Sir Julius Chan, the Australian Prime Minister, John Howard, said he thought a mercenary strike had been planned against the Bougainville rebels.

The crisis in Bougainville was playing havoc with Australian–PNG relations. Hospitals in northern Australia were put on alert to handle increased casualties from any renewed fighting in Bougainville. Papua New Guinea is Australia's closest neighbour and is seen in Canberra as vital to the country's security. According to Sir Julius Chan the possibility of using non-government soldiers to train the PNG forces had been canvassed in a defence paper drawn up in consulation with Australia but Alexander Downer, the Australian Foreign Minister, denied this. In the Australian parliament a bi-partisan motion condemned the mercenary plan and urged Australia to warn Papua New Guinea that the use of mercenaries would 'prejudice our bilateral relationship'. Amnesty International claimed that the PNG defence force was responsible for more than 40 deaths and 'disappearances' in Bougainville during 1996. The report also condemned 'deliberate and arbitrary' killings by the BRA.

On a visit to Port Moresby, the capital of Papua New Guinea, Australia's Foreign Minister, Alexander Downer, briefed diplomats of Britain, New Zealand and the United States about Australia's strong opposition to the use of mercenaries in Bougainville and Britain also expressed its concern at the use of Sandline. On his return to Australia Mr Downer told parliament that he had asked Britain, New Zealand and the United States to raise the mercenary issue with the PNG government. In the face of gathering opposition to his mercenary plan, Sir Julius Chan admitted that 40 foreign soldiers whom he described as military advisers had arrived in Papua New Guinea; he said that 30 of them would train PNG soldiers while the remaining 10 would be 'back-room advisers'.[6] The issue of foreign mercenaries now led to a rift between the PNG Prime Minister and the Commander of the PNG Defence Force which threatened to bring down the Chan government.

The new row revolved round the PNG military whose soldiers, on low pay and poor conditions, had been fighting in Bougainville for nine years and resented mercenaries being called in to do their job. As the argument between the military and the government developed it became plain that the blame for hiring the mercenaries lay as much with the military as with the government. On 17 March 1997, Brigadier-General Jerry Singirok, Commander of the PNG Defence Force, called upon Prime Minister Sir Julius Chan to resign, saying his government was guilty of 'corrupt practices' in hiring the Sandline mercenaries. He insisted he was not mounting a coup:

> As armed forces commander, I believe the strategy of the government is wrong, and I have basically told the Prime Minister and the Minister for Defence that what they have done is incorrect. We don't have a coup. I believe in a very strong democratic country, that the country should be run for the people by the people. It's a matter of principle and ethics.[7]

At this point the army had taken into custody more than 40 Sandline mercenaries most of whom came from South Africa. Brigadier-General Singirok said the hiring of mercenaries had been a quick fix solution. After a cabinet meeting the Prime Minister said he would not resign and that, constitutionally, though Brigadier-General Singirok could disagree with the government he had to carry out orders. It was not clear, at this point, how much support Singirok could depend upon from the army or the police for though he claimed to have the support of Bob Nenta, the PNG police commissioner, Nenta dissociated himself from Singirok's manoeuvres. Brigadier-General Singirok interpreted the Prime Minister's deal with Sandline as an attack upon his position as army commander and as a vote of no confidence in his forces. The appearance of mercenaries in Papua New Guinea, however Sandline and Executive Outcomes prefer to describe their personnel, was viewed with apprehension by Australia which had ruled PNG until independence in 1975 and John Howard, the Australian Prime Minister, had held talks in Sydney with Sir Julius Chan early in March in a bid to persuade him to end the Sandline involvement in Papua New Guinea.

Violence then erupted in Port Moresby as police used teargas on anti-government rioters and 2,000 civilians demonstrated outside the army barracks in opposition to the plan to pay mercenaries to crush the Bougainville rebellion. The rioters refused to disperse until their petition for the resignation of the Prime Minister had been presented. Inside the barracks 1,000 soldiers demanded that the mercenaries be sent home. There were also attacks upon government corruption and part of the demonstrating crowd turned to looting the Asian-owned department stores close to the army barracks. The Australian Prime

Minister, John Howard, sent the head of his Foreign Affairs Department, Philip Flood, and two other emissaries to try to persuade Sir Julius Chan to abandon his contract with Sandline International and its affiliate, Executive Outcomes.

Under the pressure from within and without as well as the publicity Prime Minister Chan appeared to weaken and intimated that he might cancel the Sandline contract. He said:

I think we should not be too premature about making that decision. But the situation, whether you like it or not, has been compromised by publicity. As a result of that, we may have to look at the whole situation again – the security aspects of their engagement.

Meanwhile, six Sandline International personnel had left the country while four more were accomodated at the Port Moresby Taurama army barracks 'for their own protection'. In London Sandline International would only say 'We are in direct contact with the Prime Minister and we are confident that the situation will be resolved amicably in the interests of the country'.[8] In Port Moresby the Prime Minister faced a mutinous army whose soldiers demanded the reinstatement of Brigadier-General Singirok whom he had sacked while university students boycotted classes and joined in the demand for the Prime Minister to resign. Amid rumours and counter-rumours it was claimed that the contract with Sandline had been cancelled. Brigadier-General Singirok said he accepted his dismissal but he remained in the main army barracks where 1,500 protesters had arrived to support him in his stand against the Prime Minister.

Sandline then announced in London that it would withdraw its personnel from Papua New Guinea and claimed that it was 'caught in the middle of a deep political wrangle between the government [of PNG] and parts of the military'. Sandline claimed that Brigadier-General Singirok's actions had taken them completely by surprise. The Prime Minister, Sir Julius Chan, said the Sandline contract would be suspended pending a judicial inquiry. The mercenaries then flew out of Port Moresby, expelled by the soldiers they had supposedly come to assist, and went via Hong Kong back to South Africa. They left behind a capital city in turmoil with the government and the army in confrontation and spreading violence and rioting which by then had reached towns outside Port Moresby. Australia had placed its troops on increased readiness in case the crisis got worse.[9]

A consequence of the crisis was to bring down unwelcome publicity upon both Sandline International and Executive Outcomes. Lt-Col. Tim

Spicer, the leader of the Sandline operation who described himself as a military adviser, was arrested just before he boarded the charter aircraft which took the last of his mercenary force, mainly black South Africans, back to Johannesburg. Spicer was charged with illegally importing firearms and 50 rounds of ammunition into PNG; then he was released into the custody of the British High Commission. The Sandline mission collapsed as a result of the confrontation between the PNG Prime Minister and his army commander Brigadier-General Singirok which had been triggered off by the arrival of the mercenaries. The crisis was the more surprising because originally Singirok had been in London to negotiate for the Sandline mission which was to include specialist counter-insurgency training, ambush drills, helicopter operations, radio communications and surveillance. Despite his strictures against the government for hiring mercenaries, in fact Singirok had been desperate for success against the rebels who throughout his fifteen months as army commander had outfought and outmanoeuvred his troops. When the mercenaries arrived, however, Singirok's troops reacted angrily because of the high salaries they received while they themselves were badly paid and poorly equipped.

The chairman of Executive Outcomes, Eeben Barlow, now entered the argument to claim that his organization only worked for legitimate governments. On their return to Johannesburg the 48 mercenaries refused to comment on what had happened. In Port Moresby Lt-Col. Spicer was to stand trial for the illegal import of arms and ammunition and was also to be called upon to testify before a judicial inquiry into the Sandline contract with the Papua New Guinea government. (Once he had appeared before the inquiry he was allowed to leave the country.) Although Sir Julius Chan survived a no-confidence motion by 58 to 39 votes, armed soldiers surrounded the parliament buildings and were searching for MPs. In the no-confidence debate the Prime Minister said that the country's ill-trained and ill-equipped soldiers had been captured on Bougainville or slain 'like sitting ducks' and that 'There comes a time when you have to act in the interest of the nation's security'. The decision to hire the mercenaries had been taken after Australia and New Zealand refused to provide either the equipment or the training needed to crush the rebellion. The Prime Minister won a tactical victory in the debate only to increase the anger of the demonstrators outside parliament and spark off further violence. Both the Commonwealth Secretary-General, Chief Emeka Anyaoku, and the British Foreign Office urged the PNG government to find a peaceful solution to the crisis. Meanwhile, the crisis was having severe economic repercussions as capital was withdrawn and foreign reserves fell. At the end of March the Prime Minister Sir Julius Chan, the Deputy Prime Minister Chris Haiveta, and the Defence Minister Mathias Ijape stepped down to await the outcome of the judicial inquiry into the Sandline affair. Brigadier-General Singirok, who at this point appeared as the hero of the army and those opposed to the Prime Minister, had in fact been involved in the negotiations to hire Sandline from the beginning. His motives were apparently straightforward: he was desperate to retrieve his and his army's reputation after the disastrous failure of his 1996 Operation High Speed 2 which had been designed to 'decapitate the rebel leadership' but instead had resulted in the capture of five of his soldiers who were still being held by the rebels when the political crisis exploded.

The Sandline contract which had finally been signed in January 1997 for £22.5m assigned 80 per cent of the expenditure to equipment and weaponry for the PNG Defence Force; otherwise the Sandline mandate was to train counter-insurgency teams to 'harass the rebel patrols and deny them freedom of movement'. The most likely explanation for Brigadier-General Siringok's *volte face* on 17 March, when he turned on the Prime Minister, was his realization that his own officers and men would see the Sandline contract as a vote of no confidence in their abilities. Further, the General's period as commander had been a disaster: his campaigns against the rebels had failed, the morale of the army was at a low ebb, discipline had deteriorated, and his command was being investigated for financial irregularities while it was roumoured that the Prime Minister wanted to find a replacement for him. In these circumstances the Brigadier-General's move was designed as much to save his own position as out of any professional or ideological opposition to the use of mercenaries as such.

The judicial inquiry cleared Chan of both the corruption charges that had been laid against him and illegal actions in relation to the Sandline contract and the Prime Minister resumed the premiership on 2 June. A general election was due to be held over the last two weeks of June and was contested by a large number of parties and candidates; when the results were announced on 15 July Chan himself had lost his seat and, following complex manoeuvring between the parties, the mayor of Port Moresby whose People's National Congress (PNC) had only won five seats out of 109 none the less became Prime Minister. In July ten days of talks took place at the Burnham army camp near Christchurch, New Zealand, between members of the government and various of the factions from Bougainville including the BRA although Francis Ona, the BRA leader absented himself from the talks. The result was the so-called 'Burnham Declaration' which called for a ceasefire, the demilitarization of the island, an end to the military blockade and the installation of a UN peacekeeping force. The new Prime Minister, Bill Skate, visited Bougainville in August when he endorsed the Burnham Declaration and said he would seek a peaceful settlement of the problem. The agreement appeared to make little difference and further talks were held in October; again Francis Ona failed to take part and at the end of the year there was no real sign that anything on Bougainville had changed or that the crisis had been resolved.

Although Sandline represented itself as a military advisory organization that would provide training and expertise on request to legitimate governments, its connections with the mining world suggested a more complex motivation for its involvement in Papua New Guinea. The British businessman, Tony Buckingham, who has extensive mining and oil interests in Africa and shuns publicity, was none the less drawn into the post-mortem discussions of the Sandline affair. He operates from the same offices in London as Sandline and had been discussing the reopening and financing of the Bougainville copper mine at the same time that Sandline was discussing its military contract. Mr Buckingham said: 'We offered to assist in identifying the right sources of capital and ownership'.[10] The Panguna copper mine on Bougainville had been operated by Bougainville Copper Ltd which was 53.6 per cent owned by the Australian mining giant RTZ-CRA and (when it was operating) generated a third of Papua New Guinea's foreign exchange earnings. Mr Buckingham said: 'The strategy recommended was for the Papua New Guinea government to buy back the mine from CRA so that they would control the equity and then get responsible groups involved in the development of the mine.' Mr Buckingham was responsible for introducing Executive Outcomes to the governments of Angola and Sierra Leone in both of which countries he has extensive mineral and energy interests. His links with both Sandline International and Executive Outcomes, as well as his mining interests, suggested an obvious mercenary–mining connexion with the future possibility that security companies are likely to become the close allies of international mining companies which often operate in countries where stability is far from guaranteed. Mr Buckingham insisted that he had no corporate link with Sandline although he had assisted Lt-Col.

Spicer in his negotiations with the government of Papua New Guinea. As he explained:

> The point is that PNG holds a major asset which no one is benefiting from, least of all the people of Bougainville. Sandline's role was to deal with the security elements, our role in conjunction with other parties and the government would have been to develop the mine which would have brought benefits not only to the investors but also to Papua New Guinea and the people of Bougainville.[11]

In this particular case the Sandline agreement with the government of Papua New Guinea was aborted yet there is little doubt that security firms such as Sandline or Executive Outcomes and mining conglomerates or freelances such as Mr Buckingham can envisage profitable potential partnerships when large mineral resources are at stake in countries troubled by civil wars or insurrections such as Angola, Sierra Leone or Papua New Guinea. Partnerships of this kind could well become the pattern in the future and offer lucrative pickings if they succeed.

9 Nicaragua and Colombia

The determination of the United States to exercise political controls over the countries of Central and South America – its own 'backyard' – has led successive governments throughout the present century to intervene in a variety of ways: with military force; by means of sanctions; with anti-drugs programmes; or by more covert operations, employing the CIA, military advisers or mercenaries, and by supporting proxies such as the *Contra* rebels from Nicaragua during the 1980s. The two themes that have most engaged the attention of Washington have been the fight against the spread of Communism, especially during the 1970s and 1980s, and the ongoing battle to stamp out the production of drugs which has been centred upon Peru and Colombia.

In the 1980s the CIA employed the German arms dealer, Ernst Werner Glatt, to deliver arms to the *Contras* in Nicaragua. In 1992 a helicopter which was shot down over Peru led to the death of Robert Hitchman, a former Marine Corps fighter pilot and covert-ops specialist, who was then working for the US Drug Enforcement Administration (DEA). Both these men were active in that shady world of special operations, arms running, military advisers (mercenaries) or CIA undercover operations that are a part of the less publicized means whereby Washington attempts to control its Latin American neighbours. When Hitchman was killed in the helicopter crash in Peru his son said that the then US Secretary of State Jim Baker had asked him to keep quiet: 'They didn't want the public to know the full extent of American involvement in drug wars in Latin America' he said.[1] The point about such operations is that American involvement in the affairs of its neighbours is far greater than Congressional authorization or public opinion would allow if all the facts were known. And since governments normally want to do more than the ordinary process of politics would allow covert unauthorized operations become the norm.

NICARAGUA

The Sandinista National Liberation Front which emerged victorious from the Nicaraguan civil war of 1979 that had brought about the downfall of the dictator Anastasio Somoza Debayle (later assassinated in Paraguay) appeared to move to the political left with the cabinet appointments made at the end of 1979. New laws brought locally owned banks, insurance companies and the mining sector under state control while the principal exports (coffee, cotton and seafoods) were also brought under state management. Given the ravages of the civil war – an estimated 30,000 deaths and damage to the economy in excess of US$2bn – stringent economy measures were to be expected but these 'socialist' measures were unlikely to meet with approval in Washington.

Supporters of former President Somoza now began to use the neighbouring state of Honduras as a base from which to launch cross-border raids into Nicaragua and the Sandinista government complained that the Honduran army was giving them active support. The United States increased its military aid to Honduras which it saw as a useful base for possible later intervention. During the course of 1981 the Sandinista government faced increasing American hostility: in April President Ronald Reagan announced the suspension of economic aid to Nicaragua. Earlier in the year it became public knowledge that about 600 Nicaraguan exiles were being given military training in Florida but when Nicaragua asked the US Government to condemn the activities of these exiles the US Secretary of State, William Haig, said that such training was not illegal unless it could be shown to be part of a plan to invade a friendly country. His reply was typical of the attitudes adopted by the United States, Britain or France when they chose to ignore mercenary or other activities of their nationals that are clearly aimed at the subversion of regimes of which they disapprove. In its turn, the United States then accused Nicaragua of supplying arms to the El Salvador guerrillas and condemned the Sandinista military build-up. It was already clear in the first years of Sandinista power that the United States was ready to provide extra aid to Nicaragua's hostile neighbours. By the end of 1981 there were an estimated 4,000 former national guardsmen across the border in Honduras. Tensions between the two countries increased through 1982 when Honduras established a new military base within 12 miles of the Nicaraguan border. Daniel Ortega Saavedra, the leader of the Sandinista junta, said war between the two countries appeared to be inevitable unless the United States stopped providing support to the former Nicaraguan national guardsmen then in Honduras.

The United States adopted an overtly threatening policy towards Nicaragua during 1983, for example, by staging ground-based military manoeuvres in Honduras throughout the year and holding naval exercises off the coast of Nicaragua in August. Towards the end of the year Washington also announced plans to establish a major military base in Honduras and increased its support for the border attacks against Nicaragua. These cross- border raids slowed down the national reconstruction programme which the Sandinista government was implementing. Additonal attacks were now also being mounted from Nicaragua's southern neighbour, Costa Rica. The *Contras* from Honduras were especially active in September and October when they attacked economic targets such as ports, fuel installations and industrial sites. This shift by the *Contras* from military to economic targets represented a change in strategy since the early attacks had neither eroded public support for the Sandinista government nor inflicted any significant military damage. The American government admitted that the CIA was involved in sabotage operations in Nicaragua but justified this covert aid to the *Contras* as a means of preventing the spread of the Sandinista 'socialist' revolution to its neighbours. In both July and August the US House of Representatives voted to stop further funds for these CIA operations but the more right-wing Republican-dominated Senate overturned the House bill in November and voted instead to continue aid to the *Contras* although cutting it from $50m which President Reagan had asked for to $19m. Daniel Ortega accused the United States of waging an undeclared war on Nicaragua to destroy its revolution.

During 1984 the *Contras* in Honudras continued to receive substantial support from both the CIA and private backers in the United States although the CIA was to come in for severe international criticism for its part in mining Nicaraguan ports as well as for issuing the *Contras* with a manual on methods of destabilization. US politicians increased their opposition to further funding for the *Contras* and in June the House of Representatives refused to vote for the $21m which the government had requested although a later compromise reduced an October request for $28m to $14m though this was not to be made available until February 1985. Tensions between the United States and Nicaragua became sufficiently explosive that Nicaragua accused the United States of planning an imminent invasion. In May 1985 the Sandinista government began to launch cross-border strikes against the Honduran bases of the most formidable of the *Contra* groups which called itself the Nicaraguan Democratic Force (FDN). Part of the Sandinista government's strategy was to relocate tens of thousands of people from the border areas of northern Nicaragua so as to deprive the raiding *Contras* of any local support and create 'free-fire zones' where the army could operate uninhibited by the presence of civilian populations. The US response to this heightened anti-*Contra* programme by the Sandinista government was to impose a total embargo on trade with Nicaragua. Later (June 1985) the US Congress released $27m for 'nonlethal' aid to the *Contra* rebels. Even so, *Contra* raids did not result in their being able to hold on to any territory. The *Contras* operating from Costa Rica were even less successful.

Pressures exerted upon Nicaragua with both covert and overt US support became considerably more potent during 1986. Costa Rica, despite a promise by its President, Arias Sanchez, that he would prevent *Contra* forces using his country as a base from which to launch attacks into Nicaragua was obliged to admit that *Contra* forces had been operating from Costa Rican soil. In response Nicaragua filed an action in the International Court of Justice to restrain Costa Rica from sheltering the *Contras*. US military personnel operated in Honduras throughout the year assisting the *Contra* rebels and President Jose Azcona Hoyo admitted officially for the first time that *Contra* forces were operating from his territory. He also lifted the ban on aid being given to the rebels. In March Nicaraguan armed forces moved into Honduras in order to destroy *Contra* bases. On a visit to Washington in May 1986 President Azcona told President Reagan that he would accept US aid for the *Contras*, by then estimated to number between 15,000 and 20,000, because otherwise he would be unable to control them. He then insisted that Honduras should not be used as a base for attacks upon a neighbouring state and asked that the US aid should be used to shift the war into Nicaragua. The United States provided US$61.2m in aid for the Honduras economic stabilization programme.

In August 1986, after intense debate, the US Congress passed US $100m package of military aid for the *Contras* in the expectation that this would make it possible for them to establish bases in Nicaragua for the first time. The year witnessed the trial of Eugene Hassenfas, the US pilot of a *Contra* supply plane which was shot down over Nicaragua by government forces. Hassenfas told his captors that the CIA was continuing to help the *Contras* despite the veto on its activities by Congress although the US government denied this. After a trial by the People's Tribunal Hassenfas was sentenced to 30 years in prison but was pardoned by President Ortega at the end of the year and returned to the United States where the Irangate scandal revolving round Lt-Col. Oliver North was about to break.

Despite the fact that they launched a major offensive in northern Nicaragua during April 1987 the year was to prove an especially difficult one for the *Contras*. In the fighting they were heavily outnumbered by the Sandinista forces and suffered major casualties including 477 killed in June alone. According to the Sandinista government 14,914 *Contras* had been killed in the five years to 1986 as opposed to 5,066 government soldiers and civilians. In August the Sandinista government signed a peace plan with its Central American neighbours which stipulated that external powers should cease all military aid to insurgent forces in the region. In Honduras tension mounted between the government, the *Contras* and the United States when it became known that the Pentagon intended to construct military projects in the country and Honduras realized that, possibly, the United States saw its military presence there as permanent. There were 3,700 US troops in Honduras and their numbers were increased during the year when the Americans conducted a big military exercise, Solid Shield '87. As the Irangate scandal broke in Washington, threatening to end all US support for the *Contras*, Honduras became worried about ongoing US aid should the United States be obliged to cease its support to the *Contras* in the aftermath of Irangate. In Costa Rica it was revealed, again as a result of the Irangate hearings in Washington, that an airstrip which had been used by the *Contras* had been constructed with funds derived from the covert sale of arms to Iran as authorized by Lt-Col. Oliver North.

Irangate, as it came to be called, was the biggest political scandal to erupt in Washington during the 1980s. The scandal began to emerge, ironically enough, in Lebanon when on November 3, 1986, the Beirut magazine *al-Shiraa* carried an article to the effect that the United States had negotiated an arms deal with Iran. This was at a time when Washington claimed that Iran was a terrorist state – that is, one which sponsored international terrorism – and had long insisted that no arms should be sold to it either by the United States or its allies. It was also the height of the Iran–Iraq war when the major powers were claiming to stand back and not support either side in the conflict. The essence of the *al-Shiraa* article was confirmed by government officials in Washington. It was followed by the further, more damning revelation, from the US Attorney-General Edwin Meese, that millions of dollars of profits from these arms sales to Iran had been siphoned off to support the *Contras* in their attempt to overthrow the government of Nicaragua. The revelation angered Congress since it had passed the Boland Amendment in 1984 which forbad direct or indirect military aid to the *Contras*.

President Reagan appointed former senator John Tower to head a panel of inquiry and its revelations during 1987 threatened the standing of the President himself; he was criticized for failing to control the actions of the National Security Council (NSC) and in particular the National Security Adviser Robert C McFarlane, his successor Vice-Admiral John M Poindexter and Lt-Col. Oliver North who was a member of the NSC staff. Early in 1985 McFarlane had visited Iran to negotiate the sale of 2,004 TOW anti-tank missiles, 18 Hawk anti-aircraft missiles and some 200 spare parts for the Hawk missile batteries. Iran paid US$30m for this equipment which was shipped to Iran via Israel. In his later testimony McFarlane said he thought he was dealing with 'moderates' in the Iranian government and that the government wanted to open channels of communications with a view to the eventual normalization of US–Iranian relations. Still later the government admitted that the arms sale was supposedly in return for the release of hostages held in Lebanon. McFarlane resigned and took an overdose of sleeping pills though this was not fatal.

The money generated by the arms sale, supposedly for the *Contras*, was largely used for other covert purposes: after US$12m had gone to the US Treasury and US$3m had been spent on costs of transport the remaining US$15m was to be used in supporting the *Contras*. In fact only US$3.8m reached the *Contras* while most of the rest went to a retired general, Richard Secord, and an Iranian-born businessman, Albert Hakim, who had been engaged by Lt-Col. North to establish a private network for supporting the *Contras*. This network was known as Enterprise. Lt-Col. North assisted in the creation of Enterprise, after the passage through Congress of the Boland Amendment, as a means of circumventing a government prohibition on further aid to the *Contras*. Enterprise had its own airplanes, airfield, ship and Swiss bank accounts and undertook responsibility for the arms sales to Iran in 1986. In his testimony to Congress North said that William Casey, the former director of the CIA, regarded Enterprise as a 'stand-alone' organization that would be able to carry out covert activities anywhere in the world free of Congressional review. As such it was an ideal vehicle for secret arms deals, the employment of mercenaries or other clandestine activities which form the basis of international subversion. Much of the relevant information was destroyed, both North and Poindexter shredding vital documents, while Casey died before being called upon to give detailed testimony. What emerged as the most startling aspect of the whole affair was Lt-Col. North's clear belief that the cause he was assisting – in this case the *contras* – justified breaking the law and, indeed, setting himself up as above the law altogether.[2] His action, however, was of a kind that would meet with approval from many of those organizations on the fringes of the military–political establishment in the United States, Britain or elsewhere that deal in mercenaries, provide military advice or engage to carry out other acts of arms- running, protection or subversion.

A British involvement in Irangate emerged in June 1987 when the Labour foreign affairs spokesman, George Foulkes, said that a former member of the SAS, Major David Walker, should face a murder charge for his alleged participation in Colonel North's Nicaraguan operations. Mr Foulkes said the government should prosecute Major Walker under the Foreign Enlistment Act which makes it illegal for a British subject to take military action against a friendly country.[3] A document released to the Iran–Contra committee in Washington showed that Lt-Col. Oliver North considered recruiting another former SAS officer, Captain Michael Francis Webb, who in 1982 had been involved in the abortive coup attempt in the Seychelles that had been led by 'Mad Mike' Hoare. Lt-Col. North admitted that he and the *Contras* wanted to hire foreigners for dangerous missions so that the American connection could be denied if anything went wrong. He also told the hearing that he had authorized Major Walker to perform 'military actions' to assist the *Contras*. Answering specific questions about the role of Major Walker, Lt-Col. North replied: 'No, David Walker was not hired to conduct any specific operation, certainly not by me. Mr Walker was engaged to provide operational support for certain activities in the region as I understand it.' What did emerge from these and other exchanges was the fact that Major Walker was a key figure in the military undercover world. He was the head of a firm called KMS, a mercenary business run by ex-soldiers, that supplied mercenaries or other forms of military expertise. KMS stood for Keeny Meeny Services and Walker had become a millionaire as a result of his security activities. His clients had included the British government which, for example, hired his men as bodyguards for VIPs in various troublespots round the world until the function was taken over by the Royal Military Police.

When these revelations became public the London headquarters of KMS at first denied that any such person as David Walker existed while official sources in Whitehall were certain that the former SAS officer and his company (KMS) had not been either officially or tacitly sanctioned by the British government.[4] On the one hand, it was suggested that Lt-Col. North approached KMS after hearing of the reputation it had gained in the service of the British government up to 1982; on the other hand, it became clear in the mid-1980s that the British government was distancing itself from KMS and, for example, had warned KMS in 1986 not to become involved in military action in Sri Lanka. As with other successful mercenary entrepreneurs, David Walker was involved with more than one company. He was a founder director of Saladin Securities Ltd as well as the Jersey-registered KMS and both companies were mentioned in the Irangate hearings as 'Walker companies'.[5] KMS was registered as having four shareholders, all senior executives of Morgan Grenfell (Jersey) Ltd which was a subsidiary of the London Merchant Bank. The four were named as Philip Smith, Gordon Dryden, David Endacott and Raymond Apsey. Saladin Securities insisted it had nothing to do with Lt-Col. North or the *Contra* affair and that its business consisted of providing protection for VIPs visiting Britain or going abroad. KMS, on the other hand, had been involved helping to quell the Dhofar rebellion in Oman during the 1970s.

According to a story in the *Sunday Times*[6] Major Walker was paid £68,000 to supply mercenaries to fight with the *Contras* in Nicaragua; he was paid the money on 5 May 1986, through a Panama company, Albon Values. The payment was for pilots to fly covert missions from Honduras. It was also revealed that in March 1986 General Richard Secord, who was responsible for organizing the logistics of the Iran–Contra arms deal, had visited London for a secret meeting with Walker. Walker then made several secret visits to the United States when he visited the Stanford Technology Trading Group Inc, the company run by Secord and Hakim. North, under cross-examination, revealed that Walker was involved in an operation to blow up an army depot in Managua. Other information about Walker that came out at the time included the involvement of his company KMS in training *Mujaheddin* guerrillas in Afghanistan. Another aspect of the Irangate story which has particular interest in relation to the wider question of mercenary activities generally is the extent to which high-ranking former military personnel are found to be discretely involved at some level of negotiations. North, for example, had been introduced to Walker by John Lehman, a former secretary of the US Navy.

The extraordinary world-wide publicity which the Irangate affair attracted did a good deal to expose the murky world of mercenary hiring and use as well as the inter-connection between so-called security firms in the United States and Britain and the network of former military personnel who become involved in such enterprises after retiring from the services. As a comment in *The Times* said of Walker:

> Although he surfaced earlier this year in the Tower Commission Report only as one of a host of characters involved in Lieutenant-Colonel Oliver North's global army of mercenaries, arms dealers and revolutionaries, Major Walker's exploits have remained in the spotlight as the 'British connection' in the affair.[7]

The Irangate scandal did not halt American pressures upon Nicaragua and in 1988, for example, on the grounds that Nicaraguan troops had entered Honduras in pursuit of *Contras*, the United States sent 3,200 troops to Honduras, a move that threw doubt upon the commitment of Honduras to the 1987 Central American peace treaty which called for the limitation of foreign troops in the region. Relentless US pressures had their effect and Nicaragua reversed its policy and agreed to hold direct peace talks with the *Contras* although the talks collapsed in June 1988. Efforts at finding a peaceful solution to the US-backed civil war continued through 1989. The war really came to an end following the election defeat of the Sandinistas on 25 February 1990, when a 14-party coalition won 51 of 92 seats in the assembly and Violetta Barrios de Chamorro became president in place of Daniel Ortega. The following March the US Congress lifted the trade embargo which it had imposed on Nicaragua five years earlier and in May Congress approved US$300m in economic assistance to the Chamorro government. The United States, having helped to see off the left-wing Sandinista government (almost entirely by foul means) was prepared to be friendly and helpful to its successor. Even so, US pressures continued to be applied through the 1990s to reverse various economic–political decisions of the Sandinista years.

COLOMBIA

Colombia must rank as one of the most violent societies in the world. It has been bedevilled by civil strife for many years with a number of rebel groups fighting the government and each other. In 1987 the three year truce between the government and the largest of the rebel groups, the Colombian Revolutionary Armed Forces (FARC), began to collapse as skirmishes between FARC's most active groups and the

Army became more frequent until a military convoy was ambushed in June. The situation deteriorated further following the assassination on 11 October 1987, of Jaime Pardo Leal, the leader of the Patriotic Union (UP). This party had been formed in 1985 and included numbers of former guerrillas who had been amnestied. FARC vowed vengeance. Colombia controls the largest share of the world trade in cocaine and its drugs cartels such as the Medellin cartel are seen as wielding as much power as the government. Following the assassination of Guillermo Cano Isaza, the editor of the *El Espectador* newspaper which had published investigative articles on the Medellin cartel, President Virgilio Barco Vargas extradited Carlos Leher Rivas, a prominent drug baron, to the United States according to an extradition treaty which Barco had signed into law in December 1986. The extradition was challenged in the Colombian Supreme Court which voted against the treaty to make it inoperative. US determination to fight the drug cartels in Colombia added an extra dimension to the existing confrontations in a society which appeared to thrive on violence. Colombia is quite able to subvert its own political–social system without the need for any interventions from outside.

General violence intensified during 1988 with guerrilla groups seeking to cause maximum havoc. A commission was established under the auspices of the Roman Catholic Church to identify subjects on which the government and the guerrillas could reach agreement. Following the murder of the Attorney General, Carlos Mauro Hoyos, on 25 January, a new Statute for the Defense of Democracy was passed in an attempt to strengthen the powers of the security forces but it had the opposite effect, fuelling partisan violence in the rural areas instead. A report by Amnesty International in April 1988 claimed that the armed forces were pursuing a policy of terror designed to intimidate or eliminate opposition outside the process of law. There was also an increase in the activity of death squads which were believed to have close links with the security forces.

Violence arising out of the activities of the drug cartels or the various guerrilla groups dominated Colombia through 1989 presenting external mercenary organizations with openings for providing training which they were not slow to seize. The drug cartels reacted brutally to the government's crackdown on their activities, their killings reaching a climax on 18 August with the assassination of Luis Carlos Galan who had been the ruling party's presidential candidate for 1990. This was followed by the proclamation of a state of emergency: assets believed to have been purchased with drug money were seized and the government reinstated the extradition treaty with the United States which had been suspended the previous year as a result of the action by the Supreme Court. In response the drug cartels increased their violence with bombing campaigns in Bogota, Medellin and Cali. They said they would kill ten judges for every drug trafficker who was extradited to the United States but though many people were arrested the leading drug barons eluded capture. The United States provided the government with assistance in the form of military hardware, US $65m in aid and trained personnel. Violence continued and escalated throughout the year and in one week at the end of October a magistrate, a congressman, a leftwing politician and six policemen were killed while the crash of a jet with 107 on board was thought to be the result of a bomb planted by drug traffickers. Further violence was directed against the oil and gold producing regions of Arauca and Magdalena by the left-wing National Liberation Army (ELN).

There was strong suspicion in Bogota that British mercenaries had trained the killers of Senator Luis Carlos Galan and the government demanded that Britain restrain the mercenaries. The British Labour Party said that the matter had brought Britain into disrepute and the government Minister of State at the Foreign Office, Tim Sainsbury, said in a radio interview: 'We very much regret, and indeed deplore, anything that they [the mercenaries] might do of an illegal nature overseas.' This wishy-washy condemnation of possible mercenary activity was unlikely to deter anyone.[8] In Bogota the columnist Maria Jaimena Duzan wrote in the daily *El Espectador*:

> By the way in which Luis Carlos Galan was assassinated there is no doubt that the crime was committed by professional mercenaries, but not those formed in the marginalized districts of Medellin but rather in the schools for killers that have been created in the Magdalena Medio with the help of British and Israeli henchmen.

Earlier in the year (April) a detailed report by the Colombian security service (DAS) revealed that British and Israeli mercenaries who previously had trained Nicaraguan *Contras* in Central America had been taken onto the payroll of the drug cartels. The training was led by British mercenaries calling themselves 'members of the British Legion'. DAS also claimed in August that the Cali drug cartel had recruited two British mercenaries to assassinate Pablo Escobar Gavira, the head of the Medellin cartel. At least four Israeli mercenaries under a retired paratroop officer, Lt-Col. Yair Klein, were reported to be training paramilitary troops and assassination teams for a drug dealer.

One Briton, Mr Dave Tomkins, an arms dealer and mercenary recruiter, boasted of his dealings with the Colombian drug barons and was named with other British and Israeli mercenaries as hired to train the drug traffickers' private armies. He was also named, along with a former SAS trooper, Peter McAleese, as having been enlisted by Colombian government officials to eradicate key members of the Medellin drugs cartel. In a recorded tape interview Tomkins hinted that he had been 'playing' both sides in Colombia.[9] At the time of the Tomkins revelations the British government indicated that it would cooperate if Colombia produced strong evidence for the extradition of people in Britain wanted for crimes in Colombia. However, the spokesman said that the recruitment of mercenaries in Britain was not itself illegal.

According to the Colombian Administrative Security Department (DAS) at least five Israeli and eleven British mercenaries helped train teams of assassins for Colombian cocaine traffickers and their allies. The drug barons Gonzalo Rodriguez Gacha and Pablo Escobar, the leaders of the Medellin cartel, sent trainees to remote camps between December 1987 and May 1988 to be taught by these mercenaries. The DAS report also linked the drug traffickers with rightist paramilitary 'self defense' groups and private armies of assassins who carry out killings for the drug cartels. According to the report 'the drug traffickers Gonzalo Rodriguez Gacha (El Mexicano) and Henry de Jesus Perez (Don Dario) contracted for the service of foreign mercenaries to train personnel at the schools for assassins in the Magdalena Medio' which is a northern region that the cocaine cartels, rightist groups and guerrilla forces have turned into one of Colombia's most violent regions.[10] A group of five Israelis led by Yair Klein ran a course at a training camp called '50' near Puerto Boyaca. The Israelis then left to train *Contra* fighters in Honduras and Costa Rica. Back in Israel Yair Klein admitted that he led a team of instructors early in 1988 in Colombia but claimed they were only helping ranchers defend themselves against guerrilla attacks. He was subsequently questioned by the Israeli police and had his passport taken from him while the Israeli Foreign Minister, Moshe Arens, said: 'We will do everything in our power to enforce the law and prevent all aid by Israelis to the drug cartel.'

DAS stated that by early 1988 the ranchers' group ACDEGAM was firmly linked to drug traffickers and that cartel leaders, especially

Rodriguez Gacha, had purchased millions of acres of ranchland in areas such as Magdalena Medio and then forged alliances with established ranchers. Some 50 students took part in the Israli training course at which the Israelis taught the use of night-vision equipment, infrared flashlights and telescopic sights. Another similar course was run by 11 British nationals led by a retired colonel. This course included instruction in the use of grenades, plastic explosive and camouflage techniques. The 'network' of schools was linked by a radio communications system and also controlled several planes, about 120 vehicles, motor cycles, bulldozers, tractors and some boats. A senior police official, General Miguel Maza Marquez, claimed that foreign mercenaries may have played a role in the assassination of the presidential candidate, Luis Carlos Galan, on 18 August: 'They may have been involved in planning the killing or in training the people who did the killing' he said.[11]

According to a *Guardian* article[12] the role played by Israelis in helping train drug cartel militiamen cast a harsh light on Israel's 'defence exports' although these exports were not new. During 1988 alone companies which supply security services earned US$250m in Latin America alone. Altogether there were about 800 such companies in the field, some of them selling arms. As the *Guardian* pointed out, from the late 1960s onwards (reacting to Palestinian attacks) Israeli army and intelligence personnel had gained unrivalled experience in 'protective security, small arms training, interrogation, and other aspects of counter-terrorism'. As a result there were plenty of former career soldiers or one time members of the Shin Bet security service or the Mossad foreign intelligence agency who moved into this lucrative occupation. Israeli firms which export security equipment or expertise are supposed to be licensed by Sibat, the export department of the Defence Ministry, but many circumvent the regulations. Some security contracts are huge and legitimate as, for example, providing security for Kennedy and La Guardia airports in New York which were won by Israeli firms. The Colombian exposures caused deep embarrassment to the Israeli government.

Like other mercenaries under investigation, Yair Klein back in Israel was disingenuous. When questioned about the death of the Colombian politician Galan, Klein said in an interview in Tel Aviv: 'It is possible that one of the people in our course killed Galan. But I say again, we worked with farmers. If after we left, one of them worked with drug dealers, we couldn't know.' He acknowledged that a promotional tape made by his company, Spearhead Inc., which showed his students storming a building with automatic rifles, also showed people whom Colombian officials identified as important members of the Medellin drug cartel but he insisted that these people were 'visitors from outside I didn't know'. He went on to say that he did not work with drug dealers: 'If drug dealers got into the group we worked with, then God only knows.' Mr Klein said he first heard of the need for military trainers in Colombia from a business associate in Israel and went out to Colombia early in 1988. He was refused the required government permit for foreign military training but since he was training civilians he said he did not need one. He said he offered a three-month training course and the ranchers who came brought M-16 and Uzi automatic rifles, grenades, explosives and other weapons. He did not know where the weapons came from and did not ask.[13]

In a curious postscript to the sudden publicity that was focused upon British and Israeli mercenary activity in Colombia at this time, the then British Foreign Secretary, John Major, announced that Britain would not stand in the way if Colombia sought the extradition of British mercenaries alleged to have helped train drug gangs and when he was asked about reports that SAS troops would go to Colombia as part of an aid programme to assist Colombia fight the drug cartels, he replied that British soldiers with the greatest expertise in dealing with terrorism would be chosen and stressed that they would only be engaged in training the Colombians and would be few in numbers. The ironies of the internecine strife in Colombia are many; in this case it almost appeared as if British mercenaries had paved the way for the use of the regular SAS although on the other side!

The war against the drug cartels continued fiercely into 1990 and at one time deaths in the city of Medellin averaged 50 a day. In February 1990 President Barco hosted a summit conference on drugs which was attended by Presidents George Bush of the United States, Jaime Paz Zamora of Bolivia and Alan Garcia Perez of Peru who agreed to pursue concerted action against the cocaine trade. On 2 December 1993, Pablo Escobar, the leader of the Medellin drug cartel was shot dead by police but as the Medellin cartel suffered an eclipse its rival, the Cali cartel, became more active and, despite all the efforts to reduce the cocaine trade, the huge demand for drugs in the principal markets of the north ensured that the violence and the resultant need to fight it continued. The fight against the drug traffickers as well as the general violence continued throughout the 1990s. The principal Cali drug leaders were killed or arrested in 1996 yet violence was never far from the surface of Colombian life and President Ernesto Samper Pizano was fearful that an alliance would be formed between the drug cartels and the various guerrilla groups to destabilise the country, a factor which acted as a brake upon the agreement to extradite drug traffickers to the United States.

Violence during the first half of 1998, an election year, escalated steadily as left-wing guerrillas from different groups in the civil war that by then had lasted for 25 years controlled 40 per cent of the country. The United States, alarmed at the possibility that the demoralized Colombian army would soon collapse, increased its support for a force which its advisers described as 'vulnerable and incompetent'. US advisers were attached to key bases in the war zones and Washington had reached the conclusion that it could not continue treating the regime as a pariah because of its alleged links to the drug cartels. The drug business, despite the elimination of top drug barons, remained an all-pervasive factor in almost every aspect of life in Colombia; the civil war continued relentlessly and savagely with guerrilla groups in alliance with drug traffickers; the army, when it was not being defeated by the guerrillas, tried to compensate for its incompetence by resorting to death squads; and the politicians talked of peace at any price while the country remained on the brink of collapse. The US military advisers laughed at the suggestion that the election was about peace:

> One adviser, a gnarled Vietnam veteran who calls himself the 'Colonel', said: 'My days in South East Asia tell me there is no way the rebels will talk peace while they have the army and the government on the run. The only way you'll get the guerrillas to the table is to kick butt out on the battlefield, not by talking about agrarian reform.'[14]

Given the American experience in Vietnam and the state of Columbia in mid-1998 the chances of the United States being drawn into a full-scale Vietnam-type conflict appeared to be steadily increasing. Meanwhile, there seemed every possibility that more military 'advisers' from the usual western sources would move into Columbia to provide training for its various warring factions.

10 Europe

After the devastation of WWII Europe reconstructed and then enjoyed a long period of peace and this was so despite the Iron Curtain and the confrontations across it that marked 40 years of the Cold War. There was violence, of course, but it was localized and, broadly, took two forms: either it consisted of massive interventions by the Soviet Army to maintain Russian control of its East European satellites or Warsaw Pact allies as in Hungary in 1956, Czechoslovakia in 1968, Poland and East Germany; or it took the form of long-running sectarian violence by particular minorities within states as with the troubles in Ulster for Britain, the Basque separatists in Spain or the various left-wing revolutionary groups that arose during the 1960s such as the Baader–Meinhof group in Germany. These violent uprisings or longer-lasting attacks upon the status quo might, and often did, employ terrorist tactics as in Northern Ireland but did not resort to the use of mercenaries. Europe, on the other hand, was a major source of mercenaries over these years for operations beyond its own frontiers. Several western European countries, and most notably Britain and France, supplied mercenaries, either with the direct connivance of governments or, more generally, with governments doing nothing to prevent their recruitment for operations in the Third World. The Soviet Union, however, was not a source of mercenaries since the nature of its government system would not allow the recruitment of mercenaries in the way they could be recruited in the West.

The end of the Cold War was immediately followed by the break-up of Yugoslavia with its resultant wars and the disintegration of the USSR into its fifteen component parts. The break-up of Yugoslavia during the years 1991–96 with a series of especially brutal wars involving Croatia, Bosnia and Serbia which included the freshly named but old phenomenon of ethnic cleansing provided an opportunity for mercenaries to take part on one or other side in a series of European conflicts for the first time in half a century and mercenaries were forthcoming quickly enough for the purpose. The disintegration of the USSR had two immediate consequences. First, the huge Soviet war machine was in part divided between the successor states to the Soviet Union and cut down in size so that large numbers of highly skilled Russian soldiers found themselves unemployed while, at the same time, the West became fearful that a range of Soviet weapons, including nuclear warheads, might find their way on to the open market. Second, a number of wars erupted among some of the successor states of the old Soviet Union: civil wars in Georgia and Tajikistan, a war between Armenia and Azerbaijan, or the Chechnya uprising against Moscow control each provided opportunities for mercenaries to become involved while a situation of extreme fluidity in Russia itself opened up further possibilities for a new breed of Russian mercenary to appear on the international war scene.

YUGOSLAVIA

From the death of Tito in 1980 the signs began to multiply that the Yugoslav Federation over which he had presided with such skill was liable to implode. It did so at the beginning of the 1990s: despite the opposition of the Serb-dominated federation based upon Belgrade first Croatia and Slovenia in the north, then Bosnia and Herzegovina with its large Muslim population declared their independence and obtained international recognition; they were followed by Macedonia in the south and for five years (1991–96) the region was torn by a series of brutal civil wars which included measures to enforce population removals (ethnic cleansing). In 1998, after two years of precarious peace, fighting broke out in what still remained of the Yugoslav Federation when the ethnic Albanians who make up the great majority of the population of Kosovo, sought independence from the Serbs and met with bitter oppression by the Belgrade government. Peace efforts by the great powers, by NATO, and by the United Nations were greatly complicated by rivalries among the peacemakers themselves and by the added suspicions arising from the religious factor since the Bosnian Muslims claimed that their interests were discriminated against by the western powers, a claim that ensured the involvement in the war as supporters of Bosnia of several Islamic countries including Iran and Saudi Arabia. It was the first time since the Spanish Civil War of the 1930s that a major conflict (or series of conflicts) confined to one region in Europe presented an opportunity for mercenaries and volunteers to take part and they were to do so at several levels. These Balkan wars attracted the usual killer thugs who are always a part of the mercenary business, a number of self-proclaimed idealists, though in most cases their understanding of what they were fighting for or against was decidedly limited, and some professional soldiers. These latter were either adventurers who came for the thrill and the money or they were hired by security or military advisor firms, most notably to revamp the Croatian army. Yugoslavia, moreover, was within easy access for would-be mercenaries from elsewhere in Europe who could travel there overland by car or on public transport.

One unique aspect of this war, in relation to all the European mercenaries, was that they were fighting other Europeans. They were not, as in all the other instances of mercenary activity which have been examined in this book, turning up in Third World countries to 'sort out' with their implied superior skills and knowledge situations where it was often assumed that their arrival would tilt the balance. Part of the justification for mercenary involvements in the Third World has always been the assumption on their part that a small number of European or Western mercenaries was enough to change the direction of the war because of their inherent superiority as soldiers. This was not seen to be the case in the Yugoslav wars.

In Croatia as early as September 1991 an 'anti-terrorist brigade' had been formed which contained French and German mercenaries who referred to themselves as the black legion because of the black uniforms they wore for night work. The leader of these men in black was a Croat, Mladen le Noir, who had been an emigre in Sweden but returned in 1990 and used his money to equip his anti-terrorist brigade. The story of their activities was recounted by a young French recruit, Stephane Le Fauconier, and was as much about incompetence and lack of sensible instructions as anything else although their object was to kill as many Serbs as possible. The two young French mercenaries who joined the black legion, Stephane and Damien, both from Lyons, did so because they were anti-communist and wanted Croatia to be free of Serb aggression. They held right-wing political views and saw Croatia as a European country under threat and wished to work towards a future free Europe. (They did not explain how they regarded Serbia which is also a European country.) They had not gone to fight for money and had received none except for 1,000 dinars each as a present from President Tudjman.[1]

A very different story which appeared in the *Daily Telegraph* titled 'Millwall's Dave shows Croatians how to kill'[2] describes a former member of the French Foreign Legion and one time rating in the Royal Navy who had come to Croatia as a mercenary; there he was found by another former Legionnaire, a Croation whose pseudonym in the Legion had been Captain Zulu, who brought 'Dave' to Kumrovec to run the sniper course in his training programme. Dave refused to give his surname and was elusive about his background though he admitted to travelling widely. As the article pointed out, 'Although ethnic Croats from Canada, the United States, Australia and Europe have flocked back to fight, he had no family ties with the republic. "I'm from Millwall" he says. "I'm here because of the communists. I hate them".' According to Captain Zulu, Croatia had no mercenaries and only provided food, clothing and a bit of spending money for foreign volunteers. Dave said he hoped to be rewarded for his efforts with employment in the army of an independent Croatia.

In the early fighting for its independence when Croatia's position was precarious and the future uncertain, a variegated lot of mercenaries turned up to join the growing number of foreigners in the Croatian National Guard. These included a 17-year-old Briton, George Patterson, who gave up being a student in London and travelled to Zagreb by train, a 34-year-old veteran, Rob Morgan, who had previously 'worked' for the Armenians in Nagorno-Karabakh and claimed it had been a toss-up between coming to Croatia or going to fight in East Timor, and Marcus, an Austrian from Graz. This unlikely trio set off for the front to fight far better armed Serb troops. These men, at least, were not receiving much in the way of pecuniary reward. Although there were tales in Belgrade of old Nazis coming to fight against their former Serbian foes most of the foreign volunteers coming to fight for Serbia appeared to be young English or Scottish men with a smaller number of Austrians and Hungarians, Some were older with former military experience. Explaining their reasons for coming to Croatia they said they wanted to help a small country fighting for its independence. Another volunteer was the Spaniard, Eduardo Flores, a former correspondent of the Barcelona newspaper, *La Vanguardia*, who decided to give up journalism and join the Croatian National Guard. The brigade he joined included English, Austrian, Hungarian and Portuguese volunteers.

While these volunteers get what one described as 'beer and cigarette' money, other experienced mercenaries had the job of training the Croat fighters. In 1991 the Croat ultra-nationalist Party of Rights was running a paramilitary organization of 5,000 fighters known as HoS which included more than 100 foreign fighters and half-a-dozen experienced trainers, mainly English and Scots. As the HoS leader in Zagreb, Ante Djapic, said: 'Only yesterday we got a real British expert. He fought with the Australians in Vietnam, the French in Africa, the British in the Falklands and was once a bodyguard for the King of Saudi Arabia.'[3] The HoS then wanted to establish its own foreign legion and, according to Ante Djapic, got calls from would-be recruits every day, especially from England and Ireland.

The war in Yugoslavia certainly attracted a range of mercenaries, adventurers and idealists most of whom knew little about the rights and wrongs of the conflict but saw it as an opportunity to take part in what they understood best: fighting. Those interviewed, for example by *The Times* in November 1991, talked of 'taking out' Serbs whom they described as 'bastards' though hardly being more complimentary about the Croats for whom they were fighting. At that time a majority of mercenaries appeared to seek out the HoS, the para-military wing of the Croatian Party of Rights which asked few questions of mercenaries and allowed them maximum freedom of action. As *The Times* pointed out:

> In spite of rumours about lucrative pay deals, most of the men seem more attracted by the buzz of war than by mammon. They are paid an allowance in dinars and have been promised a hard- currency payment at the end of their stint. Recruitment seems to be a hit-and-miss affair, although they confirm that Croatia is now top of the popularity league for mercenaries seeking a fresh assignment. 'Croatia is a good war for us,' said Andrew, a former Green Jacket and Angola veteran. 'It's easy to get to and there's enough for everyone to do. We're individuals. We don't like to be pushed around. Here they give you a few shells and a rifle and it's off to you.'[4]

A different kind of volunteer consists of young idealists with Croat backgrounds whose parents had emigrated to countries such as the United States or Canada who decided to come back to assist the cause of Croatian independence. As an engineering student from New York, Dragan Lozancic, whose parents had remained in America, explained: 'The war has changed me; woken me up to my heritage and where I belong. Sure I am an American, but Croatia is my home-town. It is great to have a cause to fight for.'[5]

The Croatian army's First International Platoon had its headquarters in a village outside Osijek very close to the frontline. The platoon specialized in surveillance and special operations behind enemy lines and consisted of about 100 men and three women of whom about half were foreigners coming from France, Switzerland, Hungary, Portugal, Britain, Australia, the United States and Spain. Discipline was tougher than in the regular forces of Croatia and the platoon did well in fighting a rearguard action defending a strategically important village south of Osijek over several weeks. Members of this platoon insisted they were different from the soldiers of fortune who swaggered about Zagreb whose motives, they said, 'usually stink'. Jurg, a Swiss with the platoon, believed that the Croatian forces were slowly being transformed into a professional army.[6]

There was an exodus of mercenaries in early 1992 following the ceasefire which came into effect on 3 January 1992, and seemed likely to stick. Some of them felt the Croatian authorities would like to see the back of them anyway, while others were disgruntled since there was no action in which they could take part. One group of Britons, for example, was sent on enforced leave from Vinkovci to Baronga barracks in Zagreb while others drank in Osijek. An Australian, Allan Hetherington- Clebberley who had been appointed 'commander international Zagreb', estimated that English-speaking soldiers alone then numbered about 500 while Brigadier Karlo Gorinsek, commander of the Croatian first operational zone which covered 200 miles of front including Osijek and Vinkovci, said: 'In our operational zone there are few foreigners – 20 or 30 let us say' although another Australian, Tonka Jelic, a public relations officer for the International Brigade, suggested it had 70 foreign recruits.[7]

Stories of mercenaries in disintegrating Yugoslavia periodically featured in the Western press and despite implicit condemnation of mercenary activity these stories also tended to glorify the mercenaries as adventurers. In February 1993, for example, the *Daily Telegraph* carried the story of two British mercenaries who were captured by the Serbs, tortured and then executed. One of these, Kevin Skinner, had been training Bosnian Muslim forces and spoke openly in an interview of how he had killed a Serb fighter. He had told his family he was going to drive a lorry to deliver supplies. The second man, Derek Arnold, was giving medical training to Bosnian Muslims. Both had been kidnapped from their flat in Travnik close to the Serb–Bosnian front line and six miles from the forward base of the Cheshire Regiment, part of the British peacekeeping force. According to other mercenaries, the two men were the victims of infighting between the Muslim forces and had been killed for passing information to the Cheshires. Skinner had telephoned a press agency in Liverpool before Christmas 1992 when he had said that he 'assisted' the British Army as an adviser and had been semi-officially recruited by the SAS.[8]

By 1993, when Bosnia was fighting for its survival, Mujahedin mercenaries from Islamic countries had appeared on the scene. They came from North Africa – Algeria or Tunisia, from Sudan, from

Afghanistan, Pakistan, Iraq and Iran although they only numbered a few hundred and according to Bosnian army authorities few had played any decisive role on the battlefield while 'Most commanders dislike them, dismissing them as incompetent troublemakers'.[9] The changing fortunes of war in Yugoslavia attracted mercenaries in different waves. The first mercenaries arrived in the summer of 1991 to join the Croatians and many of these were described as 'the fantasy brigade' consisting either of toughs who boasted of their killing prowess or idealists with little real knowledge of the confused politics and human rights issues of the region. More important for the Croats were volunteers who came from the Croat emigre communities in North America and Germany and these, for example, helped to smuggle in much needed arms. The war in Bosnia brought another kind of mercenary including the Mujahedin from a number of Islamic countries but many of the European freebooters who came found there was little money to be earned, that the fighting could be unpleasant and that they might well be stuck there for the duration of the war.

By 1996, in the apparent aftermath of the Yugoslav wars when the American-brokered Dayton accord was in place, a very different kind of mercenary activity surfaced in the region. Already, in the United States, moves were underway to give sufficient weight to private military corporations – security firms with a large number of senior retired officers on their payrolls – so that these would be in a position to undertake important military tasks and do so with the blessing of the US government. One such organization, Military Professional Resources Inc. (MPRI) which, in its literature, boasts 'the greatest corporate assemblage of military expertise in the world' became involved in Bosnia. At the beginning of 1996 the United States believed it to be necessary to reduce the military edge which the Bosnian Serbs enjoyed over the Muslim–Croat Federation by providing the latter with new weaponry so as to achieve a military balance in the region. As Democratic Senator Joseph Biden of Delaware said: 'We will not be able to leave unless the Bosnian government is armed and prepared to defend itself. That's the ticket home for Americans.'[10] However, this policy (of arming the Federation) faced the obvious snag that the United States was supposedly a neutral party in the region and Washington feared that any move to arm and train the Bosnians could lead to Serb attacks upon its troops. In addition, President Clinton had pledged that US troops would not play any active role in rearming the Bosnians. In response to this political dilemma Washington fell back upon the use of MPRI; in other words, the private mercenary sector could do for Washington what its publicly avowed policy made it impossible to do at government level. In a sense this has always been the case: governments allow private organizations whether mercenaries or something else, to do what the diplomatic principles of engagement at any given time prohibit the government doing overtly. Such a decision means entering into a murky world but that is what the use of mercenaries has always involved. It was, therefore, decided that MPRI which had already done work for the Croats should now undertake to train the Bosnians in the use of new weaponry to be supplied by the United States and others. James Pardew from the Pentagon who had assisted negotiations that produced the Dayton accord was sent to Sarajevo by the US administration to persuade the Bosnian government to hire MPRI (or alternately one of its American competitors). Retired Army Lt-Gen. Harry Soyster, who had been the head of the US Defense Intelligence Agency and by 1996 was operations chief for MPRI, said his company was ready for work in Bosnia: 'The Bosnians need training at the company level, putting battalion staff together, that sort of thing. It can be done pretty quickly.' Over the previous year (1995) MPRI had had a group of 15 men in Croatia headed by a retired two-star General Richard Griffitts teaching the Croats to run a military force in a democracy and had then signed another contract to reorganize Croatia's Defence Ministry. When in August 1995 an apparently rejuvenated Croatian military drove the Serbs from the Krajina region, it was suggested by various military analysts that the Croats must have received outside training which placed MPRI on the defensive. However, massive American aid to Bosnia even though supplied by the private sector would have strings attached; Washington wanted Bosnia to sever all links with Iran which the Bosnians were prepared to do. As the Croat–Bosnian vice-president Ejup Ganic said: 'You bring us stuff, we won't look anywhere else.'[11]

The Bosnian government did pick MPRI over competing bids from other American companies to train its armed forces in a US $400m programme financed, in the main, by Saudi Arabia, Kuwait, Brunei and Malaysia and supplemented by large shipments of US arms. Indeed, by the end of 1997 MPRI was a major factor in retraining the Croat and Bosnian armed forces. If reports were accurate it had been deeply involved reforming the Croatian forces just prior to the Krajina campaign in which they drove 170,000 people from their homes; as Roger Charles, a retired marine lieutenant colonel and military researcher said: 'No country moves from having a ragtag militia to carrying out a professional military offensive without some help. The Croatians did a good job of coordinating armor, artillery and infantry. That's not something you learn while being instructed about democratic values.'[12]

The emergence in the United States of private sector corporations staffed by large numbers of high-ranking former military personnel – Privatizing War as it has been called[13] – represents a new phenomenon at several levels. First, such firms are openly in business and boast the military expertise at their disposal. Second, the government appears to have no qualms about turning to them to engage in activities which the Administration itself is debarred from doing by its own policy statements. This is a new departure. Governments have often allowed mercenaries or military advisers to act while denying any responsibility for them and, as a result, have got themselves into a political tangle as did Washington over the Irangate affair. In the Yugoslav situation, however, Washington appeared ready quite openly to say 'our stated policy forbids us to undertake this task – of training and arming you – but there is an alternative in the form of one of our private organizations, so use that with our blessing instead.' It is the clear readiness of the US Administration to advise the Croat and Bosnian governments to use MPRI that signals a new phase in the mercenary business. In effect, the US government has openly endorsed the activities of the various mercenary supply organizations with their staff of retired high-ranking military personnel as legitimate and acceptable alternatives to government-supplied military assistance and, no doubt, the precedent will shortly be followed by countries such as Britain and France. If this proves to be the case, as seems likely, it will undermine totally the efforts of the United Nations to outlaw mercenary activities worldwide and, instead, provide new legitimacy to all mercenary activities. Still more sinister for the longer-term future, once such organizations are seen to be legitimate and are overtly used by their own governments for tasks the governments do not wish to carry out officially, such organizations will accrue to themselves a power and status that will permit them to operate independently of governments altogether. If, for example, the Administration in Washington uses such an organization for a particular task in Croatia or some other country where this suits American policy, it will be very difficult for it to argue against the same organization acting in a different country where there is no specific US policy involved. Should this happen – and it seems likely – we are on the verge of a new era of large-scale mercenary activity that will no longer be officially condemned.

RUSSIA

Russian or Soviet mercenaries were unknown during the years from 1945 to the collapse of the Soviet Union at the beginning of the 1990s although some Czech mercenary pilots appeared on the Federal side in the Nigerian civil war. This absence of mercenaries from the Soviet Union was not the result of any moral superiority so much as a question of the tight controls that were always exercised over Soviet citizens. During the decade prior to 1990 a large number of Russian soldiers served in the civil war in Afghanistan where the USSR had up to 125,000 troops at any given time; many of these soldiers with battle experience from one of the most difficult war zones in the world found themselves unemployed in the 1990s as the Soviet Union came to an end and its armed forces were reduced in size. There were immediate opportunities for freebooters or soldiers of fortune to operate in the wars that broke out in the successor states to the USSR and, most notably, in Georgia, Armenia, Azerbaijan and Tajikistan and by 1992 a new Russian mercenary tradition was in the making.

Typical of the new breed of Russian mercenary was Arseny D., a captain in the Russian National Legion serving in South Ossetia, Georgia, during the civil war at the beginning of the 1990s. Senya, as he called himself, aged 34, was a graduate of the Russian air force training college at Ryazan, and had served two stints in Afghanistan. He was jailed for taking part in a robbery in Afghanistan, returned to the army, was discharged for attacking a colonel and faced a prison sentence when he went on the run and joined the Russian National Legion. Like US servicemen who fought in Vietnam, there are an estimated 700,000 former Soviet troops who fought in Afghanistan and are said to be affected by the Afghan war syndrome and feel that they did not have to lose the Afghan war. Senya was one of them: fairly rootless, unmarried and without responsibilities, skilled only in soldiering, he made an ideal mercenary. Russia must have a good many thousands who fall into this category and will make typical mercenaries.

A classic description of these new mercenaries came from a Russian Colonel, Vyascheslav Barsukov, who was head of the local Russian army operations group in Ossetia:

> They're scum, those mercenaries. My regiment had the first brush with these individuals in Karabakh three years ago. They are generously paid. The guys run no risks and don't take part in operations.

They pretend they are instructors. Here in Tskhinval they go by the flashy name of the Russian Legion. They are bloated from doing nothing but drinking. Having guys like that for friends only compromises the Ossets. I think they gave them shelter out of desperation.[14]

Such a scornful description could apply equally to many other mercenary groups; the Russians were merely falling into an all too familiar pattern of behaviour.

As with mercenaries from other parts of the world the Russian volunteers have the usual mixed motives: money, adventure, idealism, using their war skills. Russia wanted to ensure that Ossetia remains Russian rather than being absorbed into Georgia and some mercenaries answered a call made by the National Republican Party of Russia for volunteers to defend Tskhinval. Ivan, a Moscow student, secured leave from his college and signed a six-month contract for 5,000 roubles a month with the National Republican Party of Russia; the Ossetians were to pay his fare, provide bed and board, a uniform and weapons. Other volunteers – legionnaires – signed similar contracts. They deny they are mercenaries and want to be called volunteers or members of an international brigade.[15] The arguments were all too familiar; the denial of being mercenaries automatic if unconvincing.

The National Republican Party of Russia came into being in April 1990; it is right-wing in its politics and supported Saddam Hussein during the 1991 Gulf War. An official of the party, Sergei Maltsev, explained the party's interest in assisting the Ossets who, he said, were Alani, a people very close to the Russians: 'By defending them we also uphold Russia's interests and protect its southern border. To us South Ossetia is as much part of Russia as Trans-Dniestria, where we're also sending legionnaires.' If a Russian political party in the post-Soviet era can create its own mercenary movement within the generally chaotic conditions that persist in much of Russia, the possibilities for mercenary activity would appear to be extensive. Because of conditions in Ossetia, Maltsev said the party would probably stop sending legionnaires; he went on to describe the legion:

> some legionnaires are real pros who can each do the job of ten in battle. The Russian National Legion is an organization controlled by the party and devoted to martial sports. It has units in Rostov-on-Don, Krasnodar, Magadan, Yekaterinburg and Chelyabinsk. There are two companies in Moscow and five in St Petersburg.... The time will come when these forces play a stabilizing role in the

country and, jointly with the other patriotic forces, they'll stop the chaos.[16]

This interview took place in 1992 and if it was possible for a marginal political party openly to flaunt its Legion the prospects for Russia more generally to field mercenaries must be very great indeed and this would be the case whether they are members of such a legion or offer their services as individuals. Given the unsettled political state in the countries on Russia's southern fringe – not just the former Soviets but also Afghanistan, Iran, Iraq, Pakistan – the possibilities of wide-scale Russian mercenary activity in the region will remain extensive at least until the Moscow government is able to exert far more stringent controls over its citizens than seemed likely at the end of the 1990s.

Another, similar military force appeared in Ukraine at this time and was involved in the struggle in Trans-Dniestria. This was the Ukrainian National Self-Defence Forces (UNSDF). The commander of one UNSDF unit, Major Vladimir Solovei, formerly of the Soviet Army, said:

> I fought in Afghanistan and I'm well aware that when there's a civil war it is conducted by terrorist methods. Terror like that in Yugoslavia or Nagorno-Karabakh can crush the enemy. A free Ukraine can only be a Great Ukraine, and for that one has to fight.

This mixture of right-wing patriotism and militarism is a staple of much mercenary motivation and these Russian or Ukrainian nationalist mercenaries are very similar to those from Britain or elsewhere in the West who claimed throughout the Cold War to be motivated by hatred of Communism. The UNSDF was created in 1991 by the extreme right Ukrainian National Assembly and was being trained by members of the Ukraine's Union of Officers under a special programme. Whether or not such an 'independent' force could be called a mercenary force must be debatable.

When Cossacks appeared to fight in Trans-Dniestria in 1992 Moscow was obliged to take action and investigate the alleged participation of Russian citizens in armed formations in Moldova though little progress was made. It appeared that the Russian government had little chance of controlling those of its citizens who wished to become mercenaries and operate as such in neighbouring countries. All the available evidence suggests that Russia has become a new and potent source of mercenaries.

11 South Africa and Executive Outcomes

The policy of apartheid – separating the races – which the South African government pursued with relentless dedication from the 1948 election which brought the National Party (NP) to power under Dr Malan until the collapse of the system at the end of the 1980s meant that South Africa was increasingly isolated until its 'pariah' status in the international community became an important factor in hastening the end of the apartheid system. When Britain's Prime Minister, Harold Macmillan, visited South Africa in February 1960 and gave his 'Wind of Change' speech he was trying to persuade his hosts to move with the times; they did not accept his message, instead answering it six weeks later with the Sharpeville massacre which focused world attention upon the iniquities of the apartheid system. In 1960 17 African countries became independent. In 1961 South Africa was obliged to leave the Commonwealth – whose members said its apartheid policy was incompatible with continuing membership. And when in 1963 36 independent African countries formed the Organization of African Unity (OAU) they insisted that none of their members should engage in diplomatic or trade relations with South Africa until that country had abandoned its policy of apartheid. From this time onwards South Africa became more and more isolated and, as a result, adopted a defensive 'laager' mentality which became increasingly important as the countries on its periphery also became independent. Even so, South Africa was to enjoy a period of relatively high prosperity until major political and military changes in neighbouring Angola, Mozambique and Rhodesia during the mid-1970s forced Pretoria to review its position and its policies. The withdrawal of the Portuguese from Angola and Mozambique in 1975 meant that South Africa was faced with two independent Marxist-oriented states on its Atlantic and Indian Ocean flanks while in Rhodesia across the Limpopo the guerrilla war was beginning to turn against the white minority Smith regime and in favour of the ZANU forces which could operate freely from an independent and friendly Mozambique. In Namibia, which South Africa had controlled ever since 1920 when it received the mandate for former German South West Africa from the League of Nations, the

SWAPO guerrilla fighters in the north of the territory were now able to receive assistance from Angola. In response to these new pressures South Africa embarked upon its policy of destabilizing its African neighbours. This policy had four main aims: first, to keep Angola and Mozambique in turmoil so that they could not develop into overt threats to South African hegemony in the region; second, to wreck the transport lines and most notably the railways which passed through these countries and served the landlocked states of Malawi, Zambia and Zimbabwe (once Rhodesia had become independent in 1980), so that they would be obliged to trade through the Republic; third, to dissuade them from giving support to the African National Congress (ANC) which wanted to operate from bases in South Africa's neighbours; and fourth, to demonstrate South Africa's power and create a permanent sense of threat and unease. Destabilization meant constant cross-border raids into the neighbouring territories (or the threat of such raids), a process that was maintained throughout the 1980s; in order to carry out such a policy successfully South Africa created a number of special military or other subversive units for the purpose. It is one of the ironies of the Southern African story in the 1990s that Executive Outcomes (set up in 1989), the highly effective military advisory services organization which supplies mercenaries and other assistance to independent African countries, is largely staffed and led by the same white soldiers who had formerly been part of the destabilization forces responsible for cross-border raids and other subversive activities against South Africa's neighbours during the 1980s. Thus the Angolan government, which staged its highly effective trial of mercenaries in 1976 in order to condemn their use had, by 1993, turned to Executive Outcomes for assistance in its war against the UNITA rebels of Jonas Savimbi.

By 1996 Executive Outcomes had become one of the best known of the private mercenary companies operating in the world. In both Angola and Sierra Leone at that time its combat units – made up principally of members of the former special forces, which had been dissolved by the Mandela government – were involved protecting mining installations from rebels in both countries; while a notable beneficiary of their operations was the South African mining giant, De Beers, whose diamond interests in those two afflicted countries had been and still were at risk. Executive Outcomes offers a range of services to potential clients (legitimate governments which normally means troubled and weak African governments under threat from rebellions); these services include training in conventional or guerrilla warfare, the creation of bases, mechanized units, parachute training, artillery, military police, the formation of special units – in fact almost anything of a military nature. That the Mandela government of the so-called new South Africa should permit so obvious a mercenary organization as Executive Outcomes to operate at all must come as a surprise to those idealists who always expect new governments to act out of the character which belongs to all governments. Various statements in the South African press suggested that Executive Outcomes was not a mercenary organization although these were contradicted by the special rapporteur for the UN Human Rights Commission, M. Enriques Bernales Ballesteros.

When Executive Outcomes (EO) was created in 1989 the end of apartheid was already in sight and it must have been clear to members of the South African Defence Force (SADF) and the South African Police that their future was in doubt, at least for those of their members who had been engaged in the more overt racist and anti-Communist activities which had characterized their operations under the apartheid regime. Just as the end of the Cold War released on to the market many potential Russian mercenaries so the end of apartheid and the emergence of the new South Africa made redundant some highly trained military or para- military personnel who would need to seek fresh employment. Executive Outcomes offered such personnel employment and, moreover, as they were soon to discover, outside South Africa in the very countries they had formerly helped to destabilize. Executive Outcomes draws its personnel from some of the most notorious former white military formations such as the Rhodesian Selous Scouts or the special units of SADF. Eeben Barlow, its director, a former white Rhodesian, had served in the notorious '32 Buffalo' battalion which had been stationed on the Namibia–Angola border, had moved on to the Directorate of Covert Collection (DCC) and then in 1989 to the Civil Cooperation Bureau which was responsible for the assassination of anti- apartheid activists. The CCB was dismantled in 1991 on the orders of President de Klerk, the same year in which Eeben Barlow began to offer the services of Executive Outcomes in Africa generally. The first big breakthrough came in 1992 when its forces were engaged by the oil companies – Gulf-Chevron and Petrangoil – to guard the oilfields near Soyo in Angola. This was followed by a further contract in 1993 to restructure and retrain the Angolan army. Then Executive Outcomes took part in operations to secure the northern diamond fields from UNITA and some of the officers and soldiers from South Africa who in previous years had been most successful in destabilizing Angola were now assisting the same government fight UNITA which Pretoria had supported from 1975 until 1990. According to Nick Van Den Bergh, another senior member of Executive Outcomes, there was no paradox in its activities. Executive Outcomes was only concerned with profit and was not interested in ideological wars.

An anonymous member of Executive Outcomes who joined it for a second time in 1994, said:

> When I was in the South African Army we fought alongside Jonas Savimbi's UNITA. The Fifth Reconnaissance Regiment to which I belonged was very different from the rest of the conventional army; it only had the best soldiers. It would never have occurred to me to join the ordinary army because its soldiers were too limited. But where I served was different: above all, the reconnaissance units, like all the special forces, were anti- Communist. We were allowed far greater initiative and freedom of action. Later, however, I became curious to discover what the MPLA was like and it was this curiosity which persuaded me to rejoin EO.[1]

According to the South African journalist Al J. Venter EO functions are twofold:

> The essential task of members of Executive Outcomes in the endless African conflicts [in which it is involved] is to instruct, to protect and to organize. They also take part in operations. When they are fired upon they respond vigorously. They are prepared to launch preventive attacks if these help save lives.[2]

The new South African government, perhaps understandably, has been ambivalent in its attitude towards the activities of Executive Outcomes although Kader Asmal, the highly respected member of the government who is minister of water resources and also chairs the national committee on the sale of arms, adopts a pragmatic attitude towards EO activities:

> Our committee has decided that the correct way to approach this question [of Executive Outcomes] was to accept that its activities should be given government approval. I think that the recruitment of personnel for or by a foreign military force should be regulated in the same way as the sale of arms. If an organization seeks to sell its services to the legal government of another country, you regulate

your permission according to the reality of the legitimacy of the government in question and according to its human rights and democratic record. I do not see any difference between the export of arms and that of advice and military services. They are the same thing.[3]

In 1996 between 200 and 500 soldiers made up the core of Executive Outcomes and most of these were former members of the apartheid era special units though in the mid-1990s some Russian recruits had been added to the force. According to the British NGO International Alert, Executive Outcomes consisted of about 2,500 mercenaries. When operating in countries like Angola and Sierra Leone Executive Outcomes also recruits local soldiers to make up its required complements but these only receive about a tenth the pay of its regular soldiers.

In New York the United Nations was deeply disturbed by these new mercenary developments which Executive Outcomes so obviously represented. Enrique Bernales Ballesteros, the UN Special Rapporteur investigating mercenary activities worldwide, said: 'To suggest that some mercenary activities are illegal and others legal is to make a dangerous distinction which could affect international relations of peace and respect between states.' A United Nations report of November 1996 claimed that both Angola and Sierra Leone were using mercenaries to protect their gold and diamond mines and that in return the mercenaries (or their business affiliates) obtained stakes in these mining industries. As the report noted, these security firms sell their services:

> mainly in exchange for concessions relating to mining and energy [and that] Once a greater degree of security has been attained, the firm apparently begins to exploit the concessions it has received by setting up a number of associates and affiliates which engage in such activities as air transport, road building, and import and export, thereby acquiring a significant, if not hegemonic, presence in the economic life of the country in which it is operating.[4]

Executive Outcomes had a contract with the government of Angola to offer protection in return for a share in the profits of the country's natural resources. It had also signed contracts in Sierra Leone with the former National Provisional Ruling Council to provide support in return for cash payments and mining concessions. Affiliates of Executive Outcomes include Branch Energy, Heritage Oil and Gas, GJW

Government Relations, Capricorn Air and Ibis Airline although the companies denied any corporate links with Executive Outcomes. According to a British spokesman the recruitment of mercenaries in Britain is only illegal in very limited circumstances (when British citizens would serve in the forces of a foreign state at war with another foreign state which is at peace with Britain). The same spokesman added that legislation to give force to the UN Convention on Mercenaries would be very difficult to implement.

Africa with its numerous civil wars or disturbances, its weak ineffective governments and the low level of priority accorded to its problems by the major powers remains highly vulnerable or open to mercenary 'assistance' as offered by the growing number of private companies providing military services. These companies represent the privatization of warfare. Executive Outcomes, for example, 'is staffed by highly trained combat veterans from the defense forces that once propped up South Africa's apartheid regime'. It has seized the opportunities offered in Angola and Sierra Leone and claims, in both cases, to have brought peace while also claiming to have prevented a coup in an unnamed African country and carried out a successful hostage rescue operation. The British NGO, International Alert, condemns Executive Outcomes as 'an assortment of former assassins, spies, saboteurs and scoundrels'.[5]

Nick Van Den Bergh, the EO chief executive, welcomed the news that the South African government was to introduce a bill on mercenaries and claimed that it would not apply to Executive Outcomes: 'There is a very distinct line between what we do and what mercenaries do' he said, 'We are providing a professional military advising service.' He added that they refused to work in places like Sudan where it believed the government supports terrorism. During 1996 Sierra Leone was able to hold democratic elections, at least in part according to Executive Outcomes, because its force of 120 men had helped turn back the rebels when they reached the outskirts of Freetown. According to John Leigh, the Sierra Leone envoy in Washington, 'The government of Sierra Leone believes EO can do a better job (providing security) than the Sierra Leone army.'[6] Leigh went on to say that the deployment of EO 'in the diamond districts has permitted the resumption of diamond mining in Sierra Leone'. The government needed revenues and EO needed to be paid. As its chief executive, Van Den Bergh said: 'We are a commercial venture. We are not an aid agency'.

Proving connections between these obscure companies is far from easy. Once a diamond area is secure, for example, another company, apparently related to Executive Outcomes, Lifeguard, then offers private security to the mining companies in the area. It is also claimed that Branch Energy follows Executive Outcomes to pick up diamond concessions though proving any connection is difficult. Malik Chaka, the UNITA spokesman in Washington, says: 'If Brazil intervened in Angola on the side of the government and committed human-rights violations, we could go to the UN to protest. Who do you complain to when these independent operators are there?' The EO reply to this charge is given by Van Den Bergh: 'The fastest thing that would get us out of business is human-rights violations.'[7]

By 1997 Executive Outcomes was active in more than a dozen African countries: it was training and advising armies from Sierra Leone to Madagascar; it was involved in two military conflicts; it was providing air transport and clearing mines; it was responsible for the protection of mines, oilfields, airports and other installations; it was undertaking the construction or repair of bridges, roads, harbours and pipelines. It could argue that all these activities were legitimate and needed doing by somebody or some organization. Wherever there was warfare in Africa the chances were that Executive Outcomes would have a presence.

Executive Outcomes has a substantial if obscure British connection. It was registered in Britain in September 1993 by the British businessman, Anthony Buckingham, and Simon Mann, a former British army officer. Buckingham, a one-time member of SAS, is the chief executive of Heritage Oil and Gas which has drilling interests in Angola. Heritage which started as a British registered company was subsequently incorporated in the Bahamas and is linked to the Canadian oil corporation, Ranger Oil. Mann was an SAS troop commander (22 SAS) and specialized in intelligence work. His service included spells in Cyprus, Germany, Norway, Canada, Central America and Northern Ireland; he has also worked as an expert in intelligence systems in Saudi Arabia, Malaysia and Nigeria. Such a background would give him a wide range of useful contacts for the possible recruitment of mercenaries at high skill levels. These two men first met Eeben Barlow of Executive Outcomes in 1993. Barlow, apart from his earlier military career in South Africa (see above), had also handled operations for South Africa in Europe, developing contacts with the secret services in both East and West Europe and working to break sanctions against South Africa. When at the beginning of 1993 the oil town of Soyo in northern Angola came under the control of UNITA, Buckingham and Mann approached Barlow whom they commissioned to recruit a force of South Africans to recapture the town and less than 100 men supplied by Executive Outcomes did so. Once this force had left, however, UNITA recaptured the town and at this point the Luanda government asked Ranger and Heritage to hire a larger force in exchange for oil concessions. Ranger oil, according to British intelligence, put up US$30m for the operation and gave the contract to Buckingham and Mann who appointed Barlow and another former South African colleague of his, Lafras Luitingh, to recruit a 500-man force to recapture Soyo. Most of the men were former members of the SADF and the ANC reportedly turned a blind eye to the operation because it believed 'it would remove personnel who might have had a destabilising effect on the forthcoming multiracial elections'.[8] This ANC attitude is a classic example of political expediency and the whole mercenary story is riddled with occasions when political expediency triumphs over any stated principles in relation to the use or non-use of mercenaries. The second and subsequent Executive Outcomes operations in Angola were successful and the organization suddenly acquired a high profile in Africa.

According to the British Sunday newspaper, the *Observer*, Executive Outcomes thereafter became involved in a wide range of activities in a number of African countries. These included Kenya where it entered into business dealings with President Moi's son, Raymond Moi, Sierra Leone, and an estimated further 30 countries, mainly in Africa but also including Malaysia and South Korea. It has become patently obvious that Executive Outcomes is far more than a simple provider of mercenaries or guns for hire; rather, it appears to be the advance guard in a scramble for Africa's mineral wealth. Whatever the precise nature of the link-up with Buckingham and Mann, it seems plain that there is a close liaison between Executive Outcomes, the military advisor organization, and the various companies run from their Chelsea headquarterts in London by Buckingham and Mann which include Heritage Oil and Gas, Plaza 107 Ltd (a management services company), Air International, Branch International Ltd, Branch Mining Ltd., and Capricorn Systems Ltd. Directors include Buckingham, Mann, Sir David Steel (the former Liberal Party leader) and Crause Steyl (the South African director of Ibis Air). It was Capricorn Air which flew the Executive Outcomes mercenaries into Angola in 1993.[9]

Subsequently, Capricorn was registerd as Ibis Air in Angola and South Africa and grew to substantial size, its fleet including Boeing 727s, two MI-17 helicopters and two Hind MI-24 gunships, a plane with surveillance capabilities, two jet fighters and several private jets. Ibis has a link with the South African state arms development and procurement firm, Denel, which has stored the aircraft Executive Outcomes uses for its Africa operations. By 1997 Ibis was thought to be based in Malta. Branch International is the holding company for a number of subsidiaries that prospect for oil, gold and diamonds. According to a British intelligence report Executive Outcomes 'is acquiring a wide reputation in sub-Saharan Africa for reliability and efficiency' and appeals especially to 'smaller countries desperate for rapid assistance' (which they cannot obtain at speed from either the United Nations or the Organization of African Unity) and, therefore, that there 'is every likelihood' that the services of Executive Outcomes 'will continue increasingly to be sought'. Since the company is able and ready to barter its services for a share of natural resources and commodities in those countries which employ it there is every indication that it will become far more – in power terms – than just a provider of mercenary services. The most telling point made by this intelligence report is the following:

> On present showing, Executive Outcomes will become ever richer and more potent, capable of exercising real power, even to the extent of keeping military regimes in being. If it continues to expand at the present rate, its influence in sub-Saharan Africa could become crucial.[10]

This growing power of Executive Outcomes with its close links to British companies engaged in comparable activities threatens to become a formidable force on a continent where many countries are so weak, indebted and at risk from potential or actual rebellions that it will be able, quite easily, to tip the balance one way or another in conflicts which arise. Such an organization can only be curbed in one of two ways: either by the South African government itself; or by the major powers working through the United Nations. Neither possibility seemed at all likely in the circumstances prevailing at the end of the 1990s. If, as appeared to be the case in 1993, the ANC thought it better to allow Executive Outcomes to operate as a means of diverting former military personnel to purposes other than subverting the new South Africa, such an argument is likely to prevail for some considerable time to come. Moreover, the views expressed by the minister, Dr Kader Asmal, equating the activities of Executive Outcomes with those of arms selling would suggest that South Africa is willing to allow such mercenary activity to continue, always provided it is cloaked in a form of respectability represented by statements such as that of Eeben Barlow that:

> We are not going to help anyone that is not a legitimate government or which poses a threat to South Africa, or that is involved in activities really frowned upon by the outside world. We have had a major impact on Africa. We have brought peace to two countries almost totally destroyed by civil wars.[11]

If this arrogant and doubtfully truthful statement is believed in South Africa, then Executive Outcomes has a bright future ahead of it. In the end, however, the South African government may well find that it has allowed a monster to grow which it is unable to control.

The alternative – the major powers working through the United Nations to curb the growth and operations of Executive Outcomes – seems even less likely. The United States government appears happy to allow comparable organizations to flourish and, indeed, seems only too willing to use them, as in the case of MPRI in former Yugoslavia. There is a far greater likelihood that US organizations will be competing for business against Executive Outcomes with encouragement from the administration in Washington rather than any chance of the administration setting out to curb such organizations through the United Nations. Other similar organizations offering military advice and services are proliferating and becoming entrenched (see Chapter 12) and Executive Outcomes, if anything, is the prototype of a new, more formal approach to mercenaries that is gaining semi-official support from governments. Universal condemnation of the use of mercenaries has become as hypocritical as was earlier condemnation of apartheid by the Western powers while they resolutely refused to match their rhetoric with action.

12 The new mercenary corporations

Attitudes towards mercenaries have undergone some remarkable changes in the thirty odd years since they made so unsavory an impact upon world opinion by their brutal antics in the Congo of the 1960s. One problem has always been the difficulty of definition. Were the first US military 'advisers' in Vietnam authorized by President Kennedy in the early 1960s mercenaries or a legitimate part of military assistance to an ally, the forerunners of a massive US intervention? Similarly, how were the British officers seconded or 'lent' to assist the Sultan of Oman in his fight against the Dhofar rebels during the 1960s and 1970s to be classified? A high point of anti-mercenary sentiment was achieved when western mercenaries captured in Angola early in 1976 were put on trial later that year in the presence of eminent jurists and other observers invited from round the world. Subsequently, there were few protests when the leading mercenaries were executed and others received long prison sentences and no one argued that they had been punished unfairly. As long as the Cold War lasted the two opposed sides were prepared to give military assistance to their allies, usually on a formal government-to-government basis, so that the role of mercenaries remained peripheral. Exceptions to this rule were most likely to occur when a major power determined to undermine a legitimate government of whose policies it disapproved, and a prime example of such mercenary use emerges from the murky story of Nicaragua during the 1980s when the United States used mercenaries (and a good many other doubtful tactics) in order to undermine the Sandinista government. The end of the Cold War changed the outlook for the mercenary business as it changed the prospects in so many other fields of activity.

Those who hoped for a peace dividend when the Cold War ended were to be bitterly disappointed. It is difficult to quantify with any precision but every year on average through the 1990s there have been from 15 to 30 wars or major rebellions in progress round the world between them contributing to an annual figure of 15 to 17 million refugees. It is almost as though the relaxation of the tensions inherent in the Cold War confrontation persuaded the world's small fry in military–political terms that they were now free to pursue their own confrontations without fear of big power restraints being imposed upon them. An estimated reduction of the US military machine by 30 per cent and a comparable or larger reduction of the Soviet machine released a huge number of military personnel, at every level of skills from cannon fodder troops to two-star generals, on to the open market; a majority of these former soldiers possessed few skills and sometimes no aptitudes for civilian employment. On the other hand they were certainly in the market for some form of military employment and were to discover that market forces would offer them a good many opportunities: there are some 80 low and middle income countries (according to World Bank definitions) and a further 35 mini-states (all members of the South or former Third World) many of which have either suffered from or are suffering from some form of civil war, rebellion or insurgency, or, as in the mini-states, are so poor and small that they offer tempting targets for subversion. This is where the mercenary comes into his own, at least in theory, although subverting a small state – even one with a minimum military establishment – is not as simple or straightforward as it might appear: Bob Denard succeeded in the Comoros, 'Mad Mike' Hoare made a mess of it in Seychelles.

There will always be the individual soldier of fortune type of mercenary who will turn up wherever there is a conflict: for money, for adventure, sometimes for idealism, because he likes fighting, and these are near impossible to control. Far more important, however, has been the emergence in the 1990s of the corporate mercenary, the firms offering a range of services and claiming, whether spuriously or not, that they are only prepared to work for legitimate governments. These organizations are attempting to confer upon the ancient trade of the mercenary a veneer of respectability that poses enormous potential problems for the future. Like the international drugs trade with its criminal cartels, these mercenary firms are also a response to market forces and there is an interesting if unpleasant parallel between the two occupations. The drug producing countries of Latin America, the Golden Triangle and Golden Crescent of Asia are responding to the huge demand for drugs of all kinds in the rich markets of the North and no matter how much the constant supply of drugs to the North is condemned by the United States or the European Union, the production of these drugs will continue as long as the demand exists. The new mercenary companies, however they dress up their activities and describe themselves, are a response by the North to demands for military assistance from the weak and sometimes chaotic countries of the South and they, too, will continue to operate as long as there is a market for their services in the South. The drug producers provide employment to peasant cultivators, middle-men, Cartel barons, couriers and distributors who together make up a formidable network of employees. The corporate military services companies provide employment for the huge number of ex-military personnel that the end of the Cold War has released. In both cases market forces are the key to the continuation of the business.

A new attitude towards mercenaries also became discernible during the 1990s in a number of articles which appeared in the Western media arguing for a different understanding of the mercenary and his activities than the total condemnation of them that, in theory if not practice, has become the accepted international wisdom. These articles, or rather their arguments, represent the first moves in an increasingly overt campaign towards the legitimization of mercenary activity, provided it is 'sanctioned' by governments.

The argument runs along the following lines: there are a number of countries where law and order has all but broken down or violent civil wars and rebellions are ruining any chances of reasonable development; the security forces of those countries are ill-trained, badly led and all too often themselves resort to banditry rather than working to bring the chaos under control (even if they have the ability to do so); their governments are desperate to end the state of civil war or chaos that prevails and look outside for help; the United Nations, the OAU or other regional organizations are either unable or unwilling for complex political reasons to respond to their needs while the big powers would only be likely to do so at a price, that is, by the subsequent imposition of 'strings' which the governments in need are unwilling to pay; but there is an alternative source of aid – the mercenary.

The mercenary, the new argument continues, has changed his spots. Of course there are the 'mavericks', the individual soldiers of fortune with their rough ways and they, as ever, are to be deplored. At the same time there are a large number of highly skilled ex-soldiers around only too anxious to be employed and now, moreover, there are fully registered corporate organizations ready to emply them on a properly regulated basis. These organizations offer every kind of military and security skill along with highly trained personnel to implement them. Moreover, in a number of cases they have already proved their worth. So why not use them and forget the old taboos against mercenaries. A number of countries such as Angola, Papua

New Guinea and Sierra Leone have already demonstrated their willingness to do so and some have said openly that the mercenary organizations they have employed have proved more efficient than their own armed forces. The mercenaries, if properly controlled and regulated, answer a vital market need and one that is likely to grow in the future. Furthermore, if these organizations, such as MPRI, Sandline, or Executive Outcomes, are legitimized the energies of the mercenaries that otherwise might well prove dangerous can be channelled into much needed support services for bona fide governments that are willing to pay for their services. This way, ex-soldiers who might otherwise hire themselves out as individual soldiers of fortune can instead be controlled and given employment; legitimate governments can be provided with assistance which they would find impossible to obtain from any other source; law and order can be introduced in regions where it does not exist; and, as a result of their mercenary interventions, trade and a reasonable communal life without violence can be resumed. The new corporate mercenary organizations emphasize that they only wish to work for legitimate governments. If, in addition, these organizations are regulated by the governments of the countries in which they are domiciled everyone ought to be content. (An extra bonus that is not included in these arguments, is the likelihood that in the aftermath of a successful mercenary intervention Western companies will obtain an even larger controlling share of the mineral resources of small developing countries than they already possess – but that is another story.) This beguiling argument is being pushed to justify the emergence of a new world-wide security business that looks set to grow as fast in the first decade of the twenty-first century as the drugs trade and the NGO aid business have grown over the last decades of the twentieth century. Arguments against the deployment of mercenaries, however well presented and morally justified, appear to be in retreat in the face of a new world trend that is willing to accept almost any form of privatization that takes pressure off governments and makes money. These new mercenary organizations appear to fullfill both criteria.

The older kind of mercenary still seeks employment and magazines such as *Soldier of Fortune* will carry advertisements that say: 'Wanted: Employment as Mercenary' to be followed by a description of the applicant's past achievements. Clubs for old soldiers or would-be mercenaries such as the Wild Geese Club which 'Mad Mike' Hoare used to run in Johannesburg will also continue to have a place as mercenary recruiting grounds for the new corporations. Indeed, there is an almost comic side to the mercenary world, best represented by the annual 'Soldier of Fortune Convention and Expo'. That of 1991, for example, held in San Diego, was attended by some 600 Vietnam veterans, police officers, arms dealers and other roughnecks who came for camaraderie and booze and enjoyed a five-day programme which included marksmanship competitions, knife-fighting workshops, evasive driving training and lectures. Formerly such lectures had been about 'The Evil Empire' but with the end of the Cold War interest in that topic dropped away. 'Some of us come for God, guns and guts,' said one long-time attendee, Steve Barkley of Pebble Beach, who never served in the military. 'And some come for Uzis, floozies and Jacuzzis.'[1] This annual convention probably had more to do with nostalgia for old soldiers but is a potent reminder, none the less, that there are a lot of old soldiers around, many of whom would sign up for mercenary roles if and when these were available.

Writing in the *Financial Times*[2] Edward Mortimer argued that both international charities and mercenaries were helping to shape foreign policy. He examined what Clare Short, the new British Labour Government International Development Secretary, calls 'social audit'; in essence, if a major business is investing in a developing country it makes sense to carry out a social impact assessment to see whether the new investment is likely to damage the environment or hurt the local economy. If it does appear likely to do so then, in theory, the investor can anticipate the trouble and take action to avoid it or, perhaps, at least to avoid bad publicity by demonstrating a willingness to make special contributions to the welfare of the local community. This makes sound business sense. The next stage, in a troubled region of the world, is of course, to hire a security firm to safeguard the company's new installations. Major international companies will spend large sums of money on public relations exercises to demonstrate how their operations are a benefit to the communities in which they are situated. In the end, however, they are there to make money and if their public relations efforts fail to persuade local communities of the benefits of their presence – as Shell failed to persuade the Ogoniland people in the Delta region of Nigeria – there is always some form of military (security) protection to fall back upon and in more and more parts of the world today companies employ the services of security firms to safeguard their investments.

The sales techniques used and the size of contracts being obtained by these new security firms indicate clearly enough that a new breed of mercenary has emerged on the international scene. These corporations or security firms are careful to distance themselves from the older image of derring-do soldiers of fortune, emphasizing instead their corporate nature as sources of highly experienced expertise. Thus, the US Vinnell Corporation and a related company obtained contracts worth US$170m to train the Saudi Arabian national guard and air force; both companies are part-owned by the Washington-based Carlyle merchant-banking group whose chairman is former US Secretary of Defense Frank Carlucci. With this sort of connection it is inconceivable that the United Nations will have much success persuading the US government to ban mercenary activities. Military Professional Resources Inc. (MPRI) won the contract to retrain the military in Croatia and Bosnia and MPRI's vice-president, Harry Soyster, a former army general, has quickly learnt corporate business-speak: 'We offer expertise from the greatest fighting force on earth, the U.S. military.'[3]

It is sad and ironical and hardly an accident that the three major Western powers – the United States, Britain and France – whose propaganda over decades has presented them as the guardians of freedom throughout the world, assisted by two smaller states with efficient if brutal military records – Israel and South Africa – between them are the source of the world's most effective mercenaries.

> At a recent arms show in Abu Dhabi, an Executive Outcomes booth quietly competed for business with mercenaries from Britain, France and the U.S. Topflight mercenaries and military consultants, many recruited from elite military units like the U.S. Special Forces, Britain's S.A.S. and Scots Guards and South Africa's 32 Battalion, can command anywhere from about US$3,500 a month for enlisted men to US$13,000 a month for officers or fighter pilots. That is far more than most of those involved could make wearing a regular-army uniform, and the package is usually topped off with free death-and-disability insurance.[4]

There is a close connection between these new corporate entities and both the mining and arms businesses. The mining connection was obvious in both Angola and Sierra Leone when Executive Outcomes became involved during the 1990s. The Israeli company, Levdan, which carried out a three year contract to train troops and bodyguards for the President of Congo (Brazzaville), Pascal Lissouba, prior to his overthrow in the 1997 civil war, was also instrumental in his government purchasing US$10m worth of Israeli weapons and military equipment. These corporate interventions can end in disaster as did that of Sandline in Papua New Guinea where the very fact that the government believed Sandline to be more effective than its own armed forces led to the debacle. The army, despite its inability over ten years to end the revolt in the island of Bougainville, refused to be upstaged by the Sandline mercenaries and insisted that they should be expelled with the result that 70 mercenaries were hurried out of the country while tons of arms and equipment which were part of the deal were impounded.

For those who believe in conspiracy theories these new corporations offering military services make perfect villains. To begin with, they work outside government controls and the bigger they grow the less susceptible to controls are they liable to be. They are prepared to undertake tasks which governments cannot be seen to do and jobs, moreover, that may go contrary to the avowed policies of the governments they serve. They work hand in hand with large multinational corporations (who have long been seen as international villains anyway) helping oil or mineral companies defend their investments in countries whose citizens may see little or nothing of the value which is eventually extracted from the ground. They engage to train armies that have the most doubtful reputations in terms of their behaviour and human rights records. They are prepared to train private forces of the most dubious kind as in the case of Colombia and the drugs cartels. And, finally, many of their senior staff – apart from the mercenaries they send into the field – have backgrounds from the least savoury and often secret sides of their own country's military machines.

Against the above background which received a good deal of publicity during the 1990s through the activities of Executive Outcomes in Angola and Sierra Leone, MPRI in Croatia and Bosnia, Sandline in Papua New Guinea and Sierra Leone again or Levdan in Congo (Brazzaville) to name the most conspicuous of these mercenary companies, some detailed arguments have been advanced in favour of these mercenary organizations by Dr Ron Smith who is a senior lecturer in political science and director of defence and strategic studies at the University of Waikato. Writing in the *New Zealand International Review*[5] he asks 'Why should mercenarism be so universally condemned? Has the mercenary no part to play in the modern world?'

Before looking at some historical examples, Dr Smith says:

> Depending upon precisely what is meant by the term, it will be claimed that some kinds of mercenary force could provide a valuable and cost-effective service for states and for international

organisations, and that it would thus be desirable to allow the development of appropriate organisations and an appropriate safeguard regime.

He distinguishes between mercenaries enlisted to serve in foreign national armies – the Hessian troops used by the British in North America, the Gurkhas in the British and Indian armies, the Pakistanis in the Saudi Arabian army – and mercenaries employed by a company such as Sandline who constitute a private army, but he goes on to ask whether, morally, there is much significance in the difference. After examining the United Nations definition of mercenaries, the author suggests that, in reality, it is concerned exclusively with 'private' mercenary forces such as those of Sandline and that such mercenaries are 'promised "material compensation" substantially in excess of that paid to combatants of similar rank in the forces of the party which employs them'.

The most controversial argument advanced by Dr Smith is that mercenaries (who according to the Geneva Conventions of 1949 are not entitled to combatant status if caught) should be treated exactly the same as any other combatant: 'All belligerents without distinction should be entitled to the same protection.' Should his argument prevail it would represent an immense step forward towards legitimizing mercenaries and their use and it must be an argument that is most welcome to Executive Outcomes, MPRI, Sandline and the other burgeoning mercenary organizations. In what must be seen as a specious justification for mercenaries Dr Smith argues that since in many developing countries there is a 'significant political risk in the mere existence of a substantial military establishment' and that, apart from the possibility that they may mount a coup, such military establishments may turn out to be little use when a crisis arises, perhaps – he implies – such governments should call in mercenaries when the need arises instead of relying upon their own armed forces. The long-term logic of such an argument is appalling: what it could eventually produce is a new form of imperialism with the weak countries of the South militarily controlled by 'independent' mercenary corporations which, in real terms, will be the instruments of the major powers. This is not a prospect to be welcomed anywhere except perhaps in Washington, London, Paris, Moscow and one or two other smaller militant expansionist states.

In a world that is awash with arms, where too many countries spend far too great a proportion of their inadequate resources upon military establishments, the idea of promoting the growth of private military establishments to operate alongside the public ones appears politically grotesque. When, in addition, it is clear that only the more advanced economies and, most notably, those with major military establishments anyway, as well as recent or current reputations for some kind of colonial or aggressive activity against their neighbours will be the sources of such mercenaries, then the concept, for all its superficial reasonableness, becomes quite extraordinarily dangerous. Any moves designed to increase rather than reduce the total of the world's military establishments are surely retrograde. When, moreover, the new establishments are to be private corporations with at best only limited government controls exercised over them the prospect becomes fundamentally daunting. This does not mean it will not happen. The key to this question lies, as with so many other political decisions, with the half dozen major powers who possess, if only they would use it, the capacity to enforce a different world order through the United Nations. At present the prospect of any such action would appear to be extremely unlikely.

13 Sierra Leone, Sandline and Britain

The small West African coastal state of Sierra Leone was established in 1787 as the result of philanthropist pressures in Britain to provide a home for freed slaves; in 1896 Britain proclaimed a protectorate over the hinterland. In 1951 Britain introduced a unitary constitution providing for universal suffrage and the first elections were won by the Sierra Leone People's Party (SLPP) led by Milton Margai who became the colony's chief minister in 1953 and prime minister in 1958. Sierra Leone became independent in 1961 as a member of the Commonwealth and retained close ties with Britain. In the elections of March 1967 the main opposition party, the All-People's Congress (APC) led by Dr Siaka Stevens, gained the majority of seats although a military coup prevented Stevens taking office. This, unfortunately, set the pattern for the ensuing years with the military periodically ousting the civilian politicians.

On 30 April 1992, a small group of mutinous soldiers under Captain Valentine Strasser seized power in a coup and forced President Joseph Saidu Momoh to flee to Guinea. A National Provisional Ruling Council (NPRC) was established with Strasser as chairman and his government pledged itself to end the border war with rebels from Liberia although it soon became clear that these were only a part of the problem and that dissident Sierra Leonians were also involved and would pose a major threat to the government that would develop into a full-scale civil war over the next few years. Strasser also pledged that his government would respect Sierra Leone's obligations to the Organization of African Unity (OAU), the Economic Community of West African States (ECOWAS) and other international organizations to which it belonged. During 1993 President Valentine Strasser dismissed his vice-chairman Lieutenant Solomon Anthony James Musa and replaced him with Lieutenant Julius Maada Bio. The government planned to sell the majority state-owned National Diamond Mining Co to private interests and announced new measures to curb illegal diamond mining. The military government had originally promised to return Sierra Leone to civilian rule within a year but now set a new date of 1996. In January 1994 the government claimed a number of military successes against the Revolutionary United Front (RUF) which had launched its first attacks against the government in 1991 from bases in Liberia. The RUF established a number of positions near the diamond-mining centre of Kenema which enabled it to threaten the principal sources of the country's wealth The war against the RUF continued throughout 1995; the Strasser government claimed that the RUF was a pawn of the National Patriotic Front of Liberia (NPFL). In February government forces recaptured from the rebels the Sierra Rutile titanium mine; it accounted for more than 50 per cent of the country's foreign exchange earnings and was the country's largest employer. In April Captain Strasser lifted the ban on political parties and promised to hand over power to a democratically elected president in January 1996.

On 16 January 1996, another coup by a section of the military ousted Captain Strasser who was replaced by his deputy, now Brig-Gen. Julius Maada Bio. The elections for a return to civilian rule which had been postponed from 5 December 1995 to 26–27 February 1996 still went ahead under Bio. The SLPP won 36 per cent of the vote while Ahmad Tejan Kabbah, the leading presidential candidate, obtained 35.8 per cent of the presidential vote the first time round. He became president after a second round of voting and on 29 March 1996, Bio handed over power to President Kabbah. Fighting against the RUF continued in the countryside although in November Kabbah signed a peace agreement with the rebels. Kabbah enjoyed the presidency for just over a year until on 25 May 1997, yet another coup was mounted by junior officers and Kabbah was forced to flee the country. The coup was launched when the capital's top security prison was stormed and 600 captives, many of them dissident soldiers, were released. Major Johnny Paul Koroma declared himself head of state. He abolished the constitution and banned political parties. The coup was at once condemned by the international community. Nigeria dispatched troops to Freetown and these were joined by 1,500 troops from Guinea. By June lawlessness had spread through most of Sierra Leone, Nigeria had failed to overthrow the new regime while as many as 300,000 people out of a population of 4,424,000 had fled the country. Koroma established an Armed Forces Revolutionary Council (AFRC) and included in his government Foday Sankoh, the former leader of the RUF who at one stage had been imprisoned in Nigeria. The AFRC rejected attempts at mediation by Britain, Ghana and Nigeria and despite the fact that Nigerian troops as part of ECOMOG (the military peacekeeping force of ECOWAS) had seized Freetown's international airport and the seaport, Koroma was sworn in as president on 17 June. The Commonwealth demanded the unconditional restoration of President Kabbah but at talks in Abidjan, Côte d'Ivoire, that August Koroma insisted that he should remain in power for four years. Another meeting was held in Conakry, Guinea, during October 1997 at which the foreign ministers of Côte d'Ivoire, Ghana, Guinea, Liberia and Nigeria persuaded Koroma to agree to restore Kabbah to power in April 1998: Koroma was promised immunity from prosecution. This was the state of affairs at the close of 1997. Over the preceding four years much of the country, which in any case is one of the poorest in Africa with a per capita income of only US$180, had been devastated by civil war and the economy was in ruins.

Mercenaries had already become involved in Sierra Leone during Strasser's term of office with Executive Outcomes having been hired to guard the diamond mining operations for the government. During the fighting which followed the May 1997 coup Executive Outcomes rescued a number of American investors who were cut off while visiting the Sieromco bauxite mine. Executive Outcomes had been hired originally in 1995 after the forces of the Revolutionary United Front (RUF) had overrun the bauxite, rutile and diamond mining areas. One of the diamond companies whose employees were rescued by Executive Outcomes in May 1997 was Diamond Works whose largest shareholder was Tony Buckingham, a name that constantly crops up in relation to mining or mercenaries in Africa. He had connections with a number of other companies with mineral interests on the continent as well as with both Executive Outcomes and Sandline. Diamond Works had hired Lifeguard which is an affiliate of Executive Outcomes to guard its exploration properties in Sierra Leone at a fee of $60,000 a month.[1]

When Koroma met the West African Foreign Ministers at Conakry in October 1997 and agreed to hand over power to Kabbah in April 1998 it was also agreed, as a concession to the rebels who had suffered at their hands, that organizations like Executive Outcomes should be banned from Sierra Leone: 'Foreign troops, private armies, mercenaries and "irregular troops" were to be withdrawn.'[2] The RUF which constituted the opposition to orderly government and had done much to ruin Sierra Leone in the years of fighting since 1991 did not have the discipline, as it had discovered, to stand up to the mercenaries. Their expulsion, therefore, suited Koroma and the rebels, even as they agreed to stand down, and did not augur well for either the mining interests or the returning Kabbah. (Indeed, had all the mercenaries and foreign troops – that is, Nigerians – actually obeyed this clause and left Sierra Leone it is doubtful whether the returning Kabbah could have lasted a month which, no doubt, was Koroma's calculation.) Nigeria was not happy with this provision in the peace accord which called for the removal of all foreign troops. Britain, too, had consistently backed the hire and use of mercenaries in Sierra Leone and justified doing so by 'extraordinary circumstances'.[3] Furthermore, in 1996 the World Bank had allowed President Kabbah to use some of its money to pay Executive Outcomes while neither the OAU nor the Commonwealth criticized the Sierra Leone government at this time for hiring and employing mercenaries.

Leaving aside Britain, the attitudes of the World Bank, the OAU and the Commonwealth to the use of mercenaries in Sierra Leone can only be described as extraordinary. The World Bank, despite being a fully independent organization, is also part of the United Nations structure although it would be fair to say that its actions are always dominated by its determination to safeguard, above all, those financial institutions which are approved by the West and these would naturally include mining investments in Sierra Leone. The whole history of the OAU has been opposed to any kind of mercenary activity in Africa while the Commonwealth as an association (with Britain taking a different line) has also been opposed to such operations while Australia was then in the process of condemning the introduction of mercenaries (in the form of Sandline) into Papua New Guinea. Yet expedience and political convenience led these three organizations either to give positive support to the use of mercenaries or to say nothing.

In March 1998, prior to Kabbah's return to Sierra Leone, the London *Observer* revealed that Peter Penfold, Britain's High Commissioner to Sierra Leone who had moved to Conakry following the Koroma coup, had held talks with Sandline which had recently made international headlines as a result of its botched operation in Papua New Guinea. The British Foreign Office, while admitting that Penfold had held discussions with Sandline, justified his talks with the phrase 'extraordinary circumstances'. This revelation came as an embarrassment to the British government whose Prime Minister, Tony Blair, had championed the cause of the ousted President Kabbah (specially inviting him to attend the Edinburgh Commonwealth Conference in October 1997) and whose Foreign Secretary, Robin Cook, had recently insisted that he wanted Britain to pursue an ethical foreign policy. As the *Observer* pointed out:

The disclosure of Penfold's secret talks with Sandline also make nonsense of this week's indignant row between Cook's deputy, Tony Lloyd, and African Commonwealth heads over whether Nigeria should be congratulated for reinstating the deposed Kabbah, allegedly with the help of Sandline.

There were sharp exchanges between Ghana's Foreign Minister, Victor Ghbo, and Lloyd over the affair. Ghana wanted Nigeria officially thanked by the Commonwealth, but at a ministerial meeting in London Lloyd objected, saying the continuing military action should have had the United Nations Security Council's approval.[4]

The dilemma for the British government escalated when it became known in May 1998 that the National Investigation Service (NIS), an arm of British Customs and Excise, was investigating a massive arms shipment to war-torn Sierra Leone which had been made in defiance of a United Nations embargo; the shipment had been dispatched the previous February, apparently with Foreign Office approval. The deal took place when a strict United Nations Security Council embargo on the shipment of arms to any of the warring factions in Sierra Leone was in place. Sandline, it transpired, had supplied equipment and training to a militia working with the Nigerian force which restored Kabbah to power.

There was no possibility of the matter being hushed up because, following Kabbah's return to Freetown with Penfold in attendance, T-shirts appeared on the streets depicting Penfold who was regarded as a hero by Kabbah supporters while the restored President said: 'The British Prime Minister and his government also deserve our special thanks for their support and assistance in every respect.' Sandline had shipped some 30 tonnes of weapons and ammunition to Kabbah's supporters from Bulgaria. In a statement Sandline's Lt-Col. Spicer said that he 'understood and still believed that we were acting with the approval of Her Majesty's Government in assisting to restore President Kabbah' and, he added, 'President Kabbah's government has at all times remained the only internationally recognised lawful government of Sierra Leone.'[5]

It was then further revealed that the 'military consultants' of Sandline headed by Lt-Col. Spicer had met Foreign Office officials led by Craig Murray, the deputy head of the Africa (equatorial) department, on some three occasions at least one of which took place in the Foreign Office prior to the dispatch of arms from Bulgaria to Sierra Leone. The Foreign Office minister, Tony Lloyd, now claimed that the

Foreign Secretary, Robin Cook, and his team had been kept in the dark about the Sandline involvement.[6] Adding to the confusion while also making certain that there could be no doubt of Britain's role, the Sierra Leone government said that anyone questioning the role of British officials in returning the elected president to power should be ashamed of themselves. Dr Julius Spencer, the Minister for Information, said he thought people were 'missing the point' in the row over collusion between the Foreign Office and Sandline: 'I would have to say that if the British government and British officials were involved in supplying arms, then the British people should be proud of their government.'[7]

A new figure now enters the convoluted story in the person of Rakesh Saxena who brokered the deal between Sandline and the exiled Sierra Leone government although the contract was finally signed with Sandline either by President Kabbah himself or by Solomon Berewa, the Solicitor General, and was settled in cash. Although there were about 30,000 ECOMOG troops at Lunghi International Airport preparing to restore Kabbah when the operation began there was also the pro-Kabbah army of Kamajors in Sierra Leone, an ethnic group loyal to the exiled President which formerly had created resentment among his enemies and had been a factor encouraging the coup of 1997. Kabbah needed these men when he returned to Sierra Leone and Sandline had the task of training and arming them. Rakesh Saxena was prepared to provide US$1.5m to assist in restoring Kabbah to power. Saxena was an Indian-born former Thai banker who at the time was on bail in Canada for an alleged fraud for US$88m in Thailand; he had diamond interests in Sierra Leone. After Saxena had telephoned Sandline in London over 12/13 July 1997, Lt-Col. Spicer faxed to him details of what he could provide:

> We are certainly able to assist... as you are aware we have unique expertise and knowledge of the country, already have a very good relationship with the government and with ECOMOG, and have the resources to implement any project the government decides on in an effective, timely manner with minimum collateral damage to innocent parties.[8]

And so the operation got underway. Lt-Col. Spicer needed US$60,000 plus US$10,000 expenses to produce a full report on what he could offer. The money was sent to him in London by Saxena's aide at the Sierra Leone and Guinea-based Jupiter Mining Corporation. Mr Saxena who had recently invested in two properties in Sierra Leone said his offer to help was motivated solely by his desire to protect his business interests.

Britain now found itself in the position of having taken a morally sound action illegally and so being unable to defend it publicly. The Labour chairman of the Commons defence select committee, Bruce George, said: 'The right thing happened in the end. An illegitimate government was ousted and a legitimate government was re-established.'[9] This simplistic explanation failed to set the matter to rest; there were too many complications. For one thing there was the position of Nigeria which at the time was the pariah state of the Commonwealth because of the behaviour of its military dictatorship under General Sani Abacha; the Nigerians, however, insisted that there was no contradiction in their helping to restore democracy in Sierra Leone while denying any return to democracy at home. Britain which had strongly criticized Nigeria now found itself assisting the Nigerian military operation in Sierra Leone by encouraging Sandline to assist Kabbah's restoration, despite the UN embargo and despite government's formal reluctance to either approve the use of mercenaries or use them itself. In fact, despite denials, once it was clear that MI6 had known of the Sandline operation and that Tim Spicer, Sandline's chief executive, had met both the British High Commissioner to Sierra Leone, Mr. Penfold, and Foreign Office officials, the Foreign Secretary had little option except to promise an independent inquiry into the whole affair.

The affair became even more complicated when solicitors for Sandline released a letter to the Foreign Secretary in which it was revealed that representatives of the mercenary organization had not only met officials at the Foreign Office but also members of the US departments of state and defence. Extracts from the letter (from Richard Slowe of S J Berwin & Co – 24 April 1998) are as follows:

> Dear Foreign Secretary,
> We have been consulted by Lieutenant Colonel Tim Spicer and Mr Michael Grunberg in relation to... their involvement with affairs in Sierra Leone... Some disturbing developments in recent weeks involving the activities of Her Majesty's Customs and Excise appear to have occurred without the knowledge of the Foreign and Commonwealth Office, the Department of Trade and Industry or the Ministry of Defence.
> As you will be aware, the coup in Sierra Leone last year which removed President Kabbah was roundly condemned... and you, Sir,

were widely reported as offering President Kabbah the full support of Her Majesty's Government in restoring the lawful government to power in Sierra Leone...

Mr Spicer is an executive of a company called Sandline International which is in the business of providing military assistance to lawful governments, and Mr Grunberg is a consultant to that company.

At the suggestion of your High Commissioner in Freetown, Mr Peter Penfold, President Kabbah asked our clients to provide such assistance. Thereafter negotiations proceeded with President Kabbah and...full briefings were given both personally and by telephone to representatives of Her Majesty's Government.

At the Foreign and Commonwealth Office those briefed include John Everard, Craig Murray, Linda St Cook and Tim Andrews and our clients were led to believe that clearance was given at Head of Department level. The Ministry of Defence personnel who were briefed included Lieutenant Colonel Peter Hicks in Conakry and Colonel Andrew Gale, the British Army military adviser to the UN Special Envoy in Sierra Leone.

Further, Mr Penfold himself called at our client's office premises on 28 January 1998, just three weeks before the equipment now in issue was delivered, and was given full details of the arrangements...

Our clients were assured...that the operation had the full support of Her Majesty's Government.

At the same time, our clients kept informed the US State Department at the highest level, including John Hirsch, the US Ambassador in Sierra Leone, Charles Snyder, Director, Office of Regional Affairs and Dennis Linskey, Chief, West and Southern Africa Division.

Furthermore, following support having been given for the proposed operation by both the US Department of State and the US Department of Defence...we understand that Michael Thomas, the Country Desk Officer for Sierra Leone at the US Department of State met with Philip Parham, the Africa Watcher at the British Embassy in Washington indicating the US Government's full support for Sandline International's involvement.

Accordingly, it is quite apparent that the involvement of Sandline International...had...the approval of Her Majesty's Government and, should it become necessary, we would contend that a licence had been given within the meaning of the Sierra Leone (United Nations Sanctions) Order 1997...

Sandline International's involvement was quite open and indeed their personnel were invited aboard HMS Cornwall where they provided tactical and operational advice.

Further, engineers from HMS Cornwall assisted in the repair of a helicopter which Sandline International was operating in support of President Kabbah...

Needless to say, our clients find the actions of the Customs Officers [who are carrying out an inquiry] to be at complete variance with the policy of Her Majesty's Government...[10]

No one reading this letter, or learning that the US State Department had been informed of what was happening, could possibly believe that the British Government had not given the go-ahead to the mercenary organization, Sandline, to assist in the return to power of the ousted Sierra Leone President. The sequence of events presented in the letter raises a number of questions: why did the Foreign Secretary not know what his department was doing; why was it necessary to inform the US State Department; if it was so important to restore Kabbah, why did not Britain do it openly by sending a Brigade of British troops and informing both the United Nations and the Organization of African Unity that it was responding to the request for help from a legitimate head of state who was a friend of Britain and a member of the Commonwealth? How much, it might also be asked, was the action dictated by the fact that though Sierra Leone is a tiny, poor and largely unimportant country there are a lot of diamonds there and a good many interested parties from outside who are anxious to see the diamond mining regions protected?

Few affairs are more likely to visit trouble upon the British Foreign Office than questions relating to the sale of arms or questions relating to the activities of mercenaries and the combination of the two here faced the Foreign Secretary, Robin Cook, with a substantial crisis, more especially as he had gone on record saying he wanted Britain to pursue an ethical foreign policy. The Foreign Secretary denied that ministers were in any way involved in the decision-making process that led to the Sandline involvement in Sierra Leone but initiated an inquiry into the whole affair. What was most important about the Sandline position was its assertion that it was legitimately serving the British state, an assertion which was equivalent to claiming that the British state is prepared to employ mercenaries when to do so serves a particular policy.

As the story unravelled it appeared first that civil servants in the Foreign Office were initiating policies of their own without informing their ministers and secondly that Tony Lloyd, the junior Minister for Africa, had been misinformed when he told the House of Commons that *The Observer* report which cited Sandline involvement in Sierra Leone was scurrilous. He was wrong.[11] More information kept coming to light. It transpired that four British air companies (two air brokers and two airlines) shipped arms to Sierra Leone including 150 tonnes of AK-47 rifles, 60mm mortars and ammunition and that the original story of a single shipment of 30 tonnes of arms was incorrect. While Sierra Leonian supporters of the restored President Kabbah were referring to Mr Penfold as a 'saint', Mr Cook in London was emphasizing: 'We stood full-square by the UN resolution... which imposed an arms embargo on Sierra Leone. That is the Government's policy and I would expect that government policy to be followed through by everyone.' The British Prime Minister, Tony Blair, now came to the assistance of his Foreign Secretary. An official spokesman from Downing Street said:

> While of course any deliberate breach of United Nations sanctions would be wrong, we can be absolutely robust in reminding people that President Kabbah was toppled and had United Nations and Commonwealth opinion united in support of him. Indeed the Prime Minister... invited Kabbah to the Commonwealth Heads of Government meeting in Edinburgh as a way of signalling that.[12]

Much to the irritation of the British government, the Sierra Leone–Sandline affair would simply not go away. The Foreign Office, it transpired, had invited key members linked to the mercenaries to a conference on 20 October 1997, to discuss the restoration of President Kabbah, at which Mr Lloyd was a guest speaker. Mr Lloyd then said: 'The message to the rebels, and let me make this absolutely clear, must be to get out while the possibility of doing so peacefully still remains.' Others present at the conference included Rupert Bowen, a former diplomat then employed by Branch Energy, a mining company partly owned by Tony Buckingham who is closely linked to Sandline; and John Hirsch, the US Ambassador to Sierra Leone whom Sandline claimed to have briefed regularly. There were also present members of Kabbah's exiled government.[13] Lt-Col. Graham McKinley, the former defence attache in Sierra Leone, was debriefed by the Ministry of Defence Staff about the terrain in Sierra Leone and he believed that the information he gave may have been passed on to ECOMOG.

It also became increasingly clear that Mr Tony Buckingham with his network of companies in the diamond–mercenary area had a deep interest in the Sierra Leone affair. According to a newspaper report:

> For the past 10 years, Mr Buckingham and his companies have been linked to a series of mercenary military operations launched on behalf of governments in power or exile and multinationals, in return for cash. He has always denied that some payments have been in the form of mineral concessions.[14]

He set up Executive Outcomes in 1989 and it was Ranger Oil which employed Executive Outcomes in Angola. Ranger Oil had links to Buckingham's company Heritage Oil and Gas. Other Buckingham companies are Diamond Works and Branch Energy. Executive Outcomes was employed by the Strasser government in May 1995 to train his army and four months later Branch Energy had taken over a diamond mine in an area then being fought over. According to reports, Executive Outcomes was also rewarded with mineral and diamond concessions. Whether or not Sandline and Executive Outlines have formal links – this is denied by Spicer – they certainly appear to work closely with each other while Spicer and Buckingham admit to passing work to one another.

In mid-May 1998 the British Foreign Secretary, Robin Cook, was on the defensive although he insisted that Foreign Office staff had not been involved in a plot to breach the UN arms embargo. The Permanent Under-Secretary at the Foreign Office, Sir John Kerr, was obliged to admit that the junior minister, Tony Lloyd, had not been fully briefed while Mr Lloyd himself said: 'I was not then briefed, told, advised or in any other way informed either orally or in writing either of alleged arms shipments or of the Customs and Excise investigation.'[15] It must appear extraordinary to any outsider that despite so many government denials in relation to Sandline, Sir John Kerr could yet also tell a House of Commons committee that the Foreign Office kept in contact with Spicer and had received a number of telephone calls from him:

> He might have some intelligence that would be useful to us. These conversations were one way – he rang a number of times. It is clear to me that the department decided not to put the phone down on Spicer because they wanted to hear what he had to say about the situation in Sierra Leone.

As the foreign affairs spokesman for the Liberal Democrats, Menzies Campbell, commented: 'These events are now taking on an *Alice in*

Wonderland dimension. The conduct of the Foreign Office is curiouser and curiouser.'

The line taken by both the Prime Minister, Tony Blair, and the Foreign Secretary, Robin Cook, made it virtually impossible for the Customs and Excise to proceed with any prosecution for breaking sanctions although it was quite clear this had happened. According to a source within Customs any prosecution would fail since the Prime Minister had referred to the whole matter as a 'hoo haa'.

> How could we convince the 12 people in a jury when the Prime Minister said the High Commissioner, Peter Penfold, had 'done a superb job'. We would not have stood a chance.[16]

The Foreign Secretary announced that an inquiry into the possible involvement of FCO officials would be conducted by Sir Thomas Legg, a former permanent secretary at the Lord Chancellor's Department. Later in May it was announced that Lt-Col. Spicer would not be prosecuted for an apparent breach of sanctions. In response Spicer said that he had had clear government approval to ship arms to Sierra Leone. He went on:

> My major irritation is that I have spent a great deal of my time working for the Government, in different political persuasions. What we did in Sierra Leone was designed for the good rather than the bad of the country. If one believes you acted with the approval of the Government, as represented by officials or whoever, it's pretty galling to be involved as part of a criminal investigation.
> That being said, I am delighted that there are going to be no criminal charges.[17]

Dropping the charges was the least the government could do in the circumstances.

During June the Foreign Secretary defied demands by a Commons select committee to disclose to MPs five telegrams which could prove officials knew about the involvement of British mercenaries in Sierra Leone. He was able to hide behind the Legg committee which he had recently established: 'The Government cannot disclose information which falls within the remit of Sir Thomas Legg's investigation while it is in progress because to do so could prejudice it' he said. Later he said he would let the Commons committee see the telegrams when Sir Thomas Legg had completed his inquiry. In July the Foreign Secretary said adamantly that ministers had not been involved in the Sandline arms-to-Africa affair although he failed to exonerate fully public servants.

The Legg report appeared at the end of July 1998 and its criticisms of the Foreign Office for incompetence, poor internal communication and failure to warn against sanctions busting persuaded the Foreign Secretary to announce a number of reforms. These would include the creation of a Sanctions Enforcement Unit, an upgrading of communications chains within the department, reinforcement of the Equatorial Africa Desk and improvement of information technology. While admitting management failings in the Foreign Office, Mr Cook said: 'There was no ministerial policy to break the arms embargo. There was no ministerial approval for any action by Sandline to break the embargo, and there was certainly no conspiracy by Foreign Office officials or Ministers to undermine the policy.'[18] According to the Legg report the staff of the Foreign Office Equatorial Africa Desk, defence advisers, the British High Commissioner to Sierra Leone and the most senior official in the Foreign Office knew what was happening but failed to tell ministers. Sandline was not prosecuted for selling military aid and arms to Kabbah's exiled regime because officials knew about the contract. It said that Mr Penfold, the High Commissioner, had been 'unwise' and had shown lack of caution in his dealings with Tim Spicer of Sandline and had also failed properly to read a copy of the UN arms embargo and so was unaware that it also covered President Kabbah's government. However, Sir Thomas Legg said, despite failures and misjudgements most of the civil servants were loyal and conscientious; the trouble had arisen out of systemic and cultural factors. At the same time ministers and senior Foreign Office staff had deliberately played down the UN embargo. The inquiry found little evidence that ministers were informed of what was happening. Finally, the quality of parliamentary briefings to ministers needed 'serious attention'.[19]

It was a classic British report of its kind: a UN embargo had been broken, mercenaries had been used against every principle that supposedly the government stood for and yet no one was seriously to blame; rather, the problem was one of 'systemic and cultural factors'. The only real justification that the government could advance for what had happened was the fact that the legitimate President had been restored to power. This might satisfy members of the public who would ask what all the fuss was about yet it revealed enormous loopholes in the way the Foreign Office was run, sufficient at least to make the Foreign Secretary promise swift reforms and, more importantly, left the impression that the government was quite ready to use mercenary organizations when to do so suited its purpose and was only really upset because its double standards had been revealed.

Other questions remained unanswered. Why was the United States kept informed of what was happening by Spicer? According to one observer: 'We know it was a joint operation. At least in West Africa, we know Britain takes no step without America's hand in it, or vice versa. The two have always operated as one in West Africa.'[20] There is also the likelihood that the United Nations colluded in the breaking of its own embargo; the Secretary-General, Kofi Annan, favoured the use of force as a last resort. More tortuous, perhaps, than either of these connections is the role of the Commonwealth. According to *New African*:

> Dr Amrit Sarup, the mother of Rakesh Saxena, the Indian-born Thai banker who had a contract with President Kabbah to bankroll the Sandline operation to the tune of US $10m in return for US $150m diamond concession, works as a senior official at the Commonwealth Secretariat in London. She is reputed to have held meetings at the Commonwealth Secretariat with both Sandline and Kabbah officials at which the US $10m deal was brokered.[21]

The question at issue here is whether the Secretary-General, Chief Emeka Anyaoku, knew what was going on and gave any Commonwealth blessing to it.

At the end of July 1998 the resurgent rebel movement, the RUF, launched a surprise attack on the northern town of Kabala while, more generally, the ECOMOG forces, consisting principally of Nigerians, had been fighting the rebels ever since Kabbah was restored to power. If, as seemed at least possible, the rebellion was going to continue so that the fortunes of Kabbah might face a second reverse such an event would raise the most important question of all: what was the point of the entire exercise (with all its adverse side effects) if it did not succeed in ending the rebellion permanently and ensuring that President Kabbah was truly in control of Sierra leone?

At best it is a convoluted story and few people or institutions come well out of it. Sierra Leone remains desperately poor and continues war-ravaged while there appears every likelihood that its government will emerge with even less control over its diamonds than it had before Kabbah was initially ousted. The intervention of Sandline demonstrated, once more, the growing influence and determination of the new 1990s mercenary organizations, and their capacity to intertwine their activities with governments in their efforts to obtain legitimate standing. The British Government, apart from obvious incompetence with one department (or section of a department) not knowing what another one was doing, demonstrated its usual ambivalence towards the use of mercenaries. Neither the United Nations nor the Commonwealth which were both actors in the drama made much impact or came out of it with any honour. And always in the background are the new power-brokers: Mr Saxena after diamond concessions, Mr Buckingham and his obscure companies and the relationship such individuals and their companies have with the new military power brokers, the mercenaries.

14 Western attitudes

As the twentieth century approaches its end the increasing collapse of formerly accepted frameworks and patterns of behaviour represented, for example, by the growth of ethnic cleansing, the breakdown of law and order in an ever lengthening number of small and not so small states, the increase of both fundamentalism and terrorism with their accompanying violence and the emergence of semi-autonomous, and often highly dangerous, groups such as the drug cartels within states between them put at risk communities, minorities, mining and other vested interests and sometimes the state itself. In such a deteriorating climate the need for military establishments which are both loyal and effective is at a premium and if, as we have seen in Angola, Comoros, Nicaragua, Papua New Guinea or Sierra Leone law and order breaks down to whom or to what may such governments turn for assistance? There are a number of choices available though, on examination, their availability is either a mirage or it depends upon a bargain with a price tag that even a country in trouble is unwilling to pay. Assistance may be obtained, in theory if not always in practice, from the following: the major powers, either working in concert or individually; regional powers such as Nigeria or South Africa on the African continent; the United Nations; immediate neighbours; major regional organizations such as the Organization of Africam Unity (OAU), the Organization of American States (OAS), the Association of South East Asian Nations (ASEAN), or sub-regional organizations such as the Economic Community of West African States (ECOWAS). Most of these powers or organizations have shown a greater or lesser willingness to intervene when called upon to do so, depending upon the circumstances, the extent of their own interests in the affected area or, in the case of organizations, the inhibitions placed upon them by their charters.

Mercenaries, on the other hand, do not face the same restraints to action although a feature of their behaviour during the 1990s has been an insistence by the more prominent military services companies that they are only prepared to act on behalf of legitimate governments and that they will not take on tasks that are unacceptable to the countries in which they are domiciled: that is, they will not act against the interests of the West generally or, for example, the United States, Britain, France or South Africa in particular. Statements to this effect have been made by the leading US companies such as MPRI, by

Britain's Sandline, and by South Africa's Executive Outcomes and these statements represent the determination of the organized mercenary establishment to provide itself with a new image that will make it acceptable to those governments which otherwise might be tempted to put a stop to mercenary activities.

There is little real danger that Western governments will do anything of the sort, however, although they do require mercenary organizations to put on a 'front' of regulated behaviour that will make it easier to justify leaving them free to operate as freelance military representatives of Western interests for that, in essence, is what they are seen to be by the rest of the world. None of this is really new; the patterns of behaviour have changed, that is all.

The provision of clandestine support to mercenary activity, the turning of a blind eye and the provision of 'off the record' encouragement to mercenaries as, for example, the French did over many years with Bob Denard has characterized Western attitudes towards mercenaries ever since the early 1960s. There have always been circumstances in which it has suited governments to allow the private sector to act while government itself remains at one remove from the action until its likely outcome is apparent. In recent times the aid agencies or non-government organizations (NGOs) have often fulfilled this role, stepping into dangerous and politically awkward situations with humanitarian aid while governments decide whether or not to become involved with more massive economic assistance or other forms of political persuasion. Mercenaries can undertake a similar role in violent or war situations.

The ambivalence of Western governments towards the activities of their nationals acting as mercenaries has been glaringly obvious, particularly in situations where the enemy were either left-wing communists as in Angola or where there was a racial element involved as in the Congo or Rhodesia, although the reluctance to take any action was always cloaked in a range of feeble excuses about the inadequacy of the law or natural 'democratic' unwillingness to interfere with the liberty of the subject. Moreover, reluctance to control mercenaries has been maintained even when their actions in the field have been overtly racist or otherwise damaging to the good name of the countries from which they come. This Western determination not to act has a profound racism at its roots; the unspoken assumption (though sometimes it has been loudly trumpeted by the right-wing press) is one that in effect says 'our boys are out in that Third World jungle sorting things out; they may be a bit crude but what can you expect in the circumstances.'

These mercenaries have almost always been seen as neocolonialist representatives of Western interests in those regions of conflict where they have put in an appearance rather than simply individual hard men seeking high pay and thrills although it has suited the Western media to portray them as such. Britain, France, Belgium and Portugal must each be held responsible – at varying levels – for the mercenaries who appeared in the Congo and then Angola during the crises of the 1960s and 1970s, while in the Nigerian civil war a form of mercenary nationalism emerged with Britain and British mercenaries supporting the Federal Military Government (FMG) and France and French mercenaries supporting Biafra. The humanitarian relief organizations or NGOs which provided supplies through Ulli airstrip to Biafra right up to the end of the civil war hired mercenaries to fly their planes although in other circumstances they would be the first to condemn absolutely the use of mercenaries.

During the Cold War the West was especially ready to turn a blind eye to any mercenary activity that was seen to be opposed to Communism. The appearance in substantial numbers of British and American mercenaries fighting on behalf of the illegal Smith regime in Rhodesia was conveniently defended by Rhodesia's chief army recruiting officer, Major Nick Lamprecht, when he denied that foreigners serving with the Rhodesian army were mercenaries at all and described them instead as volunteers whose motive was 'enthusiasm for fighting communism' and both Britain and the United States found reasons not to invoke their laws to prevent their citizens going to Rhodesia to fight as mercenaries. From a Western racist viewpoint they were on the right side. The Angolan government was certainly correct when it brought the thirteen captured mercenaries to trial in 1976 to include in its indictment the accusation of 'acquiescence and complicity of various Governments, particularly those of Britain and America, in the preparation and development' of the mercenary operation.

The emergence in the 1990s of the new, sophisticated big- business mercenary corporations and the fact that Western governments allow them to exist openly is tantamount to granting them permission to carry on their trades with impunity. MPRI in the United States or Sandline in Britain have not come into being in order to carry out military operations within their own countries; their target markets are in the Third World and objections to their existence for such purposes appear to be on the wane. States most open to mercenary activity are those which are wracked by civil violence and interventions can be of two broad kinds: in direct support of the legitimate government; or, in a security or training capacity, in support of mining and other vested interests such as the Colombian drug cartels. There is also growing evidence of close liaison between the different mercenary organizations and, in particular, of readiness to cooperate between the United States and Britain, the 'special relationship' in a new form as in Nicaragua or Sierra Leone.

More disturbing even than the open readiness of Western governments to permit these mercenary organizations to flourish is their willingness to use them in order to circumvent awkward policies which have been publicly accepted as with the United States and MPRI in Croatia and Bosnia or Britain and Sandline in Sierra Leone. Another new factor, most obviously exemplified by the activities of Executive Outcomes in Africa, is the growth of what can be characterized as 'concessions for protection', payment for mercenary services rendered by a mineral concession to a related company. Should this trend continue, as seems likely, much of the mineral wealth of Africa could well be put up to auction with the help of mercenary interventions.

Another aspect of Western mercenary activity, perhaps best exemplified by the actions of Portugal in relation to Angola in 1975–76, has been one of 'sour grapes' or revenge for defeat. As Portugal fought its bitter rearguard wars to hold on to its African empire, so Lisbon became a centre for mercenary recruitment with many ex-settlers possessed of an ideological grudge against their African successors ready to return to Africa as mercenaries if only to destabilize the new governments. The ELP, the Spinolist Portuguese Liberation Army, and its political counterpart, the MDLP or Democratic Movement for the Liberation of Portugal, were the creation of right-wing army officers who were implicated in Spinola's abortive coup of 11 March 1975, and his subsequent successful assumption of power though this was to prove short-lived. Even so, it was from the ranks of such supporters that substantial numbers of mercenaries were sent to Angola to support Holden Roberto's FNLA and Jonas Savimbi's UNITA in their fight against the MPLA successor government of Agostinho Neto, less one suspects because of their inherent anti-communism although that was important than from sheer anger at their loss of imperial control: destabilization rather than ideology was the driving force behind the readiness of many of these Portuguese volunteers to return to Angola

International awareness of mercenaries as a problem of the second half of the twentieth century dates from the Congo crisis at the beginning of the 1960s and though the most obvious retrospective reaction to the Congo mercenaries may be one of anger or disgust at the image which *les affreux* projected of casual brutality and racism, in fact the affair tells us a good deal more concerning Western attitudes which still persist a third of a century later. Large sections of Western opinion then and subsequently resented the end of the European empires and were prepared to go to very considerable lengths to undermine the political structures which replaced the colonial system. Moise Tshombe could not have mounted his secession in Katanga – and certainly would not have been able to sustain it as long as he did – without the support of the huge mining interests represented by *Union Miniere* and Tanganyika Concessions, the sustained backing provided for mercenary interventions by the Belgian government and the readiness of Britain, France and Portugal to reinforce these Belgian efforts. Western propagandists used every occasion when European lives were at risk in the Congo to emphasize the barbarism of the Africans and to reinforce the claim that independence had been granted too soon. In the process the utterly abysmal record of the Belgians in the Congo – first as the Free State under the control of King Leopold with its attendant atrocities and then as a colony under direct rule by the Belgian government – was carefully forgotten: what the Congolese did in rage against Europeans in the early 1960s could not match the years of atrocities and oppression under Belgian rule that had preceded this explosion. The mercenaries who became household names at this time for their performance in the Congo – Bob Denard, 'Mad' Mike Hoare or Black Jack Schramme – were later to be turned into a species of folk hero in Western mercenary mythology as the image they had cultivated saving whites at risk from black barbarians, sorting out failed or useless states and doing so with a kind of 'boys' own' derring-do was projected in the Western media so as to offset their brutalities. It would be difficult to think of another post-independence state of this period in which Western conduct was generally so cynically self-serving and corrupt. Belgium did its best to break up the state which it had so ill-prepared for independence and did so with the connivance of British and French financial and political interests; the Americans adopted Mobutu as their man in central Africa and supported him for a third of a century despite every form of malpractice and corruption that he perpetrated so that they could use Zaire as a base from which to subvert another African state, Angola; and France in its constant quest to increase its influence on the continent also supported Mobutu to the very end, raising a force of mercenaries on his behalf even as his long and disastrous stewardship of his country was coming to a close. In a real sense the story of Western relations with the Congo (subsequently Zaire) is the story of the West's determination to manipulate the Third World to its advantage, regardless of the cost to the peoples of those countries, and mercenaries appear and reappear throughout the sordid relationship. The alacrity with which, in November 1967, the West exerted pressures upon President Kayibanda of Rwanda to allow them to evacuate the mercenaries who had fled across the border from their final fling in the Congo tells more of the real attitude towards such soldiers of fortune from the West than all the rhetorical condemnations of their activities mouthed from time to time by politicians.

At least throughout the years of the Cold War the American resort to the use of mercenaries could be justified in terms of the defence of democracy against the threats of communist subversion. The fact that the performance of the CIA in masterminding mercenary interventions was, by and large, unbelievably inept is beside the point. The CIA recruitment of mercenaries for service in Angola during 1975 and 1976 with the open connivance and assistance of Britain, France and Belgium was a disaster which brought huge discredit upon the West while doing nothing to upset the balance of power in Angola. The use of mercenaries in Nicaragua may ultimately have helped tip the balance against the Sandinistas though the Irangate scandal again sullied the American image. Perhaps it was the sheer amateur incompetence of the CIA on the one hand and the impression of arrogant disregard for the laws of the United States displayed by the principal actors in the Irangate affair on the other that persuaded the US government to encourage the emergence of mercenary corporations during the 1990s. In the future the private sector working for profit might be entrusted with tasks of subversion by contract; this, at any rate, appeared to be the case when the MPRI was engaged to retrain the forces of Croatia and Bosnia during the 1990s.

When Ken Silverstein, a US journalist, approached the State Department's Office of Defense Trade Controls for information about these newly emerging firms he was refused an interview and told, instead, that the 'proprietary information' of the companies protected them which is an adroit way of getting round the US Freedom of Information Act. Even so, Silverstein did obtain a great deal of information about this new breed of company which offers military training or other assistance to foreign governments 'at the bidding of the United States'. As a former high-level official at the Defense Intelligence Agency (DIA) told him: 'The programs are designed to further our foreign policy objectives. If the government doesn't sanction it, the companies don't do it.'[1] As the author also points out:

> For the government, privatization offers a number of advantages. In addition to providing plausible deniability about overseas entanglements, it allows Washington to shed military personnel while simultaneously retaining the capacity to influence and direct huge missions. Firms on contract can train an entire army.

The rapid proliferation of these private firms staffed by recently retired senior military personnel with direct links to the Pentagon and State Department means Washington has at its disposal a new series of agencies through which to conduct foreign policy wherever the military content is of primary importance. Washington can now provide training for a foreign army at one remove from direct government involvement and though the conventional wisdom at the end of the 1990s was that such firms would only operate with the direct agreement of the administration the more powerful and experienced such firms become the less likely that this state of affairs – government control of their activities – will continue. At present it may be possible to argue that such firms do not consist of mercenaries though they are tending, with their greater resources and expertise, to replace the older freebooter mercenary who hired himself out as an individual but as soon as they enter into contracts that have not been arranged by the government so soon will they become mercenary firms pure and simple. As the MPRI brochure states succinctly:

> Military Professional Resources Inc. was created in 1987 specifically to bring together former military professionals to perform worlwide corporate contractual functions requiring skills developed from military service.

The brochure goes on to list the firm's capabilities as: 'Doctrine Development, Force Management, Mobile Training Teams, Wargame Support, Officer and NCO Development, Democracy Transition and Military Training.'

According to Loren Thompson of the de Tocqueville Institution: 'The only difference between what these firms do and what mercenaries do is that the companies have gained the imprimatur of government for their actions.'[2]

The British mercenary tradition goes back a long way and the practice of seconding officers to foreign regimes or giving leave of absence so that they could take up mercenary appointments was still operating in the 1960s, allowing British officers to serve in the various Gulf states. These recently retired or leave-of-absence officers were what might be described as Britain's official mercenaries at that time. Others, those who went to the Congo for example, came into a different category. When on 9 November 1967, the British ambassador to the United Nations, Lord Caradon, described the mercenaries as 'the curse of the Congo' it might have been pertinent to ask what the British government had actually done to prevent its citizens going to the Congo to act as mercenaries. The answer was little or nothing and Lord Caradon's censure was typical of the British habit of lofty condemnation unaccompanied by deterrent action. Nor did Britain make any efforts to prevent its citizens going to Rhodesia and enlisting in Smith's army; they were, after all, whites fighting blacks who were both 'terrorists' and 'communists' and that satisfied the British authorities that nothing ought to be done even though the army in which they enlisted was that of an illegal regime which was in revolt against the British Crown. So much for principles.

The romanticizing of mercenaries is often in the poorest taste. An article which appeared in the *Daily Telegraph* in 1990[3] titled 'The tough and the toff' by Christy Campbell told the story of two British mercenaries: 'Peter MacAleese, who fought his way out of the Glasgow slums, is a bulldog. His friend Roy Kaulback, an aristocratic Cambridge graduate, is a ridgeback.' After this colourful opening the writer went on to describe their mercenary careers – they claimed to be among the best in the world – and described their participation in an attack upon a 'communist guerrilla headquarters' in Colombia in 1988; in fact it was a front for the cocaine wars. Such men ought to be officially discouraged from participating in the Colombian cocaine wars or in any other similar venture; in fact they make good copy. The feebleness of the British response to its mercenaries was illustrated by the response of the Junior Minister at the Foreign Office, Tim Sainsbury, when it was suggested that British mercenaries had trained the assassins of the Colombian Senator Luis Carlos Galan: 'We very much regret and indeed deplore anything that they might do of an illegal nature overseas' he said. The minister sounds more like a supercilious student participating in a debate than a politician determined to put a stop to a vicious practice.

Leaving aside the mess the British government got itself into over the Sierra Leone–Sandline affair, with its half-truths and incompetence, what came across very strongly was the fact that Sandline and its ilk represent an acceptable means of pursuing policy aims. During the 1990s information emerged about secret British training missions in different parts of the world during the Cold War. These included British secret agents training a shadowy Swiss resistance army to counter a Soviet invasion and military training for Cambodian guerrillas fighting with the Khmer Rouge against the Vietnam-imposed Communist regime in Phnom Penh during the 1980s. In 1991 the Armed Forces Minister, Archie Hamilton, admitted that Britain provided training for the Khmer People's National Liberation (army) and the Armee Nationale Sihanoukienne by SAS personnel and though these operations could not be described as mercenary they fall into a murky half-way category that could just as easily be carried out by mercenaries and, should Britain follow the path of the United States by allowing and encouraging private firms to undertake military advisory tasks based on the Sandline pattern, then such tasks would naturally fall to these firms in the future.

The make-believe quality of the mercenary–arms sales world was vivdly highlighted by an odd story which surfaced in July 1998. A certain Peter Bleach, described as a small-time arms dealer from North Yorkshire, found himself in jail in Calcutta and on trial for 'abetting the waging of war against India'. If found guilty Bleach faced a minimum sentence of life imprisonment or possible death by hanging. Mr Bleach was arrested in Bombay in December 1995 after the plane in which he was flying, which was crewed by five Latvians who were also standing trial with him, had dropped a large consignment of arms into the Purulia countryside of northern India. The consignment included AK-47s, rocket launchers, anti-tank grenades and ammunition. What seemed so odd about this particular story was Mr Bleach's surprise that he should be on trial at all after dropping arms for insurgents in a sovereign country. The arms had been destined for the Ananda Marg Hindu sect which has been in dispute with the government of West Bengal for years over land. The West Bengal government is Communist and possibly Mr Bleach felt he was still fighting the Cold War. He did not deny that he was dropping arms into India; however, he pleaded that it was a sting operation that went wrong! He was a former officer in British intelligence who, on leaving the service, had established his own 'defence supply service'. His story was that in July 1995 he was contacted by a Danish firm to give a quote for the delivery of four and a half tons of AK-47 rifles, ammunition and rocket propelled grenades to an unnamed destination in South Asia. Mr Bleach went to Denmark where he realized that it was not a legitimate operation though he does not define what would be legitimate. Back in Britain he informed the Ministry of Defence Export Service Organization; later in the story MOD officials and Special Branch officers claimed they told him not to go ahead with the deal. However, Mr Bleach did go ahead with the deal and said that he was encouraged to do so by the British authorities in order to find out for whom the arms were destined. He says: 'My assumption was that the British would tell the Indian authorities right away. In fact they didn't tell them until November 1995.' In a most unconvincing explanation for why he went ahead with this most dubious operation, Mr Bleach told *The Independent* that though the deal was risky he saw no easy way out of it, claiming that 'If I had dropped it like a hot potato and it had all come out in the open six months later, my phone and fax numbers would have been in the records.' So he proceeded to Bulgaria to pick up the arms where a shadowy figure, one Kim Davy, apparently forced him to go through with the operation against his better judgement.[4] So, in July 1998 Mr Bleach found himself on trial in Calcutta with a far from clear or rosy future ahead of him. This unlikely story and the odd behaviour of Mr Bleach are characteristic of one part of the mercenary world some of whose idiosyncratic members emerge as Walter Mitty wish-fulfillment figures who undertake dangerously foolish adventures and then fall back upon doubtful conspiracy explanations for their plight. If the mercenary world only contained such people it would be relatively easy to control. Unfortunately, it also contains far more professional types capable of creating powerful and well financed military services corporations and it is these that present problems for the future.

The French African empire was always more important to France than the British African Empire was to Britain because it represented a greater absolute proportion of total French overseas interests; apart from French Indochina which was lost after the traumatic defeat of the French army at Dien Bien Phu in 1953 and half-a-dozen island territories or departments the great concentration of France's imperial power lay in Africa. The French Foreign Legion, the most elite of mercenary forces, had been created originally to take part in the long series of wars fought between 1830 when France found a pretext for invading Algeria and the 1880s when the whole of that vast territory had finally been brought under French control. The bitter war to hold on to Algeria (1954–62) left many psychological scars as well as producing a generation of Frenchmen who were prepared to fight in other parts of Africa in order to prolong French influence. During the 1960s, following the independence of almost all France's African colonies, Paris evolved a new African policy: this included a relatively massive concentration of French aid upon the countries of Francophone Africa as well as other policies such as the strengthening of the Franc Zone to bind these newly independent territories closer to France. In the early years of the European Economic Community (later the European Union) France persuaded her partners to grant generous aid terms to affiliated territories (which in the main meant ex-French colonies) through the Yaounde Conventions. In addition to these measures, France made considerable efforts to draw the former Belgian African territories – Zaire, Burundi and Rwanda – within her sphere of influence and, for example, invited them to participate in the annual Francophone summits while also providing support for Mobutu throughout his inglorious career as the ruler of Zaire. When the largest black state in Africa, the Anglophone Nigeria, collpased into a civil war in 1967 France was open in its support for breakaway Biafra, working on the cyncial power principle that the break-up of the largest Anglophone state in West Africa would be likely to weaken Britain's influence in the region and, conversely, might therefore strengthen that of France.

In the years from 1960 onwards French mercenaries were to appear in Angola, Benin, the Congo (later Zaire), Congo Brazzaville, Nigeria while French troops were to be stationed in half-a-dozen African states throughout this period, some 3,000 members of the Foreign Legion, for example, remaining in Djibouti after independence in 1977 where their presence in that tiny state was described, quaintly, as being 'at the disposal of the government'. France rarely appeared reluctant to sanction the use of mercenaries and certainly made fewer disclaimers about them than did the British.

The ubiquitous Bob Denard was involved in the Congo, in Benin, and in Angola. France supported him in 1967 when, with the acquiescence of the Portuguese, he crossed from Angola into Katanga. It indicted him for the aborted mercenary invasion of Benin in 1977 but admitted in retrospect that had he succeeded in bringing down the left-wing government of President Mathieu Kerekou this would have been welcomed in Paris. When the CIA embarked upon its hasty recruitment of mercenaries at the end of 1975 to support Holden Roberto's FNLA in opposing the Marxist MPLA government of Angola the secret service insisted that all French mercenaries had to be recruited through Bob Denard. The French government actively recruited mercenaries to serve in Biafra in the late 1960s and Jacques Foccart, the secret service chief, personally recruited Roger Faulques for this purpose. French support for Mobutu was unwavering – French paratroopers intervened in 1978 to assist the Zairean army recapture Kolwezi in Shaba Province from rebels – and as late as December 1996 when the collapse of the Mobutu regime could be measured in months French officers recruited a mercenary legion to send to his assistance though it made no difference to his coming downfall. When towards the end of Bob Denard's colourful career he was finally brought to trial for his part in the Benin fiasco of 1977 high-ranking French military, intelligence and diplomatic chiefs who formerly had kept at arms length from him, perhaps for reasons of maintaining a sort of international decorum, now came forward to testify on his behalf. He was discharged as a free man, more honoured as a hero by the French for his mercenary activities which he claimed and the government equally clearly accepted had always been carried out in the interests of France.

Cynical French openness about and support for the use of mercenaries to achieve its ends is perhaps more refreshing than British reticence and hypocrisy although in the end both powers are ready to turn to mercenaries when it suits their governments to do so. In the aftermath of the Cold War, with only one superpower (the United States), changing attitudes to the old world power structures and, for example, growing demands for an enlargement in the permanent membership of the Security Council, both Britain and France have been tempted to 'punch above their weight' in international affairs. They want to prolong the residual worldwide influence they still possess from former imperial days and their considerable capacity to mount military operations is one way of doing this. Both countries are prepared to support the United Nations when to do so does not interfere with their more important national interests though both will also circumvent or ignore UN resolutions if these are seen to be contrary to their interests. Like other members of the world body Britain, France and the United States have accepted in principle many of the aims of the United Nations which they do little to implement in practice. The United Nations wants to bring about an outright ban on the use of mercenaries but it has not got the faintest chance of achieving anything of the kind unless it can obtain the full backing and active support of these three countries in this aim. In 1998 there was little indication that the world body would obtain any such backing for its anti-mercenary policies.

15 The United Nations

In principle the United Nations is opposed to the recruitement and use of mercenaries; in practice it can do little more than highlight the dangers that mercenaries represent since its capacity for action on this issue (as on many others) is circumscribed by the wishes of the major powers. They show little inclination to ban mercenaries, they claim they cannot control them anyway, and are only too ready to employ them – or at the least permit them to be employed – when to do so suits their political objectives. This means that the United Nations is reduced to denunciation: it may draw up rules for the regulation of mercenary activity but has little or no power to enforce them.

The Congo crisis of the early 1960s which helped define many subsequent attitudes towards mercenaries had a profound impact upon the United Nations which was then dealing with its first major peacekeeping operation in sub-Saharan Africa. Mercenaries affected this UN operation in four broad ways: first, their presence in significant numbers prolonged the chaos which the United Nations force had been sent to bring to an end and enabled Moise Tshombe to maintain the secession of Katanga for three years; second, their conduct, which was often savage and brutal, created human rights problems and precedents for the future; third, the fact that the mercenaries were white and came from Britain, France and Belgium in Europe or Rhodesia and South Africa on the African continent exacerbated already complex race questions associated with the end of empires and the determination of the white minorities in Southern Africa to perpetuate their rule over the black majorities in their countries; and finally, the failure of the European powers to prevent their citizens enrolling as mercenaries for service in the Congo and the thinly disguised encouragement they or the mining interests gave to these mercenary activities were a major slap in the face for the United Nations. If two members of the Security Council, Britain and France, either would not or could not prevent their citizens becoming mercenaries in order to oppose a UN peacekeeping operation this augured ill for the future of the world body.

The Congo in any case presented the United Nations with a range of near insuperable problems: its vast size and poor communications, its ethnic diversity and rivalries, its lack of trained personnel or an educated population were enough in themselves to make its task a formidable one. Then, the Security Council in New York and the UN personnel on the spot had to deal with the Cold War rivalries which the United States and the Soviet Union with their respective allies had injected into the crisis. In addition to all this there were at any one time throughout the years of crisis between 500 and 1,500 mercenaries in the Congo and they, automatically, were operating against the United Nations.

Following the defeat of Central Government forces in early November 1961 by Katanga parachute commandos led by European mercenaries, the United Nations Security Council adopted a resolution (24 November 1961) which included a clause aimed at securing the immediate withdrawal from the Congo of all foreign troops including mercenaries and authorizing the Secretary-General to take requisite action, including if necessary, the use of force to ensure that such foreign forces and mercenaries were removed from the country. This was little more than a year after the Congo had collapsed into chaos and already the mercenary factor had become of central importance to any resolution of the crisis. Six years later, in November 1967, the Security Council was to meet at the request of the Congo to condemn the actions of the mercenaries who were still very much of a problem despite the 1961 resolution; the mercenaries, so the Security Council was told, had 'caused ruin and devastation' in the country. At least at the time of the Congo crisis it was possible to condemn the activities of mercenaries unequivocally: partly, this was because the major powers still believed that if intervention had to take place they should do the intervening; and partly, because as yet there were no security companies like Sandline or Executive Outcomes to organize the mercenaries who then appeared much more obviously to be individual soldiers of fortune and made little pretence of acting on behalf of anyone except themselves. Thirty years later when the United Nations was considering the rise of mercenary companies such as Sandline and Executive Outcomes the climate of world opinion had greatly changed.

In 1998 the world appeared to have become an even more violent place than it had been in the 1960s while its civil and other wars posed greater threats to peace and were less easy to control than at any time since 1945. Moreover, the major powers were showing increasing reluctance to become directly involved in peacekeeping operations. The Gulf War that followed Saddam Hussein's annexation of Kuwait in August 1990 had, it is true, seen the assemblage of a huge army including nearly half a million US troops in the region and this response was glibly hailed at the time as the beginning of a new world order and yet in 1998 Iraq was still defying the United Nations while Saddam Hussein remained in absolute control of his country and appeared as truculent and dangerous as ever. The US intervention, as the new world 'policeman' in the internecine Somali conflict in 1992 had turned into a disaster as far as US intentions and prestige were concerned and undoubtedly played its part in persuading Washington to stand clear of the Rwanda genocide of 1994. Although the US-brokered Dayton Accord had brought a precarious end to the wars which had destroyed Yugoslavia, yet by 1998 Slobodan Milosevic, undeterred by earlier setbacks, had embarked upon a new wave of ethnic cleansing, this time directed against the Albanians of Kosovo, while NATO stood by wringing its hands. In Afghanistan the extremist Taliban mujahedin seized Mazar-i-Sharif, the last important outpost of their coalition opponents, and appeared to have won control of the entire country while in Israel Prime Minister Benyamin Netanyahu determinedly destroyed the Oslo Peace accords without the United States, the United Nations or anyone else making any serious move to stop him. Elsewhere terrorism and civil wars flourished and appeared, more and more, to have become the norm rather than the exception. In such circumstances it hardly seemed out of place for the new breed of security firms to offer military services where the major powers no longer wished to operate as peacekeepers and nor did it seem especially out of place for the British government to signal the go-ahead to Sandline International to assist in restoring to power in Sierra Leone the legitimate head of state, President Kabbah. The new mercenaries might be anathema to the United Nations but they were clearly gaining credibility where it mattered – in Washington, London and Paris.

The 1990s, in any case, were a bad period for the United Nations. Briefly, in the euphoria which followed the end of the Cold War, it had been hoped that at last the United Nations would come into its own and fullfill the role for which it had been created as world peacemaker but the hope was soon dissipated. Although the super power stalemate of Cold War years which had generally crippled the possibility of effective United Nations action had disappeared this was replaced by endless wrangling about UN reforms, a determined campaign by the United States to undermine the Secretary-General Boutros Boutros Ghali who had made the fatal mistake of antagonizing Washington, and a growing reluctance upon the part of its principal members including the five permanent members of the Security Council to give the world body the full authority it required, including adequate military and financial resources, to resolve problems. Moreover, without the Cold War to concentrate their efforts the major powers reverted to an older pattern of international behaviour, each pursuing its own objectives and in the process stymying effective collective action. This became obvious in relation to the crises in Somalia, Rwanda and Yugoslavia. In these circumstances, with the added impetus to disorder that the disintegration of the Soviet Empire had contributed, it is little wonder that the decade witnessed a revival of mercenary activity, this time made all the more formidable and sinister by its organization along corporate business lines.

The Geneva Conventions of 12 August 1949 covering humanitarian law in armed conflicts stripped mercenaries of any combatant or prisoner-of-war status. According to Article 47 (2) of Protocol 1 to the Geneva Conventions of 1949, a mercenary is any person who:

a. is specially recruited locally or abroad in order to fight in an armed conflict;
b. does, in fact, take a direct part in the hostilities;
c. is motivated to take part in the hostilities essentially by the desire for private gain and, in fact, is promised, by or on behalf of a Party to the conflict, material compensation substantially in excess of that promised or paid to combatants of similar rank and functions in the armed forces of that Party;
d. is neither a national of a Party to the conflict not a resident of territory controlled by a Party to the conflict;
e. is not a member of the armed forces of a Party to the conflict;
f. has not been sent by a State which is not a Party to the conflict on official duty as a member of its armed forces.

The subject of mercenaries was first considered in the General Assembly of the United Nations in 1979 on the initiative of Nigeria following the adoption of the 1977 Protocol which was additional to that of Geneva. The President of the 1979 assembly session which considered the topic for the first time was Major- General Joseph N Garba of Nigeria. He told the Assembly that the adoption of the Convention symbolized 'the political will of the international community, despite initial differences, to outlaw once and for all the activities of these soldiers of fortune, who have not only contributed to the destabilization of the affected States but also plundered and looted villages and farms in Africa, Latin America and Asia.'[1] Despite the fact that mercenaries had been deprived of combatant or prisoner of war status their activities were not regarded as unlawful under international law.

In 1980 the General Assembly established a 35-member Ad Hoc Committee on the Drafting of an *International Convention against the Recruitment, Use, Financing and Training of Mercenaries*. This committee negotiated the text of the Convention at eight sessions between 1981 and 1989 and then submitted a draft Convention to the Assembly's Sixth (Legal) Committee for final negotiation and transmittal for adoption.

The Convention requires States to refrain from recruiting, using, financing or training mercenaries and to prohibit their activities; in addition, it obliges them to extradite or prosecute any mercenaries found in their territory, regardless of whether the offence was committed there or elsewhere. The State prosecuting the mercenary is to notify the United Nations Secretary-General of the result of the prosecution proceedings and transmit the information to the other States concerned.[2] The Convention was originally open for signature until 31 December 1990 and was to enter into force one month after it had been ratified by 22 States. By the end of 1997 it had still only been ratified by seven states.

Article 1 of the Convention defines a mercenary in the following terms:

1. A mercenary is any person who:
    a) Is specially recruited locally or abroad in order to fight in an armed conflict;
    b) Is motivated to take part in the hostilities essentially by the desire for private gain and, in fact, is promised by or on behalf of a party to the conflict, material compensation substantially in excess of that promised or paid to combatants of similar rank and functions in the armed forces of that party;
    c) Is neither a national of a party to the conflict nor a resident of territory controlled by a party to the conflict;
    d) Is not a member of the armed forces of a party to the conflict; and
    e) Has not been sent by a State which is not a party to the conflict on official duty as a member of its armed forces.
2. A mercenary is also any person who, in any other situation:
    a) Is specially recruited locally or abroad for the purpose of participating in a concerted act of violence aimed at:
    i) Overthrowing a Government or otherwise undermining the constitutional order of a State; or
    ii) Undermining the territorial integrity of a State;

b) Is motivated to take part therein essentially by the desire for significant private gain and is prompted by the promise or payment of material compensation;

c) Is neither a national nor a resident of the State against which such an act is directed;

d) Has not been sent by a State on official duty; and

e) Is not a member of the armed forces of the State on whose territory the act is undertaken.[3]

It may well be asked why the United Nations should spend so much time and effort drafting a Convention that has so little chance of being ratified, let alone observed. In part the answer to that question is simply that the existence of such a Convention in itself represents a statement of principle that can be referred to whenever, for example, the question of mercenary excesses becomes important as it both has from time to time since the United Nations came into being in 1945 and undoubtedly will do again in the future. At least, it can be argued, an instrument for the control of mercenaries does exist; all that remains is for member nations to ratify the Convention and help implement it. Forlorn as such a hope may appear in the late 1990s circumstances change and it may suit members of the United Nations to take action in a few years time: if it does, the instrument is ready to hand.

One factor which always operates in the favour of mercenaries is simply desperation. Governments which condemn the intervention of mercenaries or outside military forces in one set of circumstances reverse their attitude when conditions change.

Angola provides a classic example of such changing concerns. The MPLA government which took power in Luanda at independence when the Portuguese left in November 1975 was at once challenged by the forces of Holden Roberto's FNLA and these were reinforced by mercenaries recruited on his behalf by the CIA. The mercenaries in question turned out to be especially brutal as well as incompetent and the capture of 13 of them allowed the government to stage a show trial in which it was possible to emphasize the repellent nature of the conduct of those particular mercenaries and, by association, the repellent nature of mercenary activities as a whole. At that time there were plenty of precedents to draw upon from the Congo and elsewhere. Thus, the new Angola made a principled stand against the use of mercenaries and one that received much sympathetic attention, especially in other Third World countries at the time since they could envisage, easily enough, circumstances in which they too might become the victims of mercenary depredations. During the 1980s as the Angolan government fought its long civil war against the UNITA forces of Savimbi it was to suffer from further interventions though this time from special units of the South African security forces in support of UNITA. By the 1990s, after Savimbi had refused to accept the peace process or the 1992 election results and had returned to the bush to renew the civil war the government became desperate, especially when UNITA forces captured the northern oil town of Soyo. So it reversed its earlier principled stand against the use of mercenaries and turned to the South African company, Executive Outcomes, which it employed, first to recapture Soyo and then to capture the diamond mining regions which UNITA controlled in the north of the country. Such an about-turn will make it difficult for Angola to denounce the use of mercenaries in the future.

Mercenary activity world-wide escalated during the 1990s. Conflicts in former Yugoslavia, Armenia, Azerbaijan, Georgia, Moldova and Tajikistan which had been either hastened or sparked off by the end of the Cold War and collapse of the Soviet Union were one series of magnets for mercenary enrollment and deployment and in these central Asian conflicts the majority of mercenaries were drawn from former officers and soldiers of the Soviet military. Other conflicts included the civil wars in Africa which still attracted the largest contingents of mercenaries and the drug wars in Latin America. The United Nations Special Rapporteur on mercenary questions, the Peruvian Enrique Bernales Ballesteros, produced a new study for the Commission on Human Rights which called for the urgent elimination of what it described as this growing 'market for crime'. The report called for the ratification of the convention outlawing mercenaries and also proposed the use of extradition treaties to prosecute bounty hunters and hired guns. The report referred to mercenary attempts to overthrow the legitimate governments of at least three of its member states – Benin, Comoros and Maldives which were particularly vulnerable because of their small size and even smaller armed forces.[4]

Other demands advanced in the report included the tightening of dual citizenship laws which mask the 'criminal assignments' of hired guns as well as the strengthening of extradition laws to 'prosecute and punish' both mercenaries and their paymasters. At the time of this Ballesteros report the 1989 Convention on mercenaries remained a dead letter with only six countries having ratified it and another 14 having signed but not ratified when a minimum of 22 ratifications were needed. Britain refused to sign: the Foreign Office had argued when the Convention had been drafted that it was not compatible with British domestic law even though the recruitment of mercenaries in Britain is illegal. France and the United States also refused to sign and a cynical Whitehall source remarked 'Perhaps mercenaries are one of our most successful exports.'[5] Arguably the best way for the United Nations to restrict mercenary activity would be to criminalize recruitment; as the report claims: 'The act of recruitment is a key element in making the ensuing act unlawful. No one crosses a border in order to apply spontaneously to become a mercenary.' This may be true although as far as the conflicts raging in Yugoslavia at that time were concerned a considerable number of young European 'thrill seekers' were going there to enroll as mercenaries.

The enrollment of individuals seeking employment as mercenaries in the 1990s was perhaps of less concern to the United Nations than was the proliferation of security firms with increasingly open links to their governments. As the report says – 'member states must control or prohibit intelligence machinery that establishes relationships between government agents and organisations that recruit mercenaries.' This, as later events relating to the US MPRI or the British Sandline demonstrated, was exactly what governments did not wish to do. The tireless efforts of the United Nations both to expose the growing use of mercenaries and to shame governments into controlling them is matched by the determination of governments, and especially those of such countries as Britain, France and the United States which ought to know better to thwart UN restrictions and ensure that mercenaries (through the new security firms) are available for use in covert operations that support the more dubious aspects of their respective foreign policies.

Three years later, in 1996, the tireless UN Special Rapporteur, Enrique Bernales Ballesteros, still investigating mercenary activities worldwide, returned to the attack:

> To suggest that some mercenary activities are illegal and others legal is to make a dangerous distinction which could affect international relations of peace and respect between states.[6]

Mr Ballesteros argued that mercenary initiatives by companies registered as 'security firms' in a third country threatened national sovereignty. On this occasion, in a new report, the Rapporteur was especially concerned with the fact that two African countries, Angola and Sierra Leone, were hiring mercenaries from the South African firm Executive Outcomes to protect their gold and diamond mines. A crucial aspect of this new use of mercenaries was that the security firms sell their services 'mainly in exchange for concessions relating to mining and energy.'

In the end the United Nations faces three sets of formidable obstacles to achieving agreement to an international convention that would not only ban the recruitment or use of mercenaries but also be universally observed. The first concerns the nature of the power at the disposal of the United Nations. As long as the principal members of the United Nations, beginning with the United States, are unwilling to provide the world body with the authority, finances and military capacity to peacekeep effectively appeals to the United Nations cannot obtain the responses they deserve. When the Congo government appealed to the United Nations in July 1960 it obtained an immediate response in the form of a substantial peacekeeping force even though its subsequent efforts were bedevilled by Cold War divisions. Had the Angolan government been able to obtain a similar UN response in 1992 when Savimbi refused to stand by the election results and returned to the bush to wage a further war, perhaps he and UNITA could have been finally crushed and there would have been no need later in the decade for mercenaries to be called in, on both sides, in a messy and prolonged conflict. If the United Nations cannot mount an adequate response to resolve conflicts because the major powers refuse to give it the means to do so, then beleagured politicians have to look for help elsewhere. Since the deposition of Sierra Leone's legitimate President, Ahmad Tejan Kabbah, by Major Johnny Paul Koroma in 1997, was condemned by the world community it would, in a better ordered world, have been automatic for a United Nations force to restore him to power. That this did not happen is largely the fault of the major powers, in particular the permanent members of the Security Council, which have always been so jealous of giving real power to the United Nations as to emasculate it and render it largely useless except on rare occasions when it suits them to invoke and then support its full authority. Since, especially in the 1990s, this has usually been the case political leaders in trouble such as President Kabbah have been obliged to look elsewhere for help.

The second obstacle to an effective UN policy on mercenaries comes from the major powers themselves: despite periodic condemnations of mercenary behaviour they see mercenaries as a useful weapon of policy and have no intention of depriving themselves of it. This readiness to use mercenaries has become even more certain during the

1990s with the rise of the corporate security firm with its clandestine links to government military and foreign affairs establishments. Available evidence at the end of the 1990s would suggest that such corporate entitities as MPRI, Executive Outlines or Sandline are set to flourish in the course of the next decade and, moreover, to be joined by other similar security companies who between them will provide employment for the large numbers of post-Cold War military veterans seeking employment.

The third obstacle to UN inspired reform is the simple one of immediacy. If, as we have attempted to demonstrate, small countries beset by civil war or some other threat to their national survival are unable to obtain the assistance they require from the United Nations or some other bona fide regional or international body they will turn elsewhere and the mercenary, especially if now cloaked in corporate respectability, is the obvious answer. Since, in addition, these modern mercenaries are likely to have the backing of powerful governments which may even be prepared to act as guarantors of their good faith it is unrealistic to imagine either that those in trouble will not turn to mercenaries or that the United Nations will be able to persuade them not to do so.

16 Conclusions – the future

The 1990s have witnessed a steady growth of violence whether in the form of civil wars, ethnic cleansing, border wars, religious fanaticism and related terrorism or in connection with highly organized international crime such as the drugs business. There is little evidence that such violence will abate and much to suggest that it will become worse and, if anything, more widespread in the early years of the twenty-first century. If, indeed, this turns out to be the case the market for mercenary interventions and the demands for military security services will increase commensurately. At the same time the prospects for ordered interventions by the United Nations or other organizations backed by the major powers seem at the very least problematic; there will, of course, be interventions but their effectiveness will be determined according to the extent of the big power interests involved in any particular conflict. Many conflicts are likely to be of marginal importance as far as the major powers and UN policy-makers are concerned; as in the case of Sierra Leone and the restoration to power of President Kabbah in 1998 Britain was sufficiently involved to encourage intervention by ECOMOG and Sandline though it was clearly unwilling to go further. Such interventions by proxy may well become the norm in the future and if this proves to be the case there will be a sharp increase in the numbers of military advisory security firms with little attempt to curtail their activities beyond what are likely to be the increasingly frustrated efforts of the United Nations.

One aspect of mercenary activity which has long been taken for granted consists of the private security provided for the protection of the rich or well-to-do in most of the world's big cities. The word ghetto formerly referred to districts set aside for Jewish communities; today the term is often used more broadly to denote the poor quarters of inner cities, the crumbling 'no hope' areas passed over by prosperity which has moved elsewhere. In fact, there are now two kinds of ghetto in the world's big cities: the inner city ghettos of the poor and the suburban ghettos of the rich who live in fear of robbery or other violence behind high walls and electrified fences and employ private guards or security firms to protect them.

Johannesburg has earned an unenviable reputation for violence. At one end of the scale is the black-on-black violence to be found in the huge African town of Soweto which was long regarded by the apartheid regime as a ghetto that could be cut off and controlled by the police and military or the growing number of 'informal settlements' as they are now called – the former squatter camps. At the other end of the violence scale are the northern suburbs of Johannesburg where the rich or well-to-do whites live. Anyone who takes the trouble to walk down one of the quiet residential streets of these suburbs will be hard put to spot a single residence behind its high walls and strong gates that does not have a sign on the outside warning of 24 hour patrols, or not to set off the deep baying of large dogs simply by passing. Signs bearing the names of the appropriate security companies show a dog's head (of the Rottweiler kind) or depict a hand holding a gun. Anyone who breaks in – and many do – cannot claim not to have been warned. One of South Africa's largest and fastest growing 'armed response' security companies, Paramed, is ready through every twenty-four hours to respond to someone pressing the panic button and scarcely a home in the sprawling northern suburbs of Johannesburg does not have some kind of 'Immediate Armed Response' warning. Johannesburg, indeed, most obviously displays the huge gap that exists in the new two- ghetto cities of our violent age and a flood of new security companies have sprung up in the 1990s. According to one account:

> Protecting the well-being of South Africa's haves – who remain overwhelmingly white – from the newly enfranchised but still economically deprived black population, swelled by returning former guerrillas with no job skills save their ability to use a gun, has become a 130bn rand (£13.5bn) business.[1]

Johannesburg may appear to be an extreme case and certainly it has a unique history of violence with its roots in the apartheid years of racial segregation as well as the huge and obvious disparity in wealth between haves (who still largely equate with the white population) and have-nots who are mainly blacks yet the problems of Johannesburg described above can be found repeated in most major cities in the Third World and, increasingly, in cities of the North: security services for the rich in North America have been big business for years. Firms such as Britain's Securicor which is responsible for the safe transport of money, for example between banks, or provides bodyguards and property guards for the rich and well to-do may not qualify as mercenaries yet the line that can be drawn between their activities and those of a firm such as Executive Outcomes, which among other tasks, provides guards for mines, is not an easy one to draw. We live in an increasingly security conscious age and the security industry has become one of the world's major growth sectors. We also live in an age where the gap between rich and poor or 'haves' and 'have-nots' is fast expanding while the disparities between the two extremes become ever more apparent. In such circumstances it is unsurprising if the poor and those who feel that they have become marginalized in their own societies see the rich as natural targets for robbery and violence; in return, the rich, only a few of whom are plagued by a sense of guilt, feel the need to buy protection. Unfortunately, the very act of buying protection and retreating behind high walls makes it even more certain that the gap between the two extremes becomes even wider.

If the rich in the United States, the world's most powerful as well as its wealthiest country, feel the need to guard themselves against the possible depredations of their fellow citizens then it is even more certain that the rich in poor countries and perhaps most of all those rich who are foreigners and are often regarded as exploiters will feel a similar need. Hence, in a city like Nairobi, the capital of Kenya, the expatriate business and aid community as well as diplomats are to be found living in guarded premises, set apart from the people among whom, in theory, they have come to live and work. From this kind of situation it is only one step to hire security guards – or soldiers – to defend a valuable investment such as a diamond mine or oilfield and this is the point when the new security companies step into the picture.

If military security firms of mercenaries are not going to be banned to what extent can they be controlled? By mid-1998 South Africa's National Conventional Arms Control Committee under the chairmanship of Kader Asmal had been working for over a year on a bill to regulate Foreign Military Assistance and it is intended 'to prohibit South Africans from rendering military or military related services abroad without the government's authority'. This anti-mercenary bill defines foreign military assistance as 'engaging in combat or providing military advice, training or cooperation, various forms of support, recruitment, medical or paramedical service, procurement of equipment and also providing the services of individuals.' The bill is intended to apply both to South Africans and permanent residents who are not South Africans and failure to comply with the law as proposed could result in fines of up to one million rand (US$215,000) and/or imprisonment for 10 years.[2] The crucial phrase from the above description of the proposed bill is 'without the government's authority'. It is one thing to define what mercenary assistance abroad may comprise; it is something else to forbid its provision and if government permission to operate outside South Africa for organizations such as Executive Outcomes is too easy to obtain the legislation will be meaningless. On the other hand, if South Africa sees rival security firms from elsewhere obtaining business on the continent that otherwise could have earned it good income the temptation to compete is likely to prove stronger than the urge to control.

One estimate suggests that there are now more than 1,000 companies offering protection services in the former Soviet Union alone while an increasing number of international companies operating in countries which they regard as unstable hire their own form of protection. In Colombia British Petroleum hires soldiers to battalion strength to safeguard its oil operations while the British company Defence Systems Limited (DSL) employs former commandos to protect Angola's offshore oilfields. DSL which was formed in 1981 has become one of the world's largest suppliers of specialist security services and has become an important support company for BP's worldwide oil operations. The list of its clients which includes De Beers, Texaco, Chevron, Anglo-American and Bechtel is impressive and its operations cover an equally wide range of countries – Algeria, Angola, Russia, Mali, Colombia, Nigeria, Pakistan, Saudi Arabia, Brunei and elsewhere – and it has offices in ten countries. Of particular interest is the fact that DSL staff are not armed. As its chief executive officer, Richard Bethell (a former SAS veteran) claims:

> We work closely with the security forces of the countries where we are active. They provide whatever protection we need, military or otherwise. They secure the areas where we are active, beforehand. It is our job to indicate what, where and how that is done, which is part of the contract. DSL never gets involved in other people's wars. It's simply not an aspect of our business, and business is good.[3]

In almost every country where there is civil strife or some other form of institutionalized violence foreign defence companies employing former soldiers (mercenaries) are to be found safeguarding installations or proferring military advice. Moreover, the companies at the top end of the business such as MPRI or Sandline make sure they have their own means of supply and support: to be effective they have to mount self-contained operations and the more successful they are at achieving this all-in capacity the harder they will be to control if their original employers in any particular situation subsequently wish to dispense with their services. Executive Outcomes, for example, only goes into a combat situation when it is able to provide its troops on the ground with air support from helicopter gunships: 'In Angola and Sierra Leone, the company deployed its own MiG-17s and MiG-24s fitted with gatlings, cannons and automatic grenade launchers. EO officers reckon that they could never have done what they did without air support.'[4] This kind of sophisticated operation is a long way removed from the slapdash arrival of groups of mercenaries in Angola during 1975 and early 1976.

By the late 1990s an increasing proportion of military or semi-military functions in an ever widening number of countries and situations were being discharged by security companies rather than by the states themselves. This change in role liability represented a world-wide trend to outsource military and police functions to private organizations so as to relieve government, police and military establishments of tasks for which formerly they would automatically have been responsible. The reasons for this outsourcing are complex. Partly, as always, it is a question of cost and convenience; partly it represents a continuation of a trend to privatize that was made popular in the Western world by the example of the British government led by Margaret Thatcher during the 1980s; and partly it may be seen as a new, and arguably very dangerous, phenomenon of the deliberate outsourcing of awkward tasks to the private sector in order that politicians may distance themselves from the results should anything go wrong. The trend is further encouraged by the circumstances prevailing in small weak states or those which are deeply divided by civil disturbances where it is evident that their police and military are either not up to the task of maintaining law and order or safeguarding important and valuable installations (mines for example) or are not to be trusted to do their duty on behalf of the government in power. This is where the efficient security company offers a weak government an attractive alternative to its own doubtfully reliable police and military establishments.

The proliferation of these security companies, the huge market for their services that is clearly available in the absence of government capacity to deal with the security tasks which they undertake, the adoption by such companies of a corporate identity that is intended to put them on a par with any other exporting business enterprise and the unwillingness of governments in those countries where such companies have become big business either to ban them or even curtail their activities together mean that the United Nations has little or no chance in the immediate future of either banning their activities altogether or at least having these curtailed on the grounds that they are simply fronts for mercenaries. This being the case, is there a realistic possibility of regulating security companies so as to eliminate, at the very least, the possibility that they will simply develop into a highly sophisticated means of selling the services of mercenaries to anyone able to pay for them? The insistence of the companies themselves that they are only prepared to act for legitimate governments and not against the interests of the countries in which they are domiciled at least provides an obvious entry point for state regulation of their activities. It might, therefore, make sense for the United Nations to change its tactics and press those countries like Britain and the United States that are not prepared to ratify the Convention against mercenaries at least to control their own national companies. They could do so by implementing two strict measures: the first, to insist that all such companies must have a government licence to operate anywhere whatsoever; and second, to insist that each and every contract undertaken by such companies must first be vetted by an appropriate government department or watchdog. If enforced these two conditions would prevent the companies hiring out their skills to subversive groups such as the Latin American drug cartels or, indeed, to revolutionary groups intent on overthrowing governments.

There are two obvious problems that might, in the end, prove insuperable. The first, that in the competitive *laissez-faire* atmosphere which is encouraged by the Western business ethic such companies, if successful, would simply become too big and powerful to be controlled; moreover, should strict controls over their activities really be threatened what is to stop them emulating other businesses that resent government controls and registering in non-national tax havens? The second, even more difficult problem to be overcome concerns the likely determination of governments to use such companies as informal instruments of foreign policy as Washington did by employing MPRI to train the Bosnian military and thereby bypass its own foreign policy commitments. Such covert or semi-covert use of these firms would be ruled out if they were obliged to seek a government licence for every job undertaken.

However, if such firms are neither banned nor strictly controlled by their governments now, at a time when their emergence into public view is still relatively new and their futures still uncertain, we shall face the prospect in the early years of the twenty-first century of a range of private military–mercenary establishments that will become increasingly difficult to control at all. The prospect is both dangerous and unsettling.

Notes

Introduction

1. George Thayer, *The War Business*, Simon and Schuster, New York, 1969, p 169.
2. Wilfred Burchett and Derek Roebuck, *The Whores of War*, Penguin Books, 1977, p. 156.
3. Thayer, *op. cit.*, p. 169.
4. *Defence Today*, 08/09/1990.

Chapter 1   The Congo 1960–1965

1. Thayer, *op. cit.*, p 173.
2. *Ibid.*, p 174.
3. *The Times*, 26/10/1960.
4. *Africa Digest*, June 1961.
5. *The Guardian*, 08/05/1961.
6. *The Times*, 29/08/1961.
7. *The Guardian*, 30/08/1961.
8. *The Times*, 22/12/1961.
9. *The Observer*, 29/04/1962.
10. Patrick Keatley, *The Guardian*, 17/11/1962.
11. *The Times*, 31/12/1962.
12. *Financial Times*, 08/04/1964.
13. *The Guardian*, 30/04/1964.
14. *The Observer*, 30/08/1964.
15. *The Guardian*, 25/08/1964.
16. *The Times*, 15/09/1964.
17. Derek Wilson, *Sunday Times*, 29/11/1964.
18. Colin Legum, *The Observer*, 29/11/1964.
19. *The Times*, 31/01/1965.
20. *The Times*, 27/04/1965.
21. Colin Legum, *The Observer*, 18/04/1965.
22. *The Observer*, 29/08/1965.
23. Ian Davidson, *Financial Times*, 24/08/1967.
24. John de St Jorre, *The Observer*, 27/08/1967.
25. David Paskov, *Daily Telegraph*, 28/11/1967.
26. *Le Monde*, 18/11/1967.

Chapter 2   The Nigerian Civil War

1. John de St Jorre, *The Nigerian Civil War*, Hodder & Stoughton, 1970, p 313.

2. Thayer *op. cit.*, p 169.
3. *African Digest*, February 1968.
4. Thayer, *op. cit.*, p 170.
5. *African Digest*, February 1968.
6. *Sunday Times*, 24/12/1967.
7. de St Jorre, *op. cit.*, p 313.
8. *Ibid.*, pp 316–18.
9. *Ibid.*, p 318.
10. *African Digest*, October 1969.

Chapter 3 Southern Africa (1) Rhodesia

1. *International Herald Tribune* (Paris), 23/06/1975.
2. Southern Africa: The Year of the Whirlwind, *African Contemporary Record 1976–77*, p A50.
3. Robin Wright, *International Herald Tribune* (Paris), 10/12/1976.
4. *Daily Despatch* (East London South Africa), 22/12/1976.
5. *International Herald Tribune* (Paris), 10/12/1976.
6. *The Star* (Johannesburg), 24/07/1976.
7. Bruce Oudes, The United States' Year in Africa, *Africa Contemporary Record 1976–77*, p A76.
8. *The Guardian*, 01/02/1978.

Chapter 4 Southern Africa (2) Angola

1. Burchett and Roebuck, *op. cit.*, p 27.
2. *Daily Telegraph*, 29/01/1976.
3. Burchett and Roebuck, *op. cit.*, p 45.
4. *Ibid.*, p 123.
5. *Daily Telegraph*, 02/02/1976.
6. John Stockwell, *In Search of Enemies*, Andre Deutsch, 1978.
7. Stockwell, *op. cit.*, p 221.
8. Burchett and Roebuck, *op. cit.*, p 161.
9. Stockwell, *op. cit.*, pp 184–5.
10. *The Times*, 18/06/1976.
11. *Ibid.*
12. Stockwell, *op. cit.*, p 164.
13. *Zambia Daily Mail*, 06/11/1975.
14. Angola, *Africa Contemporary Record 1976–77*, p B446.
15. *Ibid.*, p B446.
16. *The Times*, 21/01/1993.
17. Georges Marion, *Le Monde*, 08/07/1994.
18. *The Independent*, 16/01/1998.

Chapter 5 African vulnerability

1. *The Times*, 09/02/1994.

2. *Ibid.*
3. *The Observer*, 19/10/1997.
4. *West Africa*, 22/10–09/11/1997.
5. *The Times*, 21/10/1997.
6. *Ibid.*
7. Baffour Ankrah, *New African*, May 1998.

Chapter 6 Island destabilization: Comoros; Seychelles; Denard

1. Stockwell, *op. cit.*, p 220.
2. *African Contemporary Record 1977–78*, pp B616–17.
3. *The Times*, 13/12/1989.
4. *Ibid.*
5. *The Guardian*, 16/12/1989.
6. *The Times*, 16/12/1989.
7. *The Guardian*, 02/02/1993.
8. *Daily Telegraph*, 12/03/1993.
9. *International Herald Tribune* (Paris), 26/04/1993.
10. *Ibid.*

Chapter 7 The British mercenary tradition

1. John Pollock, *Gordon*, Constable, 1993, p 60.
2. *Ibid.*, p 134.
3. Fred Halliday, *Arabia Without Sultans*, Penguin, 1974.
4. Burchett and Roebuck, *op. cit.*, p 164.
5. *Statement on the Defence Estimates 1970* (Cmnd 4290).
6. Halliday, *op. cit.*, p 345.
7. *Sunday Times*, 25/06/1972.
8. *Ibid.*
9. Eric Rouleau, *Le Monde*, 16/05/1967.
10. Quoted in Burchett and Roebuck, *op. cit.*, p 162.
11. *The Observer*, 26/07/1987.
12. *Washington Post*, 18/04/1991.

Chapter 8 Papua New Guinea and Bougainville

1. A R G Griffiths, *Britannica Yearbook*, 1990, p 533.
2. *The Independent*, 25/02/1997.
3. *Ibid.*
4. *Ibid.*
5. *The Independent*, 26/02/1997.
6. *The Independent*, 27/02/1997.
7. *The Independent*, 18/03/1997.
8. *The Independent*, 20/03/1997.
9. *The Independent*, 22/03/1997.

10. *The Independent*, 04/04/1997.
11. *Ibid*.

Chapter 9 Nicaragua and Colombia

1. Ken Silverstein, Privatizing War, *The Nation*, 09/12/1997.
2. For an immediate current account of the Iran–*Contra* Affair see Donald Morrison, The Iran–*Contra* Affair, *Britannica Yearbook 1988*, pp 485–6.
3. *The Guardian*, 17/06/1987.
4. *The Times*, 10/07/1987.
5. *The Guardian*, 15/07/1987.
6. *Sunday Times*, 19/07/1987.
7. *The Times*, 19/11/1987.
8. *The Times*, 23/08/1989.
9. *The Observer*, 27/08/1989.
10. Eugene Robinson, *International Herald Tribune*, 30/08/1989.
11. *Ibid*.
12. *The Guardian*, 30/08/1989.
13. *International Herald Tribune*, 03/09/1989.
14. David Smith, *The Observer*, 26/04/1998.

Chapter 10 Europe

1. *Le Monde*, 13/09/1991.
2. *Daily Telegraph*, 02/10/1991.
3. *The Independent*, 31/10/1991.
4. *The Times*, 29/11/1991.
5. *Ibid*.
6. *Daily Telegraph*, 30/12/1991.
7. *The Times*, 07/02/1992.
8. *Daily Telegraph*, 10/02/1993.
9. *Sunday Telegraph*, 21/11/1993.
10. Mark Thompson, *The Times*, 15/01/1996.
11. *Ibid*.
12. Ken Silverstein, Privatizing War, *The Nation*, 09/12/1997.
13. *Ibid*.
14. *Moscow News*, No 24, 1992.
15. *Ibid*.
16. *Ibid*.

Chapter 11 South Africa and Executive Outcomes

1. Laurence Mazane, *Le Monde Diplomatique*, October 1996.
2. *Ibid*.
3. Quoted in *Le Monde Diplomatique*.
4. Talif Deen, *Janes' Defence Weekly*, 13/11/1996.
5. *US News & World Report*, 20/01/1997.

6. *Ibid.*
7. *Ibid.*
8. *The Observer*, 19/01/1997.
9. *Ibid.*
10. *Ibid.*
11. *The Observer*, 19/1/97.

Chapter 12   The new mercenary corporations

1. *Los Angeles Times*, 22/09/1991.
2. Edward Mortimer, *Financial Times*, 24/09/1997.
3. *Time Magazine*, 26/05/1997.
4. *Ibid.*
5. Ron Smith, *New Zealand International Review*, September–October 1997.

Chapter 13   Sierra Leone, Sandline and Britain

1. Ken Gooding, *Financial Times*, 15/09/1997.
2. *The Independent*, 31/05/1997.
3. *New African*, April 1998.
4. *The Observer*, 08/03/1998.
5. *The Independent*, 04/05/1998.
6. *The Independent*, 06/05/1998.
7. *The Independent*, 07/05/1998.
8. *Ibid.*
9. *The Independent*, 08/05/1998.
10. *The Independent*, 09/05/1998.
11. *The Observer*, 10/05/1998.
12. *The Independent*, 11/05/1998.
13. *The Independent*, 12/05/1998.
14. *The Independent*, 13/05/1998.
15. *The Independent*, 15/05/1998.
16. *The Independent*, 19/05/1998.
17. *The Independent*, 25/05/1998.
18. *The Independent*, 28/07/1998.
19. *Ibid.*
20. *New African*, July/August 1998.
21. *Ibid.*

Chapter 14   Western attitudes

1. Ken Silverstein, Privatizing War, *The Nation*, 28/07–4/08/1997.
2. Quoted in Silverstein, *op. cit.*
3. *Daily Telegraph*, 21/03/1990.
4. *The Independent*, 09/07/1998.

Chapter 15   The United Nations

1. Quoted in Introduction to the *International Convention Against the Recruitment, Use, Financing and Training of Mercenaries*, United Nations, New York, 1990.
2. *Ibid.*
3. See Appendix for full text of the Convention.
4. Talif Deen, *Jane's Defence Weekly*, 06/11/1993.
5. *Sunday Telegraph*, 21/11/1993.
6. Talif Deen, *Jane's Defence Weekly*, 13/11/1996.

Chapter 16   Conclusions – the future

1. *The Independent*, 02/07/1998.
2. *New African*, May 1998.
3. *Ibid.*
4. *Ibid.*

Appendix

INTERNATIONAL CONVENTION AGAINST
THE RECRUITMENT, USE, FINANCING
AND TRAINING OF MERCENARIES

UNITED NATIONS
NEW YORK, 1990

INTRODUCTION

Culminating nine years of negotiating efforts, the United Nations General Assembly, on 4 December 1989, adopted without a vote the International Convention against the Recruitment, Use, Financing and Training of Mercenaries.

The President of that Assembly session, Major-General Joseph N. Garba, of Nigeria, commented that the adoption of the Convention symbolized 'the political will of the international community, despite initial differences, to outlaw once and for all the activities of these soldiers of fortune, who have not only contributed to the destabilization of the affected States but also plundered and looted villages and farms in Africa, Latin America and Asia'.

The subject was first discussed at the General Assembly in 1979, at Nigeria's initiative, following the adoption of the 1977 Protocol additional to the Geneva Conventions of 12 August 1949 on humanitarian law in armed conflicts, which stripped mercenaries of any combatant or prisoner-of-war status. Yet their activities were still not regarded as unlawful under international law.

In 1980, the Assembly established a 35-member *Ad Hoc* Committee on the Drafting of an International Convention against the Recruitment, Use, Financing and Training of Mercenaries, which negotiated the text at eight sessions between 1981 and 1989, when it submitted a draft Convention to the Assembly's Sixth (Legal) Committee for final negotiation and transmittal for adoption.

In addition to an undertaking by States parties not to resort to recruiting, using, financing or training mercenaries and to prohibit such activities, the Convention also obliges them to extradite or prosecute any mercenaries found in their territory, regardless of whether the offence was committed there or elsewhere. The State that prosecutes the mercenary will notify the United Nations Secretary-General of the outcome of the proceedings. He will transmit the information to the other States concerned.

The Convention, which will be open for signature until 31 December 1990, will enter into force one month after it has been ratified or acceded to by 22 States. Its text is reproduced in this pamphlet.

INTERNATIONAL CONVENTION AGAINST THE RECRUITMENT, USE, FINANCING AND TRAINING OF MERCENARIES

The States Parties to the present Convention,

Reaffirming the purposes and principles enshrined in the Charter of the United Nations and in the Declaration on the Principles of International Law concerning Friendly Relations and Co-operation among States in accordance with the Charter of the United Nations,

Being aware of the recruitment, use, financing and training of mercenaries for activities which violate principles of international law such as those of sovereign equality, political independence, territorial integrity of States and self-determination of peoples,

Affirming that the recruitment, use, financing and training of mercenaries should be considered as offences of grave concern to all States and that any person committing any of these offences should either be prosecuted or extradited,

Convinced of the necessity to develop and enhance international co-operation among States for the prevention, prosecution and punishment of such offences,

Expressing concern at new unlawful international activities linking drug traffickers and mercenaries in the perpetration of violent actions which undermine the constitutional order of States,

Also convinced that the adoption of a convention against the recruitment, use, financing and training of mercenaries would contribute to the eradication of these nefarious activities and thereby to the observance of the purposes and principles enshrined in the Charter of the United Nations,

Cognizant that matters not regulated by such a convention continue to be governed by the rules and principles of international law,

Have agreed as follows:

ARTICLE 1

For the purposes of the present Convention,
1. A mercenary is any person who:
    a) Is specially recruited locally or abroad in order to fight in an armed conflict;
    b) Is motivated to take part in the hostilities essentially by the desire for private gain and, in fact, is promised, by or on behalf of a party to the conflict, material compensation substantially in excess of that promised or paid to combatants of similar rank and functions in the armed forces of that party;
    c) Is neither a national of a party to the conflict nor a resident of territory controlled by a party to the conflict;
    d) Is not a member of the armed forces of a party to the conflict; and
    e) Has not been sent by a State which is not a party to the conflict on official duty as a member of its armed forces.

2. A mercenary is also any person who, in any other situation:
   a) Is specially recruited locally or abroad for the purpose of participating in a concerted act of violence aimed at:
   i) Overthrowing a Government or otherwise undermining the constitutional order of a State; or
   ii) Undermining the territorial integrity of a State;
   b) Is motivated to take part therein essentially by the desire for significant private gain and is prompted by the promise or payment of material compensation;
   c) Is neither a national nor a resident of the State against which such an act is directed;
   d) Has not been sent by a State on official duty; and
   e) Is not a member of the armed forces of the State on whose territory the act is undertaken.

ARTICLE 2

Any person who recruits, uses, finances or trains mercenaries, as defined in article 1 of the present Convention, commits an offence for the purposes of the Convention.

ARTICLE 3

1. A mercenary, as defined in article 1 of the present Convention, who participates directly in hostilities or in a concerted act of violence, as the case may be, commits an offence for the purposes of the Convention.
2. Nothing in this article limits the scope of application of article 4 of the present Convention.

ARTICLE 4

An offence is committed by any person who:
   a) Attempts to commit one of the offences set forth in the present Convention;
   b) Is the accomplice of a person who commits or attempts to commit any of the offences set forth in the present Convention.

ARTICLE 5

1. States Parties shall not recruit, use, finance or train mercenaries and shall prohibit such activities in accordance with the provisions of the present Convention.

Appendix

2. States Parties shall not recruit, use, finance or train mercenaries for the purpose of opposing the legitimate exercise of the inalienable right of peoples to self-determination, as recognized by international law, and shall take, in conformity with international law, the appropriate measures to prevent the recruitment, use, financing or training of mercenaries for that purpose.
3. They shall make the offences set forth in the present Convention punishable by appropriate penalties which take into account the grave nature of those offences.

ARTICLE 6

States Parties shall co-operate in the prevention of the offences set forth in the present Convention, particularly by:
 a) Taking all practicable measures to prevent preparations in their respective territories for the commission of those offences within or outside their territories, including the prohibition of illegal activities of persons, groups and organizations that encourage, instigate, organize or engage in the perpetration of such offences;
 b) Co-ordinating the taking of administrative and other measures as appropriate to prevent the commission of those offences.

ARTICLE 7

States Parties shall co-operate in taking the necessary measures for the implementation of the present Convention.

ARTICLE 8

Any State Party having reason to believe that one of the offences set forth in the present Convention has been, is being or will be committed shall, in accordance with its national law, communicate the relevant information, as soon as it comes to its knowledge, directly or through the Secretary-General of the United Nations, to the States Parties affected.

ARTICLE 9

1. Each State Party shall take such measures as may be necessary to establish its jurisdiction over any of the offences set forth in the present Convention which are committed:
 a) In its territory or on board a ship or aircraft registered in that State;

b) By any of its nationals or, if that State considers it appropriate, by those stateless persons who have their habitual residence in that territory.
2. Each State Party shall likewise take such measures as may be necessary to establish its jurisdiction over the offences set forth in articles 2, 3 and 4 of the present Convention in cases where the alleged offender is present in its territory and it does not extradite him to any of the States mentioned in paragraph 1 of this article.
3. The present Convention does not exclude any criminal jurisdiction exercised in accordance with national law.

ARTICLE 10

1. Upon being satisfied that the circumstances so warrant, any State Party in whose territory the alleged offender is present shall, in accordance with its laws, take him into custody or take such other measures to ensure his presence for such time as is necessary to enable any criminal or extradition proceedings to be instituted. The State Party shall immediately make a preliminary inquiry into the facts.
2. When a State Party, pursuant to this article, has taken a person into custody or has taken such other measures referred to in paragraph 1 of this article, it shall notify without delay either directly or through the Secretary-General of the United Nations:
a) The State Party where the offence was committed;
b) The State Party against which the offence has been directed or attempted;
c) The State Party of which the natural or juridical person against whom the offence has been directed or attempted is a national;
d) The State Party of which the alleged offender is a national or, if he is a stateless person, in whose territory he has his habitual residence;
e) Any other interested State Party which it considers it appropriate to notify.
3. Any person regarding whom the measures referred to in paragraph 1 of this article are being taken shall be entitled:
a) To communicate without delay with the nearest appropriate representative of the State of which he is a national or which is otherwise entitled to protect his rights or, if he is a stateless person, the State in whose territory he has his habitual residence;
b) To be visited by a representative of that State.
4. The provisions of paragraph 3 of this article shall be without prejudice to the right of any State Party having a claim to jurisdiction in accordance with article 9, paragraph 1 (b), to invite the International Committee of the Red Cross to communicate with and visit the alleged offender.
5. The State which makes the preliminary inquiry contemplated in paragraph 1 of this article shall promptly report its findings to the States referred to in paragraph 2 of this article and indicate whether it intends to exercise jurisdiction.

ARTICLE 11

Any person regarding whom proceedings are being carried out in connection with any of the offences set forth in the present Convention shall be guaranteed at all stages of the proceedings fair treatment and all the rights and guarantees provided for in the law of the State in question. Applicable norms of international law should be taken into account.

ARTICLE 12

The State Party in whose territory the alleged offender is found shall, if it does not extradite him, be obliged, without exception whatsoever and whether or not the offence was committed in its territory, to submit the case to its competent authorities for the purpose of prosecution, through proceedings in accordance with the laws of that State. Those authorities shall take their decision in the same manner as in the case of any other offence of a grave nature under the law of that State.

ARTICLE 13

1. States Parties shall afford one another the greatest measure of assistance in connection with criminal proceedings brought in respect of the offences set forth in the present Convention, including the supply of all evidence at their disposal necessary for the proceedings. The law of the State whose assistance is requested shall apply in all cases.
2. The provisions of paragraph 1 of this article shall not affect obligations concerning mutual judicial assistance embodied in any other treaty.

ARTICLE 14

The State Party where the alleged offender is prosecuted shall in accordance with its laws communicate the final outcome of the proceedings to the Secretary-General of the United Nations, who shall transmit the information to the other States concerned.

ARTICLE 15

1. The offences set forth in articles 2, 3 and 4 of the present Convention shall be deemed to be included as ex-traditable offences in any extradition treaty existing between States Parties. States Parties undertake to

include such offences as extraditable offences in every extradition treaty to be concluded between them.
2. If a State Party which makes extradition conditional on the existence of a treaty receives a request for extradition from another State Party with which it has no extradition treaty, it may at its option consider the present Convention as the legal basis for extradition in respect of those offences. Extradition shall be subject to the other conditions provided by the law of the requested State.
3. States Parties which do not make extradition conditional on the existence of a treaty shall recognize those offences as extraditable offences between themselves, subject to the conditions provided by the law of the requested State.
4. The offences shall be treated, for the purpose of extradition between States Parties, as if they had been committed not only in the place in which they occurred but also in the territories of the States required to establish their jurisdiction in accordance with article 9 of the present Convention.

ARTICLE 16

The present Convention shall be applied without prejudice to:
a) The rules relating to the international responsibility of States;
b) The law of armed conflict and international humanitarian law, including the provisions relating to the status of combatant or of prisoner of war.

ARTICLE 17

1. Any dispute between two or more States Parties concerning the interpretation or application of the present Convention which is not settled by negotiation shall, at the request of one of them, be submitted to arbitration. If, within six months from the date of the request for arbitration, the parties are unable to agree on the organization of the arbitration, any one of those parties may refer the dispute to the International Court of Justice by a request in conformity with the Statute of the Court.
2. Each State may, at the time of signature or ratification of the present Convention or accession thereto, declare that it does not consider itself bound by paragraph 1 of this article. The other States Parties shall not be bound by paragraph 1 of this article with respect to any State Party which has made such a reservation.
3. Any State Party which has made a reservation in accordance with paragraph 2 of this article may at any time withdraw that reservation by notification to the Secretary- General of the United Nations.

ARTICLE 18

1. The present Convention shall be open for signature by all States until 31 December 1990 at United Nations Headquarters in New York.
2. The present Convention shall be subject to ratification. The instruments of ratification shall be deposited with the Secretary-General of the United Nations.
3. The present Convention shall remain open for accession by any State. The instruments of accession shall be deposited with the Secretary-General of the United Nations.

ARTICLE 19

1. The present Convention shall enter into force on the thirtieth day following the date of deposit of the twenty-second instrument of ratification or accession with the Secretary- General of the United Nations.
2. For each State ratifying or acceding to the Convention after the deposit of the twenty-second instrument of ratification or accession, the Convention shall enter into force on the thirtieth day after deposit by such State of its instrument of ratification or accession.

ARTICLE 20

1. Any State Party may denounce the present Convention by written notification to the Secretary-General of the United Nations.
2. Denunciation shall take effect one year after the date on which the notification is received by the Secretary-General of the United Nations.

ARTICLE 21

The original of the present Convention, of which the Arabic, Chinese, English, French, Russian and Spanish texts are equally authentic, shall be deposited with the Secretary-General of the United Nations, who shall send certified copies thereof to all States.

IN WITNESS WHEREOF the undersigned, being duly authorized thereto by their respective Governments, have signed the present Convention.

Index

Abacha, General Sani 138
Abderrahman, Ahmed Abdallah 56, 57, 58, 59, 60, 61
Abu Dhabi 128
ACDEGAM 97
Action Jeunesse xii
AdeKunle, Benjamin (The Black Scorpion) 20, 23
Aden (People's Democratic Republic of Yemen) 67, 69
Adoula, Cyrile 9
Affreux, Les 6, 16, 151
Afghanistan 93, 107, 110, 112, 161
Africa xi, 16, 17, 18, 21, 26, 28, 33, 38, 39, 40, 47, 48, 49, 61, 104, 115, 119, 120, 121, 122, 134, 135, 136, 150, 156, 159, 162, 165
African National Congress (ANC) 43, 114, 120, 121
Aftonbladet 24
Agence France Presse 72
Ahmed, Muhammed 58
Air France 14
Air International 120
Albon Values 93
Algeria xi, 1, 19, 106, 156, 172
Alliance of Democratic Forces for the Liberation of Congo-Zaire (ADFL) 54
All-People's Congress (APC) 132
Al-Shiraa 90
American Nazi Party 30
Amnesty International 79, 95
Amanda Marg 155
Andrews, Tim 139
Anglo-American Corporation 172
Angola xi, xii, xiii, 8, 14, 15, 19, 26, 27, 28, 29, 30, 33–39
  (independence and civil war), 39–40
  (Luanda trial), 40–42
  (Cabinda), 42–45
  (the 1990s), 46, 47, 49, 51, 52, 56, 61, 68, 84, 85, 113, 114, 115, 116, 117, 118, 119, 120, 123, 125, 128, 129, 147, 148, 149, 150, 151, 152, 157, 164, 165, 166, 172, 173
Angolan People's Revolutionary Tribunal 39
Annan, Kofi (United Nations Secretary-General) 49, 145

Anugu, Tony 74
Anyaoku, Emeka (Commonwealth Secretary-General) 82, 145
Arabia Without Sultans 67
Arab League 58
Arawa 75
Arens, Moshe 97
Arias Sanchez (President Costa Rica) 89
Armed Forces Revolutionary Council (AFRC) 133
Armenia 102, 110, 161
Arnold, Derek 106
Arseny, D. 110
Asmal, Kader 116, 121, 171
Association of South East Asian Nations (ASEAN) 147
Australia 29, 58, 74, 75, 76, 77, 78, 79, 80, 81, 82, 104, 105, 135
Azcona Hoyo, Jose (President Honduras) 89
Azerbaijan 102, 110, 165

Baker, Jim (US Secretary of State) 86
Ballesteros, Enriques Bernales 115, 117, 165, 166
Banks, Jon 38
Barker, John 39
Barker-Scofield, Ray 69, 72
Barkley, Steve 127
Barlow, Eeben 44, 82, 115, 119, 122
Barsukov, Vyascheslav 110
Bechtel 172
Bedford, Doctor 7
Beirut 71, 90
Belgium 1, 2, 5, 9, 10, 11, 13, 15, 16, 17, 33, 34, 54, 55, 149, 151, 152, 159
Belgrade 102, 104
Benin 56, 57, 60, 61, 157, 158, 161
Berewa, Solomon 137
Bethell, Richard 172
BHP 75
Biafra 18, 19, 20, 22, 23, 24, 25, 65, 149, 157
Biden, Joseph 107
Bio, Julius Maada 132, 133
Blair, Tony 72, 135, 141, 143
Bleach, Peter 155–56
Boavida, Diogenes 39
Bogota 96

Index

Boland Amendment 91
Bolivia 99
Bomboko, Justin 15
Bongo, Omar 49, 50, 52, 57
Bosnia 77, 101, 102, 107, 108, 128, 129, 150, 152
Botswana 30
Botswana Radio 29
Bougainville 74–85, 129
Bougainville Revolutionary Army (BRA) 74, 75, 76, 77, 78, 79, 84
Bourgeaud, Gilbert (*see* Denard, Bob)
Boutros-Ghali, Boutros 161
Bowen, Rupert 141
Branch Energy 117, 119, 141, 142
Branch International Ltd 120, 121
Branch Mining Ltd 120
Brazil 38, 119
Brazzaville 5, 41, 49, 50, 51, 52
Britain xi, xiii, 14, 17, 18, 22, 29, 30, 33, 34, 38, 39, 46, 47, 53, 66, 67, 68, 69, 70, 71, 76, 77, 78, 79, 87, 92, 93, 94, 96, 97, 101, 105, 109, 112, 113, 118, 119, 128, 132–146
(Sierra Leone/Sandline), 147, 148, 149, 150, 151, 152, 154, 155, 156, 157, 158, 159, 166, 169, 170, 174
British Petroleum (BP) 172
Brown, Michael 41
Brunei 108, 172
Brunswick, Ronny xiii
Buckingham, Tony 84, 85, 119, 120, 134, 141, 142, 146
Bukavu 12, 13, 14, 15, 16, 21, 54
Bulgaria 136, 156
Burma xii, 70
Burnham Declaration 84
Burundi 9, 13, 47, 157
Bush, George (US President) 99
Buterse, Desi (President Suriname) xiii
Byzantine Empire x

Cabinda 40, 41, 42, 43, 44, 56
Caetano, Marcello 26
Calabar 19, 23
Cali (drug cartel) 96, 99
Cambodia xii
Campbell, Christy 154
Campbell, Menzies 142
Canada 29, 104, 105, 115, 137
Capricorn Air 118, 120
Capricorn Society 68
Capricorn Systems Ltd 120
Caprivi Strip 29

Captain Zulu 103, 104
Caradon, Lord (Hugh Foot) 14, 154
Caritas 20
Carlucci, Frank 128
Carthaginians ix
Casey, William 91
Castro, (Colonel) Santos 35, 36, 38
Chad xiii, 72
Chaka, Malik 119
Chamorro, Violetta Barrios de 94
Chan, Sir Julius 77, 78, 79, 80, 81, 82, 83
Charles, Roger 108
Chazan, Naomi 48
Chechnya 102
Cheshire Regiment 106
Chevron 172
China x, 9, 27 65
Chirac, Jacques 49, 52, 53
CIA (Central Intelligence Agency) xi, 33, 34, 35, 36, 37, 38, 40, 86, 88, 89, 152, 157, 164
CID (Criminal Investigation Department) x
Civil Cooperation Bureau (CCB) 44, 115
Clinton, Bill 107
Clywd, Ann 71
Cobra Militia 49, 50, 51, 52, 53
Cold War 46, 67, 78, 101, 112, 115, 123, 125, 127, 149, 152, 154, 155, 158, 160, 161, 162, 165, 167, 168
Colombia xii, 86, 94–100, 129, 154, 172
Colombian Revolutionary Armed Forces (FARC) 94, 95
Commission on Humnan Rights 165
Commonwealth 32, 113, 132, 134, 135, 136, 140, 141, 145, 146
Comoros 56, 57, 58, 59, 60, 61, 62, 63, 124, 147, 165
Conakry 134, 135, 139
Condottieri x
Congo (later Zaire) xii, xiii, 1–17, 18, 19, 21, 22, 23, 24, 25, 26, 34, 35, 39, 40, 46, 55, 56, 61, 64, 66, 68, 70, 123, 148, 149, 150, 151, 152, 154, 157, 159, 160, 164, 167
Congo (Brazzaville) 41, 47, 48–54 (civil war), 128, 129, 157
Congolese Movement for Democracy and Full Development (MDDI) 50
Congolese National Army (ANC) 10, 12, 13, 15
Contras 86, 88, 89, 90, 91, 92, 93, 94, 96, 97
Conzine Riotinto Australia (CRA) 76, 84

Cook, Robin 135, 136, 137, 138, 139, 141, 142, 143, 144
Costa Rica 88, 89, 90, 97
Cote d'Ivoire 134
Cotonou 57
Cotonou Radio 56
Cowper, Reg 30
Croatia 55, 101, 102, 103, 104, 105, 108, 109, 128, 129, 150, 152
Cuba xiii, 41, 42, 43
Cuito Cuanavale 42
Cullen, George (Costa Georgiu) 37, 38, 39
Cyprus ix, 119

Daily News (Tanzania) 29
Daily Telegraph 33, 34, 70, 103, 106, 154
Damien 103
DAS (Administrative Security Department – Colombia) 96, 97
Davidson, Ian 13
Davy, Kim 156
Dayton Accord 107, 108, 161
De Beers 114, 172
Declary, Michel 19
Defence Analysts Ltd 71
Defence Systems Limited (DSL) 44, 45, 172
Defence Today xii
De Gaulle, Charles 19
De Klerk, F. W. 44, 115
Democratic Republic of Congo (former Zaire) 45, 50
De Murville, Couve 16
Denard, Colonel Bob xii, xiii, 13, 15, 16, 19, 22, 34, 35, 36, 38, 56–63 (career), 64, 124, 148, 151, 157, 158
Denel 121
Denmark 155
De St Jorre, John 14, 22
Dhofar 68, 69, 70, 72, 93, 123
Diamond Works 134, 142
Diario de Lisboa 29
Dien Bien Phu 156
Di Litute 14
Directorate of Covert Collection (DCC) 115
Djapic, Ante 104, 105
Djibouti 157
Djohar, Said Mohamed 56, 58, 59, 62
Dos Santos, Eduardo 43, 51, 52
Downer, Alexander 76, 77, 79
Drug Enforcement Administration (DEA) 86

Du Toit, Wynand 44
Duzan, Maria 96

East, The 61
East Timor 101
Economic Community of West African States (ECOWAS) 132, 133, 147
ECOMOG 133, 137, 141, 145, 169
Edinburgh 135, 141
Egge, Bjorn 3
Egypt ix, 70
El Espectador 95, 96
Elf 52, 53
El Salvador 87
England 36, 37
Eritrea 47
Ethiopia 47
Europe x, xiii, 15, 16, 24, 36, 38, 101–112, 119, 159
European Union 124, 157
Everard, John 139
Executive Outcomes 44, 45, 47, 78, 80, 81, 82, 84, 85, 113–122
(operation from South Africa), 126, 128, 129, 134, 135, 142, 148, 150, 160, 161, 167, 168, 170, 172

Falklands War 71, 77
FAPLA 42
Faulques, Roger 19, 22, 23, 24, 70, 157
Fifth Reconnaissance Regiment 116
Financial Times 8, 13, 127
First International Platoon 105
Flood, Philip 81
Flores, Eduardo
Foccart, Jacques 23, 157
Force Publique 1, 2
Foulkes, George 92
France x, xi, 11, 17, 22, 23, 24, 25, 29, 34, 38, 42, 46, 48, 51, 52, 53, 56, 57, 58, 59, 60, 62, 63, 87, 101, 105, 109, 128, 147, 149, 151, 152, 156, 157, 158, 159, 166
Franque, Luis Ranque 40
Freetown 133, 136
French Foreign Legion xi, xiii, 156, 157
Frente Nacional de Libertacao de Angola (FNLA) 33, 34, 35, 36, 37, 39, 40, 41, 150, 157, 164
Front for the Liberation of Cabinda (FLEC) 40, 41, 42

Gabon 24, 40, 49, 50, 52, 57
Gacho, Gonzalo Rodriguez (El Mexicano) 97, 98

Index

Gaddafi, Muammar, al- xiii, 68, 72
Galan, Luis Carlos 95, 96, 98, 154
Gale, Andrew 139
Ganic, Ejup 108
Garba, Joseph N 162
Gardiner, Robert 7
Gavira, Pablo Escobar 96, 97, 99
Gbho, Victor 136
Gearheart, Daniel 39
Geneva 15
Geneva Convention (1949) 130, 162
George, Bruce 138
Georgia 102, 110, 111, 165
Germany x, 2, 3, 24, 29, 70, 101, 107, 119
Ghana 133, 134, 136
Giheno, John 75
GJW Government Relations 117, 118
Glatt, Ernst Werner 86
Golan, Amos 55
Gomes, Francisco da Costa 26
Goosens, Marc 22
Gordon, Charles x, 65
Gorinsek, Karlo 106
Gowon, Yakubu 20
Greece ix, 29
Griffits, Richard 108
Grunberg, Michael 138, 139
Guardian, The 8, 98
Guinea 133, 134, 137
Gulf, The 66, 67, 68, 71, 72, 154
Gulf-Chevron 115
Gulf Emirates xiii
Gulf Oil 42
Gulf War (1980-88) 71, 72
Gulf War (1991) 77, 111, 160
Gurkhas xi, xiii, 44, 45, 130

Haig, William 87
Haiveta, Chris 83
Hakim, Albert 91, 93
Halidi, Ibrahim 62
Hall, Nicholas 33, 37
Halliday, Fred 67, 69
Hamilton, Archie 155
Hammarskjold, Dag 1
Hassenfas, Eugene 89
Heritage Oil and Gas 117, 119, 120, 142
Hetherington-Clebberley, Allan 106
Hicks, Peter 139
Hirsch, John 139, 141
Hitchman, Robert 86
HMS Cornwall 140
Hoare, 'Mad Mike' xii, xiii, 10, 12, 19, 21, 22, 64, 92, 124, 126, 151

Holland 29
Honduras 87, 88, 89, 90, 93, 94
Hoods (French mercenaries) 34, 35, 38
HoS 104, 105
Hoyos, Carlos Mauzo 95
Howard, John 77, 79, 80, 81
Hungary 105
Hussein, Saddam 71, 72, 111, 160, 161

Ibis Airline 118, 120, 121
Ibo, The 21
Ijape, Mathias 83
Independent, The 77, 156
India 70, 155-56
Indo-China 19
International Alert 117, 118
International Brigade 106
International Convention against the Recruitment, Use, Financing and Training of Mercenaries 17, 163-64, 165-66, 174
International Court of Justice 89
International Herald Tribune 29
International Red Cross 14, 15, 20
Iran 71, 90, 102, 107, 108, 112
Irangate 71, 90, 91, 92, 93, 94, 109, 152
Iraq 66, 71, 90, 107, 112, 161
Isaza, Guillermo Cano 95
Islamic Pan-African Legion 72
Ismail, Khedive (of Egypt) 65
Israel 48, 49, 91, 97, 98, 99, 128, 161
Italy x

Jadotville 8
Janissaries ix
Jelic, Tonka 106
Jesus Perez, Henry de (Don Dario) 97
Johannesburg 9, 45, 82, 169, 170
John Birch Society 30
Johnson, 'Jim'
Jordan 66
Julian, Hubert Fauntleroy 24
Jupiter Mining Corporation 137

Kabalo 2-3
Kabbah, Ahmad Tejah 133-141, 144, 145, 161, 167, 169
Kabila, Laurent 50, 51, 54, 55
Kamajors 137
Kamina 9, 11
Kasai Province 2
Kasavubu, Joseph 3, 8, 9, 12, 13
Katanga Province (Shaba) 1, 3, 4, 5, 6, 7, 8, 9, 11, 13, 15, 16, 19, 41, 42, 55, 56, 69, 151, 157, 159, 160

194   *Index*

Kaulback, Roy   154
Kaunda, Kenneth   18
Kayibanda, Gregoire   15, 152
Keatley, Patrick   8
Kelly, 'Blue'   71
Kemal, Said Ali   58
Kennedy, John   34, 123
Kenya   120, 171
Kerekou, Ahmed   56, 157
Kerr, Sir John   142
Khartoum   65
Khmer Rouge   155
Kin Me, General   9
Kindu   10, 12
Kinshasa   14, 16, 21, 35, 36, 37, 38, 40, 42, 50, 51, 54
Kirkuk   72
Kisangani   12, 54
Klein, Yair   97, 98, 99
KMS (Keeny Meeny Services)   92, 93
Kolelas, Bernard   49, 50, 51
Kolwezi   8, 42, 56, 158
Koroma, Johnny Paul   133, 134, 135, 167
Kosovo   102, 161
Kurds, The   71, 72
Kuwait   108, 160

Lagos,   19, 20, 24
Lamprecht, Nick   29, 149
La Vanguardia   104
Leal, Jaime Pardo   95
Lebanon   xi, 48, 71, 90, 91
Le Carro, Alain   54
Le Fauconier, Stephane   103
Le Figaro   59
Legg, Sir Thomas   143, 144
Legum, Colin   10, 12
Lehman, John   93
Leigh, John   118
Le Monde   70
Le Noir, Mladen   103
Leopold, King of Belgium   66, 151
Leopoldville (Kinshasa)   3, 7, 10, 11
Levdan   48, 128, 129
Liberia   47, 49, 133, 134
Libreville   50
Libya   68, 70, 72
Lifeguard   119, 134
Linskey, Dennis   139
Lisbon   19
Lissouba, Pascal   48, 49, 50, 51, 52, 53, 54, 128
Livingstone, David   65
Lloyd, Tony   136, 141, 142

Lopes, Henri   40
Lorez, Pierre   19
Lozancic, Dragan   105
Luanda   34, 37, 39, 40, 42, 44, 120, 164
Lucien-Brun, Maurice (Paul Leroy)   24
Luitingh, Lafras   44, 120
Lunda (North and South)   43
Lusaka   31, 32
Lynn, Hugh   28

Macedonia   102
MacLeese, Peter   37, 154
Macmillan, Harold   113
Madagascar   62, 119
Magdalena Nedio   97, 98
Mahmoud, Ali   60
Major, John   99
Malan, Daniel   113
Malawi   114
Malaysia   108, 119, 120
Maldives   165
Mali   172
Malta   14, 121
Maltsev, Sergei   111
Mancham, James   63–64
Mandela, Nelson   43, 45, 114, 115
Mann, Simon   119, 120
Marcus   104
Margai, Milton   132
Marquez, Miguel Maza
Masirah   69
Matrix-Churchill   71
Mawere, Jason   27
Mayotte   57, 59, 62
Mazar-i-Sharif   161
Mbochi, The   48
McAleese   47
McFarlane, Robert C   91
McKenzie, Andrew   39
McKeown, General   3
McKinley, Graham   141
Medellin   95, 96, 99
Medellin Cartel, The   95, 96, 97, 99
Meese, Edwin   90
Meretz Party   48
Mesopotamia   ix
Miami   11
Middle East   71
Military Professional Resources Inc. (MPRI)   107, 108, 109, 122, 126, 128, 129, 130, 147, 149, 150, 152, 153, 166, 168, 172, 174
Millwall's Dave   103, 104
Milosevic, Slobodan   161

Index

Miriang, Theodore 76
MI6 138
Mission Marissal (MM) 5–7
Mitterand, Francois 34, 60
Mobutu, Joseph (Sese Sheko) 3, 8, 13, 14, 15, 34, 37, 40, 41, 42, 45, 51, 54, 55, 56, 151, 158
Moem Barracks 76
Moi, Raymond 120
Moldova 112, 165
Momis, Father John 75
Momoh, Joseph Saidu 132
Monga, Colonel 13
Montoya, Robert 54
Moore, Sir Jeremy 71
Morgan, Rob 104
Morgan Grenfell (Jersey) Ltd 93
Morocco 57
Moroni 56, 58, 63
Mortimer, Edward 127
Mossad 98
Movimento Popular de Libertacao de Angola (MPLA) xi, xiii, 27, 33, 34, 35, 37, 39, 40, 41, 42, 116, 150, 157, 164
Mozambique 26, 29, 30, 31, 59, 113, 114
Msinda, Emmanuel 9
Munongo 3
Murray, Craig 136, 138
Musa, Solomon Anthony James 132
Muzorewa, Abel 31

Nagorno-Karabakh 104, 110, 112
Namaliu, Rabbie 74, 75
Namibia 39, 43, 113, 115
Nasser, Abdul 70
National Diamond Mining Co (Sierra Leone) 132
National Investigation Service (NIS) 136
National Liberation Army (ELN) 96
National Party (NP) 113
National Patriotic Front of Liberia (NPFL) 133
National Provisional Ruling Council (Sierra Leone) 132
National Republican Party of Russia 111
National Security Council (NSC) 91
Nenta, Bob 80
Nepal 44
Netanyahu, Benyamin 161
Neto, Agostinho 39, 41, 42, 43, 150
New York 42
New York Times 34
New Zealand 29, 74, 77, 79, 82, 84

New Zealand International Review 129
Ngouabi, Marien 41
Nicaragua 86–94, 123, 147, 150, 152
Nicaraguan Democratic Front (FDN) 88
Niesewand, Peter 71
Nigeria xii, 18–25, 46, 47, 119, 127, 133, 134, 136, 138, 147, 149, 157, 162, 172
Nkomo, Joshua 31
Noel-Baker, Philip 4
Noriega, Manuel Antonio 49
North, Oliver 89, 90, 91, 92, 93, 94
North Atlantic Treaty Organization (NATO) 102, 161
Nubians ix

Observer, The 5, 6, 7, 12, 71, 135, 141
Ojukwu, Chukwuemeka 19, 20, 21, 24
Oman xiii, 66, 68, 69, 70, 71, 93, 123
Ona, Fred 74, 84
Onitsha 22, 24
Organization of African Unity (OAU) 14, 15, 21, 58, 62, 63, 113, 121, 125, 132, 135, 140, 147
Organization of American States (OAS) 147
Ortega Saavedra, Daniel 87, 88, 89, 94
Osijek 105, 106
Oslo Peace Accords 161
Ossetia 110, 111
Ottomans ix
Oumarou, Ba Alpha 57

Pakistan 107, 112, 172
Palestine xii, 66
Papua New Guinea xii, 74–85, 125–126, 129, 135, 147
Paraguay 87
Paramed 170
Pardew, James 108
Parham, Philip 139
Patterson, George 104
Penfold, Peter 135, 136, 138, 139, 143, 144
Perez, Alan Garcia 99
Peru 86, 99
Peters, John 18, 19, 22
Petrangol 115
Pharoahs ix
Philippines 38
Picket, Lucien 20
Pierre, Mouton 41
Pizano, Ernesto Samper 100
Plaza107Ltd 120
Poindexter, John M 91

Index

Pointe Noire 51
Port Harcourt 19, 20, 22
Port Moresby 76, 79, 80, 81, 82, 83
Portugal 15, 17, 20, 26, 29, 33, 34, 38, 105, 149, 150, 151
Pummelhardt, Jacques 52

Qabus, Sultan 69
Quimba, Evarista Domingo 41

Rabin, Yitzhak 48
Radio France Internationale 50
Radio Moscow 29
Ranger Oil 119, 120, 142
Reagan, Ronald 87, 88, 89, 91
Rene, Albert xii, 63
Resistencia Nacional Mocambicana (RENAMO) 59
Revolutionary United Front (RUF) 132, 133, 134, 145
Rhodesia xi, xii, 2, 9, 11, 24, 26–32, 46, 113, 148, 149, 159
Rhodesia Herald 9
Rio Tinto 76, 78
Rivas, Carlos Lehrer 95
Robert, Maurice 61
Roberto, Holden 33, 34, 36, 37, 38, 150, 157, 164
Rochard, Michel 53
Roman Empire ix, x
Rose, Sir Michael 77
Rouleau, Eric 70
Roux, Marcel 72
Royal Marines xii, xiii, 71
Royal Military Police 92
Russia 18, 102, 110–112, 172
Rusian National Legion 110, 111, 112
Rwanda 12, 13, 14, 15, 19, 47, 152, 157, 161, 162

Sainsbury, Tim 96, 154
Saladin Securities ltd 93
Salala 69
Salisbury (Harare) 9, 26, 30
Sanctions Enforcement Unit 144
Sandinista National Liberation Front 86, 87, 88, 89, 90, 94, 123, 152
Sandline International 47, 77, 78, 79, 80, 81, 82, 83, 84, 85, 126, 129, 130, 132–146 (intervention in Sierra Leone), 148, 149, 150, 154, 155, 160, 161, 166, 168, 169, 172
Sankoh, Foday 133
Sao Salvador 37

Sarup, Amrit 145
Sassou-Nguesso, Denis 48, 49, 50, 51, 52, 53, 54
Saudi Arabia 68, 102, 104, 108, 119, 172
Saurimo 43
Savimbi, Jonas 34, 35, 38, 43, 45, 46, 114, 115, 150, 165, 167
Saxena, Rakesh 137, 145, 146
Schramme, Jean (Black Jack) 12, 13, 14, 15, 16, 21, 151
Secord, Richard 91, 93
Securicor 170
Selous Scouts 115
Senya 110
Serbia 54, 101, 103, 104
Seychelles xii, 63–64, 124
Shaba Province (formerly Katanga) 158
Sharpeville 113
Shell Petroleum 127
Shin Bet 98
Shokat, Mohammed 72
Short, Clare 127
Sicily x
Sierra Leone 47, 53, 84, 85, 114, 117, 118, 119, 120, 126, 128, 129, 132–146 (civil war), 147, 150, 154, 161, 166, 167, 169, 173
Sierra Leone People's Party (SLPP) 132, 133
Silva Ponto 35
Silver Shadow 55
Silverstein, Ken 152
Simbas 1, 8, 9
Singirok, Jerry 80, 81, 82, 83
S J Berwin & Co 138
Skate, Bill 84
Skinner, Kevin 106
Skorzeny, Otto 20
Slovenia 102
Smith, Ian 26, 27, 29, 31, 113, 149
Smith, Ron 129, 130
Snyder, John 139
Soldier of Fortune 126
Soldier of Fortune Convention and Expo 127
Solih, Ali 57
Solovei, Vladimir 112
Somalia 47, 70, 162
Somare, Sir Michael 75
Somoza Debayle, Anastasio 86, 87
South, The 124, 125, 130
South Africa 1, 9, 11, 12, 16, 19, 26, 27, 28, 29, 30, 33, 38, 42, 43, 45, 47, 59, 60, 61, 63, 64, 70, 78, 80, 81, 113–122

Index

(Executive Outcomes), 128, 147, 148, 159, 170, 171, 172
South African Defence Force (SADF) 115, 120
South Korea 120
South West Africa People's Organization (SWAPO) 29, 42, 114
Soweto 26, 169
Soyo 43, 44, 115, 119, 120, 165
Soyster, Harry 108, 128
Spain x, 8, 18, 29, 101, 105
Spanish Civil War 102
Spearhead Inc 98
Special Air Service (SAS) xii, 33, 44, 45, 67, 70, 92, 97, 99, 106, 119, 128, 156
Spencer, Julius 137
Spicer, Jim 77, 78, 81–82, 85, 136, 137, 138, 139, 142, 143, 145
Sinola, Antonio 150
Sri Lanka 93
Stanford Technology Trading Group Inc 93
Stanley, Henry Morton 66
Stanleyville 10, 11
Star, The (South Africa) 26
St Cook, Linda 139
Steel, Sir David 120
Steiner, Rolf 24
Stevens, Siaka 132
Steyl, Crause 120
Stirling, David 67, 70
Stockwell, John 34, 35
Strasser, Valentine 132, 133, 134, 142
Sudan 12, 47, 65, 66, 106, 118
Sunday Times 10, 69, 93
Suriname xiii
Sweden 29
Swiss Guards x
Switzerland 6, 105

Tajikistan 102, 110, 165
Taki, Muhammed 62
Talabani, Jalal 72
Taliban, The 161
Tanganyika Concessions (Tanks) 4, 151
Taymar, Said ibn 68
Teixeira de Sousa 8
Tel al-Zaatar xii
Tel Aviv 98
Telli, Diallo 15
Temkin, Benny 48
Texaco 172
Thacker, Gerald xii
Thatcher, Margaret 173

The Whores of War 34, 68
Third World (The South) xi, xiii, 1, 68, 101, 103, 124, 148, 149, 151, 164, 170
32 Buffalo Battalion 115, 128
Thomas, Michael 139
Thompson, Loren 153
Thompson, William 41
Tiago, N'Zita Henrique 40
Times, The 8, 11, 94, 105
Tito, Josip Broz 102
Togo 52
Tomkins, Dave 97
Tower, John 91, 94
Trans-Dniestra 111, 112
Tshombe, Moise 1, 2, 3, 4, 5, 7, 8, 9, 11, 12, 13, 14, 55, 151, 159
Tudjman, Franjo 103
Tully, Peter 71
Tunisia 106
Tuta, Jack 77

Uganda 12, 24, 47
Ukraine 112
Ukraine Union of Officers 112
Ukrainian National Self-Defence Forces (UNSDF) 112
Ulli 20, 22, 23, 149
Uniao Nacional para a Independencia Total de Angola (UNITA) 33, 34, 35, 38, 42, 43, 44, 45, 46, 51, 52, 114, 115, 116, 119, 120, 150, 165, 167
Union Miniere du Haut-Congo 1, 4, 151
Union of Soviet Socialist Republics (USSR) xiii, 1, 27, 46, 101, 102, 120, 160, 165, 172
United Nations 1, 4, 12, 14, 17, 21, 46, 49, 57, 63, 109, 117, 121, 122, 125, 128, 130, 131, 135, 136, 139, 140, 141, 145, 146, 147, 158, 159–168, 169, 173, 174
United Nations High Commissioner for Refugees (UNHCR) 76, 115
United States xi, 1, 9, 10, 13, 27, 28, 31, 33, 34, 37, 39, 46, 53, 71, 77, 78, 79, 86, 87, 88, 89, 90, 92, 93, 94, 95, 96, 100, 104, 105, 107, 109, 122, 123, 124, 128, 139, 140, 145, 147, 149, 150, 152, 155, 158, 160, 161, 166, 167, 171, 174

Van den Bergh, Nick 116, 118, 119
Vargas, Virgilio Barco 95, 99
Veillard, Max 62
Venter, Al J. 116
Venter, Dries 60
Victoria, Queen 65

Index

Vietnam 29, 33, 39, 100, 110, 123, 127, 155
Vila Luso 8
Vinnell Corporation 128
Von Rosen, Count 23, 24
Vorster, B. J. 29

Walker, David 92, 93, 94
Walle, van der 9
Walls, Peter 31
Ward, 'Sharky' 71
Warsaw Pact 101
Warton, Henry 20
Watchguard (International) Ltd 67
Wavreille, Jean-Claude 54
Webb, Michael Francis 92
West, The 27, 28, 38, 42, 61, 71, 101, 135, 147–159 (attitudes towards mercenaries)
Wewak 76
Wicks, Alistair 22, 24
Wild Geese Club 126
Williams, 'Taffa' 24
Wilson, Derek 10
Wingit, June Paias 75
World Bank 124, 135
World Council of Churches 20
World War I 66
World War II xi, 2, 19, 66, 67, 76, 101
Wright, Robin 29

Xenophon ix

Yachroutou, Caabi el 62
Yaounde Conventions 157
Yemen 19, 22, 61, 66, 67 (North), 69, 70–71 (North)
Yugoslavia xiii, 101, 102–109, 112, 122, 161, 162, 165, 166

Zachrin, Zeev 48
Zagreb 104, 106
Zaire (also see Congo) xiii, 34, 37, 40, 41, 42, 47, 49, 51, 55, 151, 156
Zambia 15, 30, 31, 114
Zamora, Jaime Paz 99
Zanettaci, Stephane xii
Zimbabwe 32, 39, 114
Zimbabwe ANC 31
Zimbabwe African National Union (ZANU) 27, 29, 113
Zimbabwe People's Army (ZIPA) 29
Zoulou, The 48, 52